Assassination and Terrorism:
Their Modern Dimensions

Assassination and Terrorism:
Their Modern Dimensions

Murray Clark Havens
Carl Leiden
Karl M. Schmitt

STERLING
SWIFT publishing company
p. o. box 188
manchaca, texas 78652

Copyright © 1975 by
Murray Clark Havens,
Carl Leiden,
Karl M. Schmitt

ISBN 0-88408-073-0

Assassination and Terrorism:
Their Modern Dimensions

Contents

Preface

Several years ago two of the present authors (Leiden and Schmitt) published a book on revolution—*The Politics of Violence: Revolution in the Modern World* (Englewood Cliffs, N.J.: Prentice-Hall, Inc., 1968). In the course of preparing that work it became evident that many kinds of political violence, not only revolutions, seriously affect political systems. One such form of violence is assassination. Political systems exhibit their characteristics more openly in stress than in repose. Assassination is certainly one way in which political systems are subjected to stress.

The third author (Havens) had already investigated the nature and activities of extremist political movements in *The Challenges to Democracy* (Austin: University of Texas Press, 1965). It seemed natural to join forces in a preliminary exploration of the nature and effects of political assassination.

We soon found that virtually no systematic research had been done on assassination. We also found out why. Not only did we encounter unexpected problems in conceptualization, but we also found that the questions about the politics of assassination were highly complex and difficult. In our initial probings we posed three questions:

1. What effect does assassination have on a political system?
2. How effective is assassination as a political tool?
3. In what kind of societies does assassination tend to occur?

Our initial researches forced us to limit so ambitious a project, but assassinations are difficult to study in any event. Data are elusive. Interpreting the data is hazardous. More importantly, the cost of collecting what data there are—on any but the most obvious level—is extremely high. We decided, therefore, to label our work *preliminary*, to restrict our task to the elucidation of our first two questions, and to attempt to discover broad patterns of distribution of assassination in space and time.

In our work we have presented ten case studies of assassination. Their political impacts range from negligible to destructive, and we have discussed our ten examples in an ascénding order of turbulence. We have not tried to measure impacts in any precise fashion, but we have made judgments as to the relative magnitude of personnel, policy, and systemic changes. Obviously where only a few persons have shifted around in office or where only minor policy changes have followed an assassination, we consider the impact low. Conversely, where a political regime has collapsed or even disappeared as a result of a political murder, we have judged the impact as high. The most troublesome cases fall in the intermediate or moderate range, and we make no brief for the infallibility of our judgments.

In attempting to explain why a particular degree of impact resulted from each of these assassinations, we have focused attention on three interrelated factors: the characteristics of the regime, the nature of the conspiracy (if any), and the quality of political opposition in each country at the time of the murder. In answering the second question, i.e., assessing the usefulness of assassination as a political weapon, we have roughly compared the expectations of the assassin (or assassins) with the actual results of the deed. Finally, in attempting to arrive at an understanding of the distribution of assassination we statistically analyzed the assassinations of heads of state over a fifty-year period from the end of the First World War; we considered only those countries that existed over the whole time span.

As part of our organizational labors, one of us (Leiden) presented a paper on assassination in the Middle East at the 1967 meetings of the Southern Political Science Association in New Orleans. Commentary at the session proved valuable; we would like to express our appreciation to those who offered thoughtful criticism on that occasion. The three of us then presented a graduate seminar on assassination at the University of Texas in the spring of 1968. This experience was also valuable to us, and we wish to express our appreciation to our students for important questions that they raised.

The tragedies of April and June, 1968, spurred President Johnson to the appointment of a National Commission on the Causes and Prevention of Violence. We wish to thank James Kirkham and William Crotty of the Task Force on Political Assassination of that commission, who invited us to work with them. In addition to the gathering and organization of data for the commission, we prepared a number of commentaries on assassination in various geographic areas for the commission's perusal. We wish to acknowledge here our debt to the ideas and data presented by James Soukup, Feliks Gross, and Rita James Simon in their papers for the commission.

If the many arguments that we have had with each other over the nature of assassination and its effects on political systems are any indication, there will be many areas in which colleagues in other universities will see fit to challenge our conclusions. There seems to be no way out for us here. This field of research is new, and disagreements over interpretation seem natural and inevitable.

We also wish to acknowledge the assistance of the following people, who helped us in various ways: Ann Kerrey, Sonia Alianak, Constance Singleton, Martha Dickson, Geraldine Gagliano, and Veronica Van Fleteren. Thanks are also due to our colleagues David Edwards and Robert Cushing for reading part of the manuscript, and to Dean John Silber and Professor William Livingston for their support of this project.

We wish also to acknowledge grants from the Center for Middle Eastern Studies and the Institute of Latin American Studies, both of the University of Texas, and from the Relm Foundation. Obviously none of these organizations, nor the National Commission on the Causes and Prevention of Violence, nor the many colleagues and students who have helped us in our research can be held responsible for what we say here. If errors of fact are to be found or if our interpretations seem unacceptable, there is no one to blame but the authors.

Preface to the Revised Edition

The 1970s have witnessed no diminution in political violence. There are still revolutions. Assassination is no less. Moreover, new forms and intensity in systematic terrorism have come into being.

An opportunity to bring this study out in a slightly revised edition has been welcomed by us. Although a number of works dealing with assassination and violence have appeared since 1970, none has approached the phenomenon from a theoretical perspective, as this one did. Neither the theory nor the empirical foundations of this study seem to have been superseded by any other work. Certainly our conclusions have not been negated. They seem as relevant today as they did in 1970.

At the same time it seems appropriate to consider, even if briefly, the newer forms of terrorism that have developed. As a result the concluding chapter (15) has been completely rewritten and lengthened. The remainder of the work, however, is substantially as it was originally written. Although the revisions have been carried out by Schmitt and Leiden, all of the authors remain fully associated with the work, in its revised edition.

The Nature of Assassination

Our world abounds in violence of every kind. Some is massive and organized; much is individual, spontaneous, and chaotic. Politics itself, a budget of power relationships, often generates violence. In fact, violence seems to be a natural companion to, and perhaps an essential part of, the political process. Governments attempt to monopolize violence and generally succeed in legitimizing it. Nevertheless, only in recent years has violence itself been studied in any detail.

The first efforts at such research dealt with macroviolence. Studies of *a* war or *The War*, although always numerous, have had to yield some ground to generic studies like Quincy Wright's classic, *A Study of War*. Revolution, too, has been analyzed apart from its specific examples. Crane Brinton, Chalmers Johnson, Harry Eckstein, and others have attempted to extract from examples of revolution some dimensions of its essence.[1] Studies of these kinds have been enormously important to the understanding of political systems in their broader perspectives.

But the same attention has not been paid to other, seemingly minor, violent activities—the microviolence of political systems—which would certainly include riots, demonstrations, political intimidations, violence at the polls, and murder for political ends. Of course, all crime, of whatever kind, affects and is in turn affected by the political system. Although political violence in the United States obviously did not begin with the death of President Kennedy in 1963, the last half-dozen years have produced a plethora of racial riots, student demonstrations,

1. See, for example, Carl Leiden and Karl M. Schmitt, *The Politics of Violence: Revolution in the Modern World* (Englewood Cliffs, N.J.: Prentice-Hall, Inc., 1968); Chalmers Johnson, *Revolutionary Change* (Boston: Little, Brown and Company, 1966); Harry Eckstein, ed., *Internal War, Problems and Approaches* (New York: The Free Press, 1964).

and assassinations—enough to prompt some to term the United States a sick society. One result has been the creation of governmental commissions to study violence, a number on the local level and two on the national level.[2] Although all of these forms of violence warrant attention, our interests lie with one form of microviolence—political murder or (with some redefinition) assassination.

What Is Assassination?

Political murder describes the general type of violent activity that concerns us, but this term can be applied as well to mass killings, blood baths, or genocide. Although important in their own right, these acts of violence go somewhat beyond our dimensions of study. The proper word to describe our interests seems to be *assassination*, but there is some looseness in its usage.

Conventionally, assassination means "the act of killing with treacherous violence . . . usually [a] prominent person . . . either for hire or from fanatic adherence to a cause."[3] Bernard Lewis points out that the first reference to the word in a Western language occurred in Dante's *Inferno* (*lo perfido assassin*) which was explained by a near contemporary commentator as "one who kills others for money."[4] Lewis himself suggests that today an assassin "means a murderer, more particularly one who kills by stealth or treachery, whose victim is a public figure and whose motive is fanaticism or greed."[5] Max Lerner, in the first edition of the *Encyclopedia of the Social Sciences*, says, "Used in a political sense assassination refers to the killing of a person in public life from a political motive and without legal process."[6] Still another writer has defined assassination simply as "the trucidation [*sic*] of a political figure without due process of law."[7] Somewhat more elaborately, Oscar Jászi argues that "political murder means the premeditated killing of an individual or group of individuals in order to get, maintain, or extend the power of the state in the interest of an

2. The National Advisory Commission on Civil Disorders and the National Commission on the Causes and Prevention of Violence.
3. *Webster's Third New International Dictionary.*
4. Bernard Lewis, *The Assassins: A Radical Sect in Islam* (New York: Basic Books, Inc., Publishers, 1968), p. 2.
5. Ibid.
6. Vol. II, p. 271.
7. Saul K. Padover, "Patterns of Assassination in Occupied Territory," *Public Opinion Quarterly*, VII (1943), 680.

individual or group. When the killing is directed to well-defined individuals, it would be more correct to speak of 'political assassination.' "[8]

Obviously assassination is not an easy term to define precisely.[9] It is apparent from usage that assassination is regarded as a subset of murder, generally committed against individuals or small groups of individuals. The term is not usually used to denote mass murder. Furthermore, the victim must be singled out *as an individual*, not merely as a member or representative of some larger group against which general terrorism is being directed. In common usage a murder or killing is more likely to be termed an assassination if the victim is prominent, is "well-defined," or is in public life. In addition, the relationship between the assassin and his victim tends to be different from that in common murder. In the latter the killer-victim relationship is more apt to be a personal one—that is, the murderer and target are more likely to know each other and the motive for the act is more likely to be personal—than in the case of assassination.[10] In assassination the assassin (whether the actual killer or the author of the crime) is less likely to know his victim and less likely to derive immediate personal benefit from his act. Of course, if the killer has been hired he will be paid or if he has acted on his own initiative he will derive emotional and psychological benefits from his deed. Moreover, there is a strong odor of the political to assassination, whether carried out by a government against its opponents or by opposition elements against government personnel. Perhaps *political* assassination is a redundancy.[11] Most assassination is politically motivated and can never be separated from the political context in which it occurs; its impact, public and systemic, is political. This impact seems to be a distinguish-

8. Oscar Jászi and John D. Lewis, *Against the Tyrant: The Tradition and Theory of Tyrranicide* (Glencoe, Ill.: The Free Press, 1957), pp. 150–51.

9. The word assassin is of Arabic origin. It derives from the Arabic *hashīshiyyīn* meaning "those who use hashish," and refers historically to one of the Shī'ite Ismā'īlī sects in Syria and Iran in the eleventh and twelfth centuries, which for a time facilitated its political aggrandizement by the violent removal of its opponents, allegedly inducing courage and fortitude among its agents by the use of drugs (hashish). See for example Freya Stark, "Assassins of Syria," *The Cornhill Magazine*, CLXII (1947), 417–26, and Bernard Lewis, "The Sources for the History of the Syrian Assassins," *Speculum, A Journal of Medieval Studies*, XXVII (1952), 475–89. See also Lewis, *The Assassins*, pp. 11–12.

10. Crime statistics in the United States indicate that the great majority of common murders occur within family or closely associated circles.

11. We recognize that, in common usage, the term assassin can be used simply to indicate a hired killer.

ing feature of assassination. Ordinary murder may be notorious and celebrated and may capture public attention, but its impact is almost never political. The ghastly murder of Mrs. Sam Shephard some years ago, for example, provided almost a generation of Americans with a *crime célèbre,* but there was no political impact.

To summarize briefly from usage, *assassination refers to those killings or murders, usually directed against individuals in public life, motivated by political rather than by personal relationships.*

But described (rather than defined) in this way, the demarcation lines remain vague; assassination itself blends gradually into other forms of violence and systemic disturbances. Borderline examples are troublesome to delineate and to classify. Was the death of Senator Percy's daughter Valerie a simple murder or can it be considered an assassination because of its political repercussions? Was Mussolini executed or assassinated? Was the death of Nadir Shah (King of Afghanistan) in 1933—an act of private, personal revenge—an assassination or a non-political murder?

Cases that are difficult to classify can easily be multiplied. Where a single case of assassination (or execution) is being studied in terms of systemic significance, it matters little how the event has been identified. But where a different sort of problem is being investigated (such as the correlation between assassination *rates* and the political process, for example) it is necessary that we be able to identify with greater precision. We shall consequently redefine assassination as follows: *Assassination is the deliberate, extralegal killing of an individual for political purposes.*[12]

Needless to say, this definition is not completely congruent with common or historical usage. But it does permit us to sort out from a wide variety of killings those of a common inspiration, those having some connection with a political system. We are not interested in all murders. The murders of prominent people, unless politically motivated, will not concern us. The murder of all sorts of "ordinary" people, if motivated by political reasons, will interest us very much indeed. The violent deaths of prominent individuals are more apt to be chronicled and investigated and it will not be easy to sort out the deaths of individuals on the more ordinary social and political levels. By our definition, murder becomes political as a result of the motive of

12. Attempted assassinations differ in that the death of the intended victim does not result. For some purposes, such as analysis of the *incidence* of assassinations, data may include unsuccessful attempts.

the murderer or the assassin. But this suggests in turn that the victim possesses some political significance. In short, the political character of the victim makes possible the political motive for killing him. The nature of the victim's political character also determines the kind of impact his death will have on the political community and its system. Thus motive and impact have a distinct if tenuous interconnection. The public and systemic impacts of assassinations may vary from nil to immense. Although this study will focus on the impacts of assassination, the extent of impact is not a defining characteristic.

A number of questions may be raised about the definition given above. Are deaths resulting from "political" crimes assassinations? Obviously, there are important differences between assassinations undertaken by governments and those undertaken by private individuals and groups; nevertheless, each has great potential impact on the political system. Specifically, if treason is a political crime, are all executions of traitors assassinations? These are excluded by the adjective "extralegal," but one should recognize that treason trials in some times and climes are shallow subterfuges for ridding regimes of troublesome individuals. The Egyptian government assassinated Hasan al-Banna on the streets of Cairo in 1949; it was too dangerous to try him. But what about the Israeli trial and execution of Adolf Eichmann in 1961–62? This is surely a borderline case. It does not matter that arguments over jurisdiction were made and lost, that a dramatic trial was created, that there was no death penalty in Israeli law; all of these or their negations cannot belie the fact that Eichmann was "executed" for potent political reasons. Clear-cut executions, whatever the motives for their consummation, are hardly assassinations. There is a no-man's-land, however, in which it is difficult to distinguish one from the other. An orderly public trial kept within procedural legal bounds may result in what is undoubtedly a legal execution. But the removal of an individual by a hurriedly concocted trial, held in camera, with little opportunity for defense, may better be classified as assassination. The world abounds in examples in this gray area. It is not surprising that many examples are found within the dictatorial political communities or as concomitants to revolutionary activity. But there are examples in the democratic community as well, such as the action of the military commission that tried General Yamashita after the Second World War.

Troublesome cases can sometimes be described as killings which are, in terms of motive, only *partially* assassinations. No doubt many killings are the result of a mixture of motives. With assassination the political motive predominates and cases in which the political motive is less significant fall on the borderline between assassination and simple murder.

The State of Our Knowledge on Assassination

Until recently most studies of assassination have been moralistic, journalistic, or historical. Relatively few have tried to relate assassination to broader social, economic, or political factors. What attempts have been made are either limited in scope or not very revealing.

The earliest writers on assassination addressed themselves to the moral question and throughout history various commentators have argued about the right (and even responsibility) of people to assassinate undesirable leaders. In both Islam and Christendom, however, the weight of opinion has condemned the practice.[13]

Those political philosophers who have defended assassination have always insisted on the tyrannical character of the victim. Before violence could be justified before God it had to be demonstrated beyond all doubt that the object of the intended violence was vile and reprehensible and that, except for killing him, *there was no other way of relieving the burden of his tyranny*. Few assassinations meet the criteria of the philosophers. Assassins make errors, often attributing to a figure an importance that he does not possess or evil qualities that do him injustice. What if the victim is not in fact a tyrant? There is, in every society, some deranged mind that views with distaste the acts of any leader. The moralists obviously cannot resolve the conflict. Moreover, assassins have often been singled out for praise. Brutus was honored by a faction in ancient Rome, and in 1964 West Germans commemorated the twentieth anniversary of the attempt on Hitler's life. Even governments have extolled the virtues of assassination, but of course in states other than their own. King Saud of Saudi Arabia apparently financed efforts to murder President Nasser of Egypt, who in turn often publicly exhorted the people of Jordan to destroy their king, Husain.

A host of writers have collected considerable data on individual as-

---

13. There is the famous argument of John of Salisbury (d. 1182) in his *Policraticus*, supported by the Old Testamentary examples, that it is right and just to commit tyrannicide. More than seven centuries later Jesuit Father Hermann Wehrle was executed for having advised one of the Rastenburg conspirators that tyrannicide under certain conditions is sinless.

sassinations and assassination attempts. Some medical scholars have studied the psychopathology of the assassin, while historians have carefully chronicled individual events and attempted to relate them to broader historical trends and patterns. Journalists have recorded events as they occurred, frequently reporting the more sensational aspects of assassinations. From these accounts it appears that assassinations run the gamut from spontaneous, unplanned acts to highly organized conspiracies. President Garfield was murdered in 1881 by an individual, a so-called "disappointed office seeker." Garfield was a symbol for his own frustration, but a political symbol nevertheless.[14] Little planning was involved; no organization or conspiracy lay behind the act. An extreme form of the highly spontaneous, individual act was Sirhan's assassination of Senator Robert Kennedy in 1968, which was made possible by a chance combination of access to the victim, a weapon at hand, and an emotional justification. At the other extreme, Lincoln's assassin, Booth, led a conspiracy; the assassination of the foreign minister of Germany, von Rathenau, in 1919, was the deliberate act of the *Freikorps*.[15] In other cases the victim may be chosen purely by chance. It seems likely that President Kennedy's assassin, Lee Harvey Oswald, was anxious to destroy some, indeed any, prominent person in order to acquire notoriety proportionate to the victim's prominence. Oswald apparently had already attempted to kill Major General Edwin Walker. Regardless of how Oswald chose his target, it is evident that the act itself was carefully planned and was not a purely spontaneous act of violence. Also highly organized was the conspiracy to kill Hitler in 1944: the time and place were chosen, the proper weapons were procured, and the assassin was carefully selected. In the Rastenburg affair, it was decided that Hitler could only be successfully attacked in his headquarters and a bomb was chosen as the most effective weapon, given the physical infirmities of Graf Claus von Stauffen-

14. See Charles E. Rosenberg, *The Trial of the Assassin Guiteau* (Chicago: The University of Chicago Press, 1968). The author states that delusion rather than rational disappointment in not obtaining office was the primary motivation of Garfield's assassin. Guiteau was probably a paranoid schizophrenic. Rosenberg's book is a remarkably thorough and penetrating account of the assassin and his subsequent trial.

15. Conspiracies vary greatly in size and character. Some involve large, well-organized entities like the *Freikorps*. The Rastenburg group in 1944 was extensive, but many of those on whom it relied were only peripherally or tangentially engaged. Booth's conspiracy was small and was organized around a single figure, Booth himself. We include as a conspiracy any effort by two or more individuals in concert to produce an assassination.

berg, a leading planner of the act and the would-be assassin. Princip, the assassin of the Archduke Ferdinand and his wife in 1914, was chosen with apparent care. On the other hand, when Catherine de Medici attempted to murder Admiral Gaspard de Coligny, she showed consummate skill in all details except the selection of an assassin.[16]

In general, the more carefully planned the act of violence the more necessary is an organization for its consummation, but even diffuse groups can give a potential killer a climate, target, and justification for assassination. The distinction should be made here between the individual assassin who organizes his own efforts and the organized group (organization) necessary to effectuate some complicated patterns of violence. As this is being written we still know relatively little about Ray's assassination of Martin Luther King, Jr. The evidence indicates considerable organization on the assassin's part, whether or not he was part of a conspiracy.[17] Where the efforts of a number of individuals are required, an organization is almost always necessary. More importantly, organizations can spew violence more efficiently; individuals may contemplate violence at one moment or another, but groups are more likely to carry such inclinations to fruition. An organization also gives the individual assassin a raison d'être; he acts now not merely in accordance with his own selfish feelings, but as the agent of something much greater than himself. He conceives himself as the savior of his people, his church, his race, or of mankind. In such a mental condition he does not think too seriously of his own personal preservation.

The motives and perceptions of assassins have interested virtually all observers of political murder. Motives have ranged from the completely rational (i.e., carefully planned and organized) drive for power to the blind and irrational blow against authority—any authority. The murder of Colonel Zaim in Syria in 1949, of General Kassem in Iraq in 1963, and of President Diem in Vietnam in 1963 preceded and perhaps were essential to successful coups d'état. The murder of Prime Minister Verwoerd of South Africa in 1966, on the other hand, was the insane act of a man with a grudge against society.

To the nihilists and anarchists of the nineteenth century, the as-

16. Sire de Maurevert was initially chosen; he fired at Coligny, but missed and killed his companion. A second attempt was made and, again, Maurevert was chosen as the assassin. He bungled again, but this time he slightly wounded his victim.
17. Even the trial judge, now dead, raised the question of conspiracy.

sassination was an end in itself. The assassination of the Archduke
Ferdinand in 1914 had no immediate object in view; hatred of King
Alexander Obrenovich and Queen Draga of Serbia probably motivated
their murder in 1903 to a greater degree than did the simple desire
for a change in government; the assassination of King Abdullah of
Jordan in 1951 was likely revenge for Abdullah's rapprochement with
Israel; and in a later case, Colonel Shishakli, sometime dictator of
Syria, was assassinated out of revenge in 1964 in Brazil, a decade after
his exile from Syria. Some assassinations have no object other than
publicity; the attempts of Puerto Rican terrorists to assassinate President Truman and assorted congressmen belong in this category, as do
most of the anarchistic assassinations of the late nineteenth century.
One victim is as good as another, so long as he is prominent enough, or
wealthy enough. His death need not solve any problems.

Most studies, however, reveal that assassination rarely accomplishes
the desired ends. Assassins seldom survive long enough to view their
deeds with historical detachment.[18] What is important, nonetheless,
is what they think to be true. Is the would-be victim the obstacle to
freedom or democracy? Has he trampled on institutions and defied
"the people?" Have the normal processes of political control proved
impotent and other political leadership proved inadequate? In short, is
the victim a tyrant who cannot be reasoned with and for whom there
is no alternative but death? How "necessary" is the death of such a
tyrant to those good ends the assassin desires? Certainly a clear
example of these problems was the murder of Jean-Paul Marat by
Charlotte Corday in July, 1793. It seems clear that Marat was a
thoroughly despicable person, responsible for a number of hideous
crimes in the name of the French Revolution; it also seems sufficiently
evident that Charlotte Corday was a sincere, dedicated Frenchwoman
who killed Marat *because he seemed to her to be the key to all that
was bad in the revolution.* With his death, she thought, mob rule

18. Gavrilo Princip (the assassin of Ferdinand in 1914) lived long enough
to be shaken by events subsequent to his act. By 1916 he "could not face the
question of the consequences of what he had done. He struggled to hold on to
the notion that his deed had not been in vain, though doubt obtruded: 'Cannot
believe that the World War was a consequence of the assassination; cannot feel
himself responsible for the catastrophe; therefore cannot say if it was a service.
But fears he did it in vain.'" (Lewis S. Feuer, *The Conflict of Generations: The
Character and Significance of Student Movements* [New York: Basic Books, Inc.,
1969], p. 83. The quotation is from Hamilton Fish Armstrong, "Confessions of
the Assassin Whose Deed Led to the World War," *Current History,* XXVI [1927],
704.)

and violence would vanish and France could be returned to the path of moderation. But what Charlotte did not live to learn was that Marat, however bad he was, was not important enough to be the key to revolutionary violence. If anything, his death hastened the destruction of the Girondins and facilitated the rise of the Terror, which engulfed France, carrying both Danton and Robespierre to the guillotine, and lasted until Bonaparte restored order to the country.

One aspect of assassination—the extralegal removal of political figures by government action—has attracted attention only in the last several decades. Governments have often provoked violence to serve their own ends and they have often used assassination when other methods of elimination were closed to them. It is sometimes necessary to eliminate individuals completely, silently, and rapidly. Trials and prison sentences are time-consuming and uncertain; moreover, they permit the victim some favorable opportunities to speak. Governments have long circumvented obstacles of this kind by the total removal of the individuals concerned. Where almost complete political control exists, as was the case in Stalinist Russia, it is possible to conjure up trials and announce the "deliberations," after the sentences have been executed. This was the case in the Stalinist destruction of Marshal Tuchachevsky in 1936 and in the later Malenkov-Molotov-Khrushchev removal of Beria in 1953. A well-known example of both individual assassination and mass extermination, sponsored and carried out by the government, was the thirtieth of June (1934) purge in Germany. In two days, about 400 individuals were killed, including Ernst Roehm (founder and head of the *Sturmabteilungen*—the Brownshirts), General Kurt von Schleicher (former Reich Chancellor), and Gregor Strasser (long-time leader of the Nazi organization).[19] Although Hitler later rationalized the purge as the quashing of treasonable conspiracy, no attempt was made to utilize the normal channels of judicial punishment (which were ample and adequate in the Germany of 1934).

For centuries political leaders have been groping for a way to protect themselves from assassination. A German priest of the fourteenth century, Brocardus, offered this advice: "I . . . know only one single remedy for the safeguarding and protection of the King, that in all the royal household, for whatever service, however small or brief or mean, none should be admitted, save those whose country, place,

19. Here is one of the borderline cases: although we exclude from our study assassinations en masse, we must consider the prominent targets in such mass slayings as individual assassinations. Certainly Roehm was such a target.

lineage, condition and person are certainly, fully and clearly known." [20]
In 1969 the National Commission on the Causes and Prevention of
Violence considered, inter alia, the degree to which political candidates
should be permitted to expose themselves to the people. The commission in effect argued that assassination is a function of political
exposure and that its incidence can be reduced by regulating that
exposure. Already the facilities of the modern state are widely used in
attempts to insulate prominent political figures from would-be attackers. Access to weapons is made more difficult, vigilant security
measures are undertaken, and contacts with the populace are diminished. All of these precautions may well reduce the incidence of
assassination of major figures, but there is hardly a way of preventing
it altogether. In highly authoritarian states with tight security measures, assassination of major political figures (except with official
sanction) is a relatively rare phenomenon. [21] In democratic societies,
security measures cannot be as rigidly enforced. Most candidates are
prepared to run some risk in the pursuit of votes. Moreover, the political system itself cannot afford to minimize contacts between candidates and their constituents. According to Sandburg, Lincoln said
"that the only effective way to avoid all risk was to shut himself up
in an iron box, where he could not possibly perform the duties of
President." Lincoln went on to say directly, "Why put up the bars
when the fence is down all around? If they kill me, the next man will
be just as bad for them; and in a country like this, where our habits
are simple, and must be, assassination is always possible, and will come
if they are determined upon it." [22] In some non-democratic systems,
too, such as in the present-day United Arab Republic, the charismatic
character of political leadership demands a high degree of public
visibility. In Stalinist-type regimes, where these demands are less imperative, tighter security measures may be more feasible. The top
leadership has no need of direct personal contact with the mass of the
citizenry. Undoubtedly the leaders of every political system will continue to seek new devices, techniques, and approaches to excise this
element of violence from the political process, but such measures
merely point up more sharply those acts of violence that either

20. Quoted in Lewis, *The Assassins*, pp. 1–2.
21. However, the alleged attempt against the Russian astronauts in early 1969
may have been directed against Soviet political leaders.
22. Carl Sandburg, *Abraham Lincoln: The War Years* (New York: Harcourt,
Brace and World, Inc., 1939), II, 210. The second quotation is in Lincoln's words.

originate within the security elite itself—it has been suggested that this was the case in the death of Huey Long—or are the products of highly organized and dedicated conspiratorial groups. It is impossible to prevent fulfillment of these types of assassination. The Rastenburg conspiracy in Germany, which resulted in the attempt on Hitler's life on July 20, 1944, could hardly have been prevented by normal security measures. The conspiracy was within the highest ranks of the German army and would have led, if successful, to a coup d'état.

In recent years a few scholars have begun to investigate the relationship between assassination and other kinds of social and political events. A host of questions may be posed along these lines: In what kinds of political systems is assassination likely to occur? Is there any connection between assassination and other forms of violence? Is there any relationship among assassinations on various levels, i.e., are low-, middle-, and high-level assassinations mutually exclusive in any society? Are mature political systems less likely to produce assassination than developing political systems or those undergoing major stress and strain? Can mature systems be divided into those least and most likely to generate assassination? In short, is there any connection between assassination and the various characteristics of political systems? Is assassination infectious in the sense that examples generate their successors? Is this multiplication restricted to a single system or can it splash over national boundaries and periods in time? Is assassination an accidental variant of murder? Is it the product of other violence? If so, what kinds?

Pioneers in attempting to get at some of these problems are Raymond Tanter and R. J. Rummel. They limit their focus, however, to the connection between assassination and the presence at the time of other forms of political violence or turbulence and do not consider the connection between assassination and types of political systems. Furthermore, Tanter's data appear to relate assassination more closely to the momentary existence of political turbulence than to the incidence of assassination in the past. Defining assassination as "any politically motivated murder or attempted murder of high government official or politician," Tanter has attempted to correlate about two dozen variables of violence one with the other in a three-year period (1958–60) for some eighty-three countries.[23] His data do not demon-

23. Raymond Tanter, "Dimensions of Conflict Behavior Within and Between Nations, 1958–60," *Journal of Conflict Resolution,* X (1965), 41–64.

strate much connection between assassination and other forms of violence, at least for the period of time and the nations studied. The only factors showing moderate correlation were the presence of guerrilla warfare ($r = .49$), riots ($r = .51$), and the total "number of people killed in all forms of domestic violence" ($r = .51$). An earlier study by R. J. Rummel indicated only guerrilla warfare ($r = .45$) riots ($r = .45$), and demonstrations ($r = .51$) as at all significant.[24] None of these correlations is very impressive.

Proceeding from the Tanter and Rummel work, Ivo and Rosalind Feierabend have undertaken a most ambitious project to study violence cross-nationally over a period of twenty years, 1948–67.[25] Their findings at the highest level of generalization seem reasonable and in line with our own observations. They hold that "violence, viewed cross-nationally, is not a random or isolated occurrence," and that assassination tends to occur most often in conjunction with guerrilla warfare. On the other hand, assassination, according to their data, correlates only "reasonably" well with revolution and not at all significantly with other less severe political events. They also find that the higher the levels of systemic frustration, external aggression, minority tensions, homicide rates, and general political violence, the higher the assassination rates. Conversely, the higher the levels of modernity and the higher the suicide rates, the lower are the assassination rates. Finally, their data indicate that both "permissive, democratic" countries, as well as "highly coercive regimes" are less prone to assassination than societies somewhere between. Significantly, one of the two countries most deviant from this pattern is the United States; the other is El Salvador. When the Feierabend studies are examined beyond this level, serious questions may be raised about their data and their method of measurement. It is out of place here to provide a detailed critique, but a few points can illustrate some problems. In their "level of modernity" index Japan is grouped with (among others) Albania, Honduras, and Ecuador as a "stable transitional" regime; the United States with Argentina as "modern unstable"; and Italy with the

24. R. J. Rummel, "The Dimensions of Conflict Behavior Within and Between Nations," *General Systems Yearbook*, VIII (1963), 1–50. The correlation between Rummel's and Tanter's data for assassination is $r = .24$. (See Tanter, op. cit., p. 47.)

25. Ivo and Rosalind Feierabend et al., "Cross-National Comparative Study of Assassination," Unpublished report prepared for the National Commission on the Causes and Prevention of Violence (edited version), Task Force I, Vol. I, chap. III (Mimeographed, 1968).

Dominican Republic and Syria as "transitional unstable." In their "external aggression" index the United States and the Soviet Union are grouped with (among others) Guatemala, Haití, and Paraguay as "high external aggression, unstable"; the United Kingdom and West Germany with Costa Rica and Mexico as high "external aggression, stable," and Canada, Japan and Sweden with Panama, El Salvador, and Ecuador as "low external aggression, stable." These groupings are patently misleading, but some of the scores assigned on the stability profile are incomprehensible. In the profile ranging from a low of 12 points (high stability) to a high of 445 (high instability), the United States rates 319—just slightly better than Bolivia with 323, but behind Colombia with 244, the Dominican Republic with 195, and Ecuador with 117!

Although we have made no such systematic study of these kinds of relationships, our own investigations have led us to some tentative observations. Like the Feierabends, we see little correlation between assassination and nonpolitical violence in a society; like Tanter and Rummel, we note some correlation with guerrilla warfare. Interestingly too, there seems to be no close connection between assassination and the simple prevalence of weapons. While it is true that assassination rates and the availability of weapons are both low in Great Britain, in Australia assassination rates are also very low but weapons exist in some profusion. Access to weapons seems to be a factor primarily where revolutionary turbulence already exists. However much they interest us, these questions have not been the focus of this study, which is much more modest in its scope.

The Scope of This Study

This book is not a study of individual notorious assassinations nor a compendium of world famous ones. Essentially it deals with the relationship between events (assassinations) and their contexts (political systems). Within this basic framework we shall attempt to answer three questions. First, is there any pattern to assassination in space and time? In an attempt to get at this problem we have compiled a comprehensive list of assassinations and attempted assassinations of chief executives and heads of state (prime ministers, presidents, kings, and so forth) from the end of the First World War to the present in countries that have existed throughout the period.[26] Second, what is the efficacy of assassination as a political tool? To answer this question we will compare the motives and expectations of assassins in ten case studies with the actual results of the murders. And third, what kinds of systemic impacts are produced by assassination? This is our primary interest and is, of course, related to the second question. To handle this inquiry we have subjected the ten case studies to close scrutiny, examining the political system as it appeared at the time of the assassination and studying the changes (and their causes) in the aftermath of the deed. We have attempted to select our case studies so as to include examples in which some political systems experienced basic systemic changes, some moderate changes in policies and personnel, and some negligible changes.

26. For the purposes of this question, attempted assassinations seem as important as successful assassinations since the difference in conclusion is the result of largely fortuitous circumstances.

## 2

The Problem of Classification

Given the frequency of its occurrence over the centuries, it is not surprising that assassination has assumed a galaxy of forms. How can these forms be classified? Oscar Jászi, in a work concerned primarily with the moral and political question of tyrannicide, has prepared a classification scheme for "political murder" based largely on the motive of the assassin:

1. " Assassination for personal motives"
2. "Murder to seize power for the gratification of power"
3. "Diplomatic assassination"
4. Murder "committed for reason of state"
5. Political murder "involving religious issues"
6. Murder where the driving motive is nationalism
7. Political murder where "the main motive . . . is class struggle" [1]

In a more recent study, Richard B. Laney basically accepts Jászi's categories, and adds several of his own. Laney does not attempt to structure his typology entirely around motive, but inquires into the nature of the victim and the circumstances of the deed itself. He offers the following distinctions among assassinations:

1. That committed by one, a few, or many conspirators
2. That involving a tyrannical or non-tyrannical victim
3. That motivated by ideology
4. "Irrational assassination, as exemplified by most of the attempts on the lives of U.S. Presidents"

---

1. Oscar Jászi and John D. Lewis, *Against the Tyrant* (Glencoe, Ill.: The Free Press, 1957), chap. 14.

5. "Mass assassination, illustrated by the slaughter of millions in Nazi Germany"
6. "Terroristic assassination," as in Algeria and Vietnam
7. "Assassination to produce a martyr to the cause" which may be the assassin himself
8. "Preemptive or defensive assassination" [2]

Laney's categories are neither complete nor uniformly useful. The very complexity of assassination—and the empirical data that we possess—makes classification a difficult thing. Assassinations can be most simply classified in terms of a *single* factor. *Motive* might be one such factor. It tells us something about assassination, but even a complete motive classification neglects elements that are vital to understanding the phenomenon. For example, King Abdullah of Jordan was assassinated in 1951. Was his death motivated by the desire for personal revenge, or for political revenge, or was it the need to remove him from the Middle Eastern scene, or something else? It is difficult to answer those who assert that motive in this case was almost (but not quite) irrelevant to the Arab "political system" in 1951. What difference did it make what motive prompted the actual assassin or those who supported and defended him (not necessarily identical)? The only motive that counts is what the public mind fastens upon as persuasive and what really was important was the impact of the assassination in the Middle East of 1951, regardless of the assassin's motive. The description of assassination based on a single factor, even such an essential element as motive, is necessarily incomplete. One solution is the creation of a multifactor classification—cumbersome, but more complete and considerably more useful.

One such multifactor classification might emphasize as the essential factors: *environment, timing, impetus, motive, nature of the victim,* and *impact* (both public and systemic). Assassinations occur in an environment; that is, they are imbedded in some political system or another. These systems could be delineated as traditional, transitional, or modern, for example. Ultimately an important question must be answered: Are some environments more conducive than others to assassination?

Whatever the nature of the system, assassinations may occur at times that are unduly propitious for violence. The system may itself

2. Richard B. Laney, "Political Assassination: The History of an Idea" (Ann Arbor, Mich.: University Microfilms, 1966), pp. 17–18, 279.

be undergoing change. Domestically, it may be characterized as being in stable or unstable equilibrium or in revolution. It may be at peace or at war with its neighbors or in a state of tension with them. Who can argue that the foreign environment had little to do with the death of Robert Kennedy? Other basic questions include: Is assassination more likely in time of peace or war? Is it a product of foreign pressures or tensions?

It also seems important to classify assassinations by the origin or source of the assassin or assassins. An assassination that is purely personal, involving only the assassin and his victim, may offer complexities in motivation, but the impetus for the act would seem more easily discerned. Is the source of assassinatory impetus domestic or foreign? Thus it seems important to know whether the assassins of King Alexander of Yugoslavia and Foreign Minister Barthou of France in 1934 were French or Croat. Foreign assassins may be sponsored by a government or by some lesser group; they are less likely to act for themselves. Was the impetus revolutionary? Did it arise from competing power blocs within the system? Was it, finally, an act arising from within the political elite itself?

Motive, of course, is a primary category. There is a temptation to erect a complicated typology of motivation, but an examination of many assassinations suggests a simple threefold classification: revenge, removal, and the symbolic slaying. Each of these may assume several forms. Revenge may well be more private than public; an individual may be removed through assassination by another individual who aspires to his position or by a government that fears his ambitions. In individual cases it is sometimes possible to trace out motivation patterns in some detail. But in broad classifications such richness in detail can only complicate.[3]

Also important in any classification scheme is the nature and character of the victim himself. The fact that a person has been assassinated is in itself a clue to his nature or position. To begin with, he is likely to be prominent. An assassin rarely singles out a victim as unknown as himself or as inconsequential and uninfluential as the great mass of people. To be sure, there are low-grade assassinations: a civil-rights worker is shot to death in Mississippi, an irate house-

3. A brief discussion of motive classification for the Middle East can be found in Carl Leiden, "Assassination in the Middle East," *Trans-Action*, VI, no. 7 (1969), 20–23.

wife kills a deputy sheriff for delivering a subpoena. On this level of influence there are many political murders which are, of course, assassinations. But it is difficult to unearth these examples, to separate them from the large numbers of ordinary murders that occur. And most important of all, the ultimate repercussions are apt to be minimal. For these reasons they are often neglected. Those assassinations that we can study and which interest us because of their impact tend generally to be those with prominent victims or those whose victims momentarily occupy *positions* of some importance. Special conditions can lend importance to an otherwise insignificant assassination, as when the Nazis chose to make significant the death of the otherwise inconsequential Horst Wessel in January, 1930. Generally, however, the victims of those assassinations that may affect political systems are likely to be prominent.

Prominent or otherwise, we must know something about the victim. Why was he singled out for death? (Why was Senator Kennedy singled out from among the many American politicians who have pursued a "soft line" on Israel, if indeed this was the motive for his assassination?) Why was the victim killed at this particular time? What position did he occupy? Was he in government or out?

By far the most important aspect of assassination is the public and systemic impact that follows the act. We are, however, apt to confuse these two impacts. Assassinations are likely to have large emotional repercussions among the populace, especially in the immediate area in which they occur, but the impact on the political system is something very different. An assassination with a large emotional and public impact may not actually alter the political system. And should alterations traceable to the assassination occur, they are likely not to be discerned in the immediate aftermath of the assassination. Robert Kennedy's death resulted almost immediately in the passage of restrictive firearms legislation, a relatively insignificant change in the American political system. Will it have more far-reaching results in the system?

Possible impacts range over a many-dimensioned spectrum. Assuming that the system itself survives, personnel and policies may be changed and institutional relationships altered. Impacts may range from the comparatively inconsequential to major alterations just short of revolution. The former—the short-run, comparatively inconsequential ones—are commonplace and are to be expected. If the victim is a

high-level member of government, his very removal (not to mention
the emotional overtones of the manner of his death) is bound to affect
the immediate operations of the system.

We shall return again and again to questions of the nature of the impact of assassination. In our case studies it will be the criterion used
to distinguish one case from another. Impact makes the problem of
assassination an interesting one in political science, just as it is often
the anticipated impact that gives the assassin his motive.

3

The Distribution of Assassination

History is filled with accounts of the sudden deaths of kings, ambitious ministers, and overactive generals. Casual inspection reveals that many of these sudden deaths were assassinations. A cursory journey in time through the eastern Caliphate, or the later Turkish Sultanate, or through the rise, decline, and fall of Byzantium or Rome would unearth large numbers of assassinations.

It is safe to suggest that many lesser figures than kings, ministers, and generals have been killed over the years, but unfortunately we know very little about them: who they were or even in what numbers they were killed. The situation is only relatively improved for the researcher in more modern times. In some parts of the world almost no public mention is made of assassinations on the lesser level. And after the event it is often difficult to disentangle what reports there are in such a way as to delineate accurately the cases of assassination.

The data that we would like to have would be accurate lists of assassinations at all levels—from national rulers to very local *politicos* —from all parts of the world and extended at least over a period of several hundred years, but it is operationally impossible to put together such lists. There is much that they might tell us: Must all political systems endure the whole spectrum of assassination or is this phenomenon to be found only at certain levels in some systems? (The latter is probably true, but we cannot support that conclusion with hard data over a long period of time.) Does the outbreak of assassination on one level generally spread in predictable ways and at predictable rates to other levels within the same political system? (There is too little evidence to give a definitive answer to this question.)

The difficulties of collecting data were made clear in late 1968 when we assembled a list of some 1,500 assassinations (and attempts) from the end of the First World War in 1918 through 1968 for the National Commission on the Causes and Prevention of Violence. This list included victims and would-be victims at all political levels (down to rural constables). Major limitations of time and resources made the list of necessity incomplete, and it seems evident that there is virtually no way to make this list reasonably complete for that fifty-year period.[1] It can easily be corrected and amplified, but there are no procedures or operations available to carry through to reasonable completion the enumeration of assassinations for this period. And this period is merely the past fifty years. If we cannot prepare such a list for this period, it seems an inescapable conclusion that no complete list for any comparable period could be prepared!

The incompleteness of our list stems from a number of factors: (1) Not all assassinations or attempts are reported in the Western press; this is especially true of secondary figures in relatively unimportant countries. (2) Press accounts are often garbled, incomplete, or otherwise inaccurate. (3) There is a continuing difficulty in distinguishing assassination from murder, especially when relatively few facts about the crime are available. (4) The spurious quality of many plots and some attempts creates difficulties.

All plots, whether genuine or not, were disregarded in our tabulation. Governments have been known to fabricate plots as an excuse to arrest opposition leaders or to destroy opposing political parties or organizations. Leaders of opposition groups may fabricate assassination plots to discredit the government. Attempts, on the other hand, were recorded. However, it is well to remember that some attempts are not reported and that there is always some question about an attempted assassination. Is a bomb placed outside the home of a prime minister a *genuine* attempt to assassinate him? Some attempts are never expected or intended to succeed. They may rather be efforts to intimidate an official or to draw attention to the seriousness of some political issue. Political figures have been known to invent or fabricate

1. We checked systematically the *New York Times Index,* the *Times of London Index, Le Monde, Facts on File,* and *Deadline Data.* A variety of other assassinations were known to us or came to our attention from other sources. This is especially true of the geographic areas of which we have special knowledge: Western Europe, the United States, the Middle East, and Latin America. The time period of fifty years between 1918 and 1968 was selected as contemporary and relatively long. It begins with one of the more conspicuous watersheds of modern history (the end of the First World War). Data for this period are far more complete than for any previous era.

attempts (as they have plots). It is impossible for us to distinguish among these possibilities.

A more serious question can be raised with respect to attempts: If an attempt in some particular case is genuine—for example, Theodore Roosevelt was fired upon and wounded during his political campaign in October, 1912—then it is distinguished from an assassination only in that it failed. In such cases the study of assassination rates becomes in part the study of the changing efficacy of medical practice and of the weapons employed. Assassination is a subset of attempts, and it is the latter that should be studied, but they elude us and we are restricted to the study of those attempts that succeed.

We are also, in the analysis that follows, limited to the study of only a part of the assassinations (during the fifty years after 1918) that we know about. We arbitrarily restrict our analysis to "chief executives" (and former chief executives) for only here are we reasonably certain that we have attained completeness. The following analysis applies therefore to chief executives and only indirectly to any other category of assassination.

The list in Appendix A has been extracted from the longer list of 1,500 assassinations prepared for the National Commission on the Causes and Prevention of Violence. It includes all those who could be termed chief executives: kings, prime ministers, regents, dictators, and so forth. It also includes former rulers. Attempts as well as successes are recorded.

Since it includes only "chief executives," Appendix A omits a number of very important killings of other types of political leaders. Some of these were probably more significant than the assassinations of chief executives in the same countries. A partial list for the same period of assassinations of political leaders other than chief executives will be found in Appendix B.

How are the assassinations of chief executives distributed in space and time? Disregarding attempts, for which our data may be less reliable than for successful assassinations, the number of cases in countries in existence throughout the fifty-year period is thirty-nine.[2] The

2. The thirty-nine cases are those indicated by asterisks in Appendix A. This fifty-year period will exclude 1918. The calculations are confined to countries that were in existence for the entire period. It would not be valid to compare the number of assassinations in countries in existence for the entire fifty-year period with the number in countries that existed for shorter periods of time, because in the latter there was obviously less opportunity for assassinations to take place.

distribution of these thirty-nine assassinations over the fifty-year period ranges from years with no assassinations to years with as many as three. This distribution is presented in Table 1.

TABLE 1: DISTRIBUTION OF 39 ASSASSINATIONS OF CHIEF EXECUTIVES BY NUMBER PER YEAR, 1919–68

Number of Assassinations per Year	Number of Years	Poisson Distribution
0	23	22.9
1	17	17.9
2	8	7.0
3	2	1.8
4	0	.4

$\bar{x} = .78$, $s^2 = .75$, $\chi^2(49 \text{ df}) = 28.96$
$\chi^2_{.99} = 28.94$

This sample has a mean of .78 assassinations per year, with a statistical variance (s^2) of .75. In a Poisson distribution, the mean equals the variance; in our sample these measurements are almost identical, indicating little departure of the actual sample from the theoretical Poisson distribution. It is possible to measure the "goodness of fit" by means of the Fisher variance test,[3] which is distributed as χ^2 (with $n - 1$ degrees of freedom). Application of this text yields χ^2 virtually at the .99 level of significance, which is to say that the random concurrence of the sample with the theoretical distribution as closely as this one would be a most unlikely event. An ideal Poisson distribution indicates the utter randomness of events in time, events which in themselves have a relatively low probability of occurrence. In this case it means that the assassination of a chief executive is a relatively improbable event and is virtually unpredictable in time. The distribution of such assassinations is utterly random.

If it can be argued that the above figures distribute themselves randomly in time, what about space? A list of sixty-five countries which maintained independent existence throughout the fifty-year period is used as a base.[4] How do the assassinations distribute themselves

---

3. For an explanation of this test see William G. Cochran, "Some Methods for Strengthening the Common χ^2 Tests," *Biometrics*, X (1954), 421–25.
4. (1) United States, (2) Canada, (3) Cuba, (4) Haiti, (5) Dominican Republic, (6) Mexico, (7) Guatemala, (8) Honduras, (9) El Salvador, (10)

The Distribution of Assassination 25

among these countries? Tables 2 and 3 offer some indications. The fit
with the theoretical distribution is not very good, and would in itself

TABLE 2: DISTRIBUTION OF 39 ASSASSINATIONS AMONG 65 COUNTRIES, 1919–68

Number of Assassinations per Country	Countries
4	Iraq
3	Guatemala, Japan
2	Afghanistan, Bulgaria, Egypt, France, Iran, Mexico, Rumania
1	Austria, Bolivia, Dominican Republic, Ireland, Nicaragua, Panama, Peru, Poland, Portugal, South Africa, Spain, Thailand, United States, Venezuela, Yemen
0	Remaining 40 countries

indicate a not quite random distribution of assassinations of chief
executives in the sixty-five countries.

One must remember that the number of countries has altered over
the years. In the spring of 1969 there existed a much larger number of

Nicaragua, (11) Costa Rica, (12) Panama, (13) Colombia, (14) Venezuela,
(15) Ecuador, (16) Peru, (17) Brazil, (18) Bolivia, (19) Paraguay, (20)
Chile, (21) Argentina, (22) Uruguay, (23) United Kingdom, (24) Ireland, (25)
Netherlands, (26) Belgium, (27) Luxembourg, (28) France, (29) Muscat and
Oman, (30) Switzerland, (31) Spain, (32) Portugal, (33) Germany, (34)
Poland, (35) Austria, (36) Hungary, (37) Czechoslovakia, (38) Italy, (39)
Albania, (40) Yugoslavia, (41) Greece, (42) Bulgaria, (43) Rumania, (44)
USSR, (45) Finland, (46) Sweden, (47) Norway, (48) Denmark, (49) Liberia,
(50) Ethiopia, (51) South Africa, (52) Iran, (53) Turkey, (54) Iraq, (55)
Egypt, (56) Saudi Arabia, (57) Yemen, (58) Afghanistan, (59) China, (60)
Mongolian People's Republic, (61) Japan, (62) Nepal, (63) Thailand, (64)
Australia, (65) New Zealand.

This list is based on Bruce M. Russet, J. David Singer, and Melvin Small,
"National Political Units in the Twentieth Century: A Standardized List," The
American Political Science Review, LXII (1968), 932–51. The basic criterion is
independent existence for the period 1918–68. However, of necessity, some alterations and interpretations have had to be made. Ireland, for example, has been
included, although she became independent only in 1922. Ethiopia and a number
of other areas suffered interludes of foreign domination but have been retained
in the list. Iraq has been included although technically she received her independence only in 1932; she had a king (Faisal I) from 1921 and was certainly
as independent in fact as Egypt (which became "independent" in 1922). Several
areas have been excluded although they are in the Russet, et al. list. These are
Andorra, Vatican City, San Marino, Liechtenstein, and Monaco. The resulting list
has sixty-five entries.

countries—126 were then members of the United Nations—than had existed at any previous time in this fifty-year period. Obviously there are more potential victims now than at any other time; ceteris paribus, we would expect the number of assassinations to rise. A reexamination

TABLE 3: DISTRIBUTION OF 39 ASSASSINATIONS BY NUMBER PER COUNTRY, 1919–68

Number of Assassinations per Country	Number of Countries	Poisson Distribution	Truncated Poisson Distribution
0	40	35.67	—
1	15	21.40	18.25
2	7	6.42	5.47
3	2	1.28	1.10
4	1	0.19	0.17
5	0	0.04	0.01

$\bar{x} = .60, s^2 = .838$

of the list in Appendix A indicates an additional seventeen assassinations of chief executives from countries not in existence throughout the whole period. If we combine these with our earlier list of thirty-nine, the distributions are those shown in Tables 4 and 5.

TABLE 4: DISTRIBUTION OF 56 ASSASSINATIONS OF CHIEF EXECUTIVES
BY NUMBER PER YEAR, 1919–68

Number of Assassinations per Year	Number of Years
0	19
1	15
2	8
3	7
4	1
5	0

It is probably more appropriate to weight the number of assassinations each year according to the number of independent countries in existence that year. This cannot be done with precision but esti-

TABLE 5: DISTRIBUTION OF 56 ASSASSINATIONS OF CHIEF EXECUTIVES BY COUNTRY, 1919–68

Number of Assassinations per Country	Number of Countries*
1	22
2	10
3	2
4	2
5	0

* The total number of countries considered is 76: the original list of 65, plus 11 other countries in which assassination occurred. Not included are countries in which assassination of chief executives did not occur.

mates can be made. Table 6 presents the distribution of fifty-six assassinations weighted in terms of numbers of political units.

TABLE 6: ASSASSINATION OF 56 (WEIGHTED 48) CHIEF EXECUTIVES BY NUMBER PER YEAR, 1919–68

Number of Assassinations per Year	Number of Years	Poisson Distribution
0	19	19.14
1	16	18.38
2	13	8.88
3	2	2.82
4	0	.84

$\bar{x} = .96$, $s^2 = .81$

What do all these tables tell us? There is considerable evidence that, taken over a fifty-year period, the assassination of chief executives tends to distribute itself randomly in time. There is must less randomness in the distribution of assassinations among political units, indicating that some political systems are more prone to the assassination of chief executives than others.

An examination of the actual year-by-year distribution reveals that assassinations tend to congregate together in pockets. About 70 percent of the assassinations (69 percent of the weighted number) during the fifty-year period took place in the four groups of years (eighteen years out of the total of fifty) shown in Table 7. The first period is the im-

TABLE 7: POCKETS OF ASSASSINATIONS, 1919–68

Period	Number of Assassinations	Weighted Number of Assassinations	Weighted Mean per Year
1919–23	9	9	1.80
1932–34	7	7	2.33
1946–51	12	10	1.67
1963–66	11	7	1.75
	39	33	

mediate aftermath of the First World War and the third period is the equivalent aftermath of the Second World War. The second period is the heart of the world depression. The fourth period is more difficult to characterize except to say that it has been a time of extreme insecurity and chaos. Those who subscribe to cyclic interpretations of history may be intrigued by the appearance of such a period of unrest, characterized by assassinations, about ten years after the period of chaos which immediately followed each of the world wars. None of these periods coincides with the great wars, although in all the periods wars of some magnitude were being fought. But all periods were characterized by turbulence, political systems in revolution or transition, and general political instability.

If the data in Table 6 are assumed to hold for the present period, then the probability of an assassination taking place within one year after the last one is .62 $(1 - e^{-\lambda x}$ where $\lambda = .96$ and $x = 1)$ and within two years, .85.[5] The probability of an assassination of some chief executive within any one year somewhere in the world is thus, on the basis of the last fifty-year period, high. In terms of space, the assassinations tend to cluster in countries and general areas marked by the beginnings of the modernization process and/or by the breakdown in political consensus. Table 8 offers a rough verification of this view.

The Middle East has been a cauldron of discontent since the end of the First World War, struggling against colonial domination and out-

5. For a full explanation of the Poisson distribution see Frank A. Haight, *Handbook of the Poisson Distribution* (New York: John Wiley and Sons, Inc., 1967). A discussion of the probability of Poisson events is found on p. 26.

TABLE 8: GEOGRAPHIC DISTRIBUTION OF 39 ASSASSINATIONS OF CHIEF EXECUTIVES, 1919–68

Middle East		Latin America		Southern and Eastern Europe		Western Europe, U.S., and South Africa		Far East	
Iraq	4	Guatemala	3	Rumania	2	France	2	Japan	3
Afghanistan	2	Mexico	2	Bulgaria	2	Ireland	1	Thailand	1
Egypt	2	Peru	1	Poland	1	Austria	1		
Iran	2	Venezuela	1	Spain	1	United			
Yemen	1	Bolivia	1	Portugal	1	States	1		
		Panama	1			South Africa	1		
		Nicaragua	1						
		Dominican							
		Republic	1						
Totals	11		11		7		6		4

moded social and economic structures. Latin America has exhibited many of the same symptoms of unrest and drive for change. Well over half the total number of successful assassinations of chief executives in our fifty-year period have occurred in these two areas. Southern and Eastern Europe, in turmoil during the interwar years, contribute another one-sixth of the total and Western Europe and the whole English-speaking world less than one-sixth. Only four cases were recorded in the Far East, but it must be remembered that much of this part of the world is taken up by China and that many of the countries of the East are excluded because they did not enjoy independent existence for the whole or major part of our time period. Japan witnessed three assassinations, all of which took place in the turbulent interwar years as Japan's old political system passed through a period of disintegration. We have made no definitive study of the correlation between politico-socio-economic factors and assassinations, so these observations are merely suggestions for further research on assassination and its relationship to political life.

4

The Impact of Assassination

Every political system faces the question of succession to public office, from the lowest to the highest positions. Mortality guarantees periodic replacement, and resignation and forced retirement of one kind or another add to the turnover of personnel. A ruler may abdicate for various reasons: Edward VIII because he was in love, Wilhelmina because of advanced age, Talal of Jordan because of ill health, Farouk because of fright. Death may likewise assume a variety of forms. The president or ruler of a state may simply die of natural causes (Franklin D. Roosevelt); he may die by accident (King Albert of Belgium, while mountain climbing); he may commit suicide (Vargas); he may be murdered, in the most ordinary sense of the term (the Roman Emperor Domitian was murdered by a freedman out of personal revenge); he may be executed (Prime Minister Menderes of Turkey); or he may be assassinated. All political systems are affected by such changes in personnel, some more than others; in some systems, the degree of change is affected by the mode of the succession process itself. Assassination, throughout history a relatively common though unpredictable occurrence, seems to result rather frequently in low or moderate political impact.

For want of better terminology we shall refer to assassinations as low-, middle-, and high-level assassinations.[1] Although assassinations, i.e., extralegal killings that are politically motivated, can and do occur at all levels of the political system, at the lower levels they are much more difficult to note and disentangle. They are not so often reported

1. The various levels of assassination may be roughly construed as follows: (a) high—chiefs and heads of state, top commanders of armed forces, important cabinet officers; (b) middle—middle-grade armed forces officers, less important cabinet officials, governors, nonofficial political leaders; (c) low—local political officials, field-grade officers, less important private citizens.

in the (world) press; they are more easily disguised as other forms of killing, and their effects are less easily noted. It must be evident that a high degree of low-level assassination, with significant impact on the immediate systemic environment, can exist alongside an absence of high-level assassination. Cuba of the 1940s and 1950s offers an excellent example.[2] Is the reverse true? Can there be a high degree of high-level assassination with a low degree of low-level assassination? A political system in which assassination has become institutionalized as a method of changing political leadership would not necessarily experience large amounts of violence on the lower levels. Indeed, every justification of tyrannicide excludes blanket endorsements of violence. Perhaps Japan of the 1930s offers an example. Japan was a rather orderly, highly disciplined society in which the high levels of assassination were exceptions to a general absence of internal violence. The impact on the system, however, was high; the assassinations destroyed the budding Japanese party and parliamentary system.[3]

However, a relatively high rate of high-level assassination has had little systemic political significance in the United States. Four American presidents have been assassinated and there have been attempts on the lives of four others. These events have varied somewhat in significance. Most historians would probably agree that the most significant of the four assassinations was that of Lincoln. Then follow (far below) those of Kennedy, Garfield, and McKinley. None of these has altered the American political system in any important ways.

How significant is assassination to the American political system? There are relatively few examples of other high-or medium-level assassinations in United States history.[4] Very few high-ranking military

2. William S. Stokes, "National and Local Violence in Cuban Politics," *The Southwestern Social Science Quarterly*, XXXIV (1953), 57–63.

3. See James R. Soukup, "Assassination in Japan," unpublished report prepared for the National Commission on the Causes and Prevention of Violence (edited version), Task Force I ,Vol. III, chap. 5, Appendix D (Mimeographed, 1968).

4. The excellent report by Rita James Simon prepared for the National Commission on the Causes and Prevention of Violence, "Political Violence Directed at Public Office Holders: A Brief Analysis of the American Scene," Task Force I, Vol. I, chap. I (Mimeographed, 1968), has been extremely useful. Miss Simon suggests that there is a "relationship between importance or prestige of position and likelihood of assassination." She adds, "One out of four presidents has been a target of assassination, compared to one out of every 166 governors and one out of 142 senators, and one out of every 1,000 congressmen." (pp. 13–14). Her figures are for 1790–1968. She records eight assassination attempts against presidents, eight against governors, eight against senators and nine against repre-

officers, cabinet members, congressmen, judges, or state governors
have been assassinated or even the targets of attempted assassinations.
In many such categories (the vice-presidency for example), there
have been none. Only one Supreme Court justice—Stephen J. Field of
California—has been attacked by an assassin. William Seward, the
secretary of state, the only cabinet member to be a target, was at-
tacked by the same group of conspirators who assassinated Lincoln.
Among senators, only Robert Kennedy and Huey Long have been as-
sassinated, although John Bricker was shot and wounded in 1947.
Eight governors have been attacked and three killed, the last in 1905.
In 1959 someone attempted to shoot Governor J. Lindsay Almond of
Virginia and in 1963 John Connally, governor of Texas, was shot by
Lee Harvey Oswald, the assassin of President John F. Kennedy. On
the other hand, a somewhat larger number of low-level assassinations
have occurred—police chiefs, mayors (an attempt was made on *Mayor*
Hubert H. Humphrey in 1947), and so forth.

Rita James Simon has conducted a thorough investigation of the
problem of assassination in this country. She concludes that, compared
to other kinds of violence in the United States, assassination rates have
been low.[5] The exception has been at the presidential level. Lincoln,
Garfield, McKinley, and Kennedy have been killed; Jackson, the two
Roosevelts, and Truman had attempts made on their lives; recent presidents endure virtually thousands of threats each year. This exception
has caused many to ascribe to the American scene a climate for assassination, a "sickness," a proclivity for this kind of violence.

The deaths of four presidents and attempts on the lives of others cannot be minimized. Nevertheless, except on this level, assassination
cannot be said to have any marked incidence or any marked political
effects in the United States.

---

sentatives. Among the representatives, five of these (in 1954) were the result of
random shots fired in the House of Representatives by Puerto Rican nationalists;
one other involved an exrepresentative. Some of the other examples listed (for
other categories) are more properly assaults—and some of these are marginal.
Miss Simon's figures represent a maximum limit of attempted assassination; we are
inclined to revise many of them considerably downward. Altogether they support
our general contention that—in spite of the American reputation for violence—
the United States is remarkably assassination-free (except on the presidential
level). It must be remembered that political opposition is free and unfettered
in the United States. Campaigns are often bitter and vituperative. Opportunities
abound for assassination among an inflated group of officeholders. And yet, few
are assassinated.

5. Ibid., pp. 4–5.

Even on the presidential level it can easily be argued that assassination has had no systemic effects of any consequence. Only in the case of Lincoln could this thesis be challenged, and in that case conclusions are not easily reached. Even Lincoln's assassin conforms to the pattern of other American presidential assassins—persons of extreme mental aberration. Undoubtedly Booth viewed his own motives as political and patriotic, but it seems clear that his mind was deranged. Not all assassins have deranged minds; but all assassins of American presidents have been so burdened.

American history has been full of "times of crises"; the present period, with its generation gaps, student revolts, and violent dissents, is only different in detail from periods in the past. And assassination as a general weapon has never characterized any of those periods.

Types of Impact: Personal and Systemic

Assassination is obviously a symbiotic relationship between persons: victim and assailant. But the public character of the victim makes it more than that. The environment, as well as the individuals involved, is affected by assassination. The degree and nature of that involvement is the concern of this chapter.

Obviously a successful assassination destroys some victim. Whether high in political circles or low, his life is gone, the lives and patterns of his family have been disrupted, and his community is without his services. His assassin, if he survives, can receive satisfaction from having accomplished his primary task. Quite often the assassin can derive no other satisfaction, for the political repercussions of the event may either move entirely beyond his control or prove repugnant or even incomprehensible to him. Even when an assassination fails, numerous effects can be discerned from the attempt. It cannot be demonstrated conclusively, given the evidence available at present, that an assassination or an unsuccessful attempt either encourages or discourages attempts by others. Evidence is available, however, to suggest that some assassinations tend to provoke other attempts. Killing some political figure becomes a challenge. The attempt kindles the imagination of other potential assassins and causes them to think of this act among *possible* alternatives of action. There seems every reason to believe that an assassination or even an attempt makes more likely, in the immediate spatial and temporal environs, another attempt against the same man or against still another victim. Anarchist propagandists in

the late nineteenth and early twentieth centuries appear to have
sparked a wave of assassinations and attempted assassinations against
prominent world leaders, including ten chiefs of state.[6] The Secret
Service does not circulate information about the many thousands of
threatening letters it receives against the president's life. Would an
examination of these records indicate threatening pulsations during
those periods when other assassinations were taking place? In another
context, a dominant though threatened political faction might be
driven by desperation to successive attempts to remove a powerful
opponent. In something over ten months (from November 1, 1963, to
September 12, 1964) five assassination attempts were directed against
the life of René Barrientos, chief of the Bolivian air force and political
power contender. In March, 1965, Barrientos, by then provisional
president and presidential candidate for a constitutional term, was the
object of still another attack. It too failed, and the attacks ceased as
Barrientos became solidly entrenched in power.[7]

An attempted assassination may change some personal patterns of
behavior among political leaders. The victim who survives an attempt
is no longer the same. He becomes more wary, more concerned with
his safety. A random shot fired over Lincoln's head in 1863 frightened
him into several days of circumspection. The attempt on Truman's
life in 1950 surely made him more aware of the danger of his position.
Undoubtedly it spurred the Secret Service to more energetic precautions. But such incidents do not seem to have changed the basic

6. Barbara Tuchman, *The Proud Tower. A Portrait of the World Before the
War, 1890–1914* (New York: The Macmillan Co., 1966) maintains that there were
no contacts between the theorists and the assassins nor among the assassins themselves, but rather that the theorists had so dramatized the division in society that
"desperate or deluded men" responded by using the extreme form of violence in
pursuit of the "enchanting vision of a stateless society." (chap. II, "The Idea
and the Deed: The Anarchists 1890–1914," pp. 63–113).

7. As the National Revolutionary Movement (MNR), which had governed
Bolivia since the revolution of 1952, began to fragment during 1963, Victor Paz,
the president of the country and the head of the party, at first encouraged
Barrientos to seek the vice-presidential nomination of the MNR as Paz' running
mate for the upcoming 1964 presidential elections. When Barrientos demonstrated
real political strength, Paz came to fear him and denied him the nomination. By
March, 1964, however, Barrientos had accumulated such strong support from
several MNR factions that he forced his candidacy on Paz. Paz and Barrientos
were duly elected and inaugurated, but the continuing disruption of the MNR
led to violence and a coup in November. Barrientos assumed office as provisional
president. Although admittedly circumstantial, the evidence points strongly to the
Paz faction of the MNR as being responsible for the six assassination attempts
against Barrientos.

political style of most American political figures in exposing themselves to the public. Thus a Robert Kennedy or Nelson Rockefeller
finds it impossible to conduct a campaign under tight security measures. Moreover, "the man who repeatedly and publicly proclaims his
vulnerability to assassination may be encouraging the delusional and
grandiose isolate who dreams of accomplishing at least one important
and publicly recognized act in his lifetime." [8]

In addition to its impact on the persons immediately involved, assassination also affects the political system and society at large. One must
distinguish, however, between what we may call "shock" and what
are true systemic alterations. Any assassination rather profoundly disturbs the emotional state of the people.[9] This "shock" manifests itself
in many ways: increased symptomatic mental disturbances,[10] enormous public displays of grief, political exhortations to remember the
fallen leader, possibly riots and demonstrations, attempts at revenge
(Ruby's murder of Oswald, for example), public trials of the assail-
ants, the public renaming of streets, airports, or parks after the dead
hero.

It may be argued, and with some justification, that some of these
actions are as much *responses* to shock as they are shock itself. But
they are *responses to shock rather than to the assassination* and as
such must be considered in conjunction with shock rather than as impact to the system. A high degree of shock and its responses permit a
system to absorb the assassination of a leader. Shock is a ritualized
substitute for change. A leader has been struck down. People are
stunned, angry, eager to do something. Public and lengthy funerals;

8. Alfred E. Weiz and Robert L. Taylor, "The Assassination Matrix," *Stanford
Today* (Winter, 1969), p. 14.

9. "Shock" is manifested in various ways. The shock displayed at the deaths of
the Kennedy brothers is instructive. First stunned disbelief, then guilt feelings and
emotional catharsis came at the heels of the violent acts themselves. For many
Americans the latter feelings could be channeled into a sentimental (but nonetheless real) attachment for the surviving Kennedys. But note also that the shock
stemming from the assassination of the President led to an "impact," the 1964
legislative program of President Johnson.

In the Middle East, shock assumes certain almost ritualistic patterns. The assassination of an Arab chief of state would typically be followed by demonstrations
(with peripheral violence perhaps being directed against Western embassies),
lamentations in the press, an impressive funeral, and then a rapid adjustment to
the political realities of the succeeding regime. The death of Gandhi in 1947 resulted in large-scale, bloody rioting but had little noticeable impact on the Indian
political system. If enough anguish is exhibited, what more is needed?

10. This phenomenon was reported by psychiatrists after the death of John
Kennedy in 1963.

numerous displays of anguish and remorse; riots, pillage, or the burning of some symbolic property: all these acts are substitutes for political change. In these ways the energies produced by an assassination may be sublimated in shock rather than result in systemic change. None of the above effects is unimportant, but to the political scientist, the environmental changes wrought in the political system compel interest. Such changes may not occur at all, or the system may collapse because of the sudden removal of some individual. The latter occurrence is certainly rare in history, but most political systems register some measurable reaction to assassinations. Assassination may force justice into more draconian channels or the government into reprisals and vengeance. Stalin, for example, used the Kirov assassination as the excuse to launch a long series of purge trials in the Soviet Union.[11]

The Problem of Assessing "Impact"

It is exceedingly difficult to measure the impact on political systems of a wide variety of events, including assassination. To a greater or lesser degree every political system is in a constant state of change. How much change may be attributed to any single event, even one as traumatic as an assassination? It must be evident that not all change, merely because of propinquity in time and space, is attributable to a given event.

A distinction must always be made, moreover, between the immediate significance of an assassination and the significance that history ultimately assigns to it. We must be judicious in assessing what

11. The evidence is overwhelming that Stalin ordered the assassination. Apparently Stalin ordered Yagoda (head of the NKVD) to organize the attempt; in turn, Yagoda chose Zaporozhets, who was the assistant to the head of the Leningrad NKVD. Zaporozhets insisted that he be given his instructions directly by Stalin; presumably this was done. At any event Zaporozhets, by combing the NKVD files on those who had been reported as making threats against the regime, found "a disillusioned and embittered young Communist," Leonid Nikolayev. He was furnished a gun and his contacts with Kirov facilitated. On his third attempt (December 1, 1934) he succeeded in shooting his victim.

Nikolayev was quickly liquidated and ultimately, of course, both Yagoda and Zaporozhets were executed by Stalin. The Kirov assassination permitted Stalin to launch the first of the big purges.

A reliable and lucid account of the Kirov assassination and its aftermath is to be found in Robert Conquest, *The Great Terror: Stalin's Purge of the Thirties* (New York: The Macmillan Co., 1968). See particularly chap. 2. (The brief quotation above is from p. 47.)

historical events might have occurred had the assassination not taken place. It is after all much easier to determine what did occur subsequent to the assassination. The assassination of Napoleon in March, 1796—the Directory had just given him carte blanche in Italy and he had just married Josephine—would not have been *at the time* very significant to the French political system. Napoleon's assassination in 1806 would of course have been enormously more significant. We must also distinguish between the systemic significance of a *particular* assassination and that of the genus *assassination*. Because individual assassinations are often so dramatic and indeed may be (as individual events) very significant to the system, it may seem tempting to argue that assassination as a dimension of violence is systemically significant. But this does not necessarily follow.

Our means of measurement are necessarily crude. We must attempt to separate what appears to be pertinent specific change from its background of general change. Where there is some great quantum of change, particularly in new directions, this becomes somewhat easier to do. But where the magnitude of change is slighter, the task becomes one of considerable difficulty. Regardless of the difficulties of measurement and classification, the following rough categories seem to have some merit:

1. Some assassinations produce *no discernible changes*. The assassination of Verwoerd in South Africa seems to be an example of this. Aside from the fact that Verwoerd was dead and someone else had taken his place as prime minister, virtually no unambiguous impact could be noted. In fact in the immediate aftermath of the assassination there were fewer cabinet shifts and changes than in the preceding year of Verwoerd's administration. It may be argued that the first response of the system was to become more rigid and inflexible; if true, this constitutes impact, but it cannot be easily demonstrated.

2. In most assassinations *personnel changes* occur that would not have taken place otherwise. The essence of this type of change is not merely the removal of the victim. Depending on the circumstances, his successor (or superior where the victim's position is low enough so that superiors rather than successors make the decisions) may dismiss a few key personnel or he may take the opportunity to sweep out all those who had been responsible for policy decisions. In other situations the successor may wish to emphasize his continuity with the regime of the fallen leader, but he may not be able to hold on to all of his high-level officers. The succession of Lyndon Johnson after the death of John

Kennedy is a case in point: Johnson went to extraordinary lengths to minimize prominent personnel changes in order to identify with the slain president. He was only partially successful.

3. Assassination impact may be measured in some cases by the degree of *policy change* brought about in the political system. Policy changes are something more than personnel changes and something less than systemic changes. Of course in a trivial sense changes in personnel usually result in changes in policy, and often policy changes can be brought about by a change in the personnel making and implementing them. The key factor here is where the emphasis is placed. Moreover, policies may be changed only instrumentally; that is, it is not goals so much that are altered as the means of attaining them. Many of the decisions of the regent, Prince Paul, in Yugoslavia after Alexander's death, reflect this type of change. On the other hand, goals themselves may be altered by an assassination—and this may indeed be the assassin's only object.

Policy may change because the victim was its most eminent and vocal supporter and there are few left to give it the energetic support it needs. But policy may also change because the assassination represents in the minds of the survivors a discrediting of the old policy. It may change as well when the succeeding regime uses the assassination as an excuse to embark on new policies that the victim himself would have endorsed had he lived. Indeed, his assassination may provide the moral authority without which his goals could not have been achieved at all. And policy changes can come about because of assassinations at lower levels of government or outside the government entirely. The assassination of the Socialist parliamentary leader Matteoti in Italy in the 1920s resulted in some basic policy changes in the government; it may even be argued that Matteoti's murder brought the end to meaningful parliamentary government in Italy.

4. A few assassinations produce profound alterations in the political system in which they occur. *Systemic changes* are not mere changes in personnel or policy but are rather more fundamental structural alterations in the political system itself. The abolition of political parties, the abrogating of constitutional civil liberties, the promulgation of new ideological fonts: all these and many more are the kinds of systemic changes we have in mind. The changes must be major alterations in the "rules" of the systemic game. The assassination of Trujillo certainly unleashed systemic changes in the Dominican Republic. So did the assassinations of Kirov in the USSR,[12] Sir Lee Stack in Egypt,

12. Stalin issued a decree dated December 1, 1934 (the day of Kirov's death), *without consulting the Politburo,* which directed that investigations against oppositionists be speeded up, that the judiciary not impede the death sentences to

Lumumba in the Congo, Francisco Madero in Mexico, and Julius Caesar in ancient Rome.

5. An extreme combination of the previous two categories is assassination that leads not only to political systemic changes (e.g., the Dominican Republic) but also to *social revolution*. We have no explicit cases, but the assassination of Obregón in Mexico apparently opened the way for social and economic innovations as well as systemic political changes. When Calles' dictatorship was forced to give way to new and younger members of the revolutionary movement, the new leadership under Cardenas, as we have seen, began to institutionalize the political system. In addition it undertook substantial socioeconomic reforms, including a vast program of land redistribution, the organization of national rural and urban labor unions, and the nationalization of several key industries like petroleum production and the railroads. In these respects the decade following the assassination of Obregón constituted the most radical period of the Mexican revolution.

One may distinguish between systemic impacts that are largely political in character and those that are more specifically socioeconomic. An assassination that brought about major economic reforms would fall into the latter category.

6. Occasionally *a political system disappears* in the aftermath of an assassination. It is not easy to locate clear-cut examples of this rare phenomenon—rare because political systems are never easily destroyed by single events. It is tempting to point to the assassination of the Archduke Franz Ferdinand and his wife as leading to the destruction of a number of political systems, including those of Serbia and Austria-Hungary. But more accurately this assassination merely facilitated hostilities among states and the ensuing war resulted in the destruction of a number of systems. The example points up the fact that political systems are generally destroyed by war with external foes or by revolution. Neither war nor revolution is easily achieved through assassination, although assassination may become an excuse for actions already anticipated. Another example in this category is the assassination of Engelbert Dollfuss, the chancellor of Austria, in 1934. Although the Austrian political system limped along until 1938, when the *Anschluss* occurred, Dollfuss' removal paved the way for the demise of the state.

---

be handed down, and that indeed these sentences be consummated immediately upon their ordering. Conquest says, "This was the first exercise in Stalin's new technique, by which the state of emergency was used to justify personal, and technically unconstitutional, action. In the circumstances any attempt at disapproval would have been extremely difficult. And thus even what poor guarantees Soviet law gave to 'enemies of the State' were destroyed" (Conquest, op. cit., p. 48). Prior to this time, Stalin had felt it necessary to act through the Politburo, but after Kirov's death the Politburo quickly faded as a restraint on Stalin's actions.

What we have tried to describe is the continuum between the extremes of no change and complete change. In actual cases it is difficult to determine precisely what systemic impacts have occurred.

What Accounts for Differences in Impact?

The inchoate nature of our research does not offer sufficient hard data to substantiate the theories suggested by the data we do possess. What of course is needed is a detailed consideration of amounts and kinds of assassinations and their *impacts* distributed among various kinds of political systems. Although there seems little doubt that the nature of the impact varies with the system, we cannot demonstrate this precisely.

In political systems where all forms of political violence are scarce, an isolated assassination is likely to have little significant impact on the system. But whatever impact it has will be that of a unique event, hardly likely to be repeated. Because it is unique a certain amount of what we have called "shock" is generated, but the impact tends to be low. It is tempting to suggest a priori, that the energy of an assassination spends itself either in shock or in impact, but rarely in both.

Far different is the political system in which assassination has become routine. In such a case the shock value of assassination tends to be minimized. But this is not to say that there is no impact on the system. Such an impact may, in fact, be very high. In many ways the Japan of the 1930s represented almost a classic case of "government by assassination." Assassination became a tool of political implementation so commonplace that its shock value was minimal.

We pose the basic question: how significant is assassination as a factor in the political process? Obviously assassination can only be significant where it has been attempted. It does not exist as a homogeneous phenomenon everywhere and at all times. But where it does exist, what is its functional relationship to the political system? Only empirical investigation can reveal the nature of the functional relationship.

It may help to make use of the term *political capability*.[13] Political

13. Terms like *capability* and *development* are commonplace in the current literature of comparative political systems. There is considerable controversy over their use and meaning, however. We owe our own predilection for the former term to its use in Gabriel A. Almond and G. Bingham Powell, Jr., *Comparative Politics: A Developmental Approach* (Boston: Little, Brown and Company, 1966) although our mutual understandings of the term perhaps no longer coincide. On

systems vary in their capability to meet challenges (which may range from economic crises to war and assassination). *Political development* may be thought of as any change which results in an increase of capability. A system high in capability is one that is able to absorb assassination with impacts clustered at the lower end of the continuum just described. This of course does not mean that capable systems, because they can absorb assassination, will or will not be burdened by that event.

We must not confuse capability with sophistication. A relatively primitive political system can be a capable one, given its traditional environment, and may appear to be less affected by an assassination than a society less capable but more sophisticated and more complicated. Such a state of affairs has led some, quite erroneously, to attribute to primitive systems a *propensity for assassination*. It disturbs these observers to discover in such systems a lack of proper (i.e., modern) shock; they view absorption ability as an element of primitiveness, when it should be thought of simply as an element of capability. Actually our data suggests that stabilized systems (whether primitive or sophisticated) show the impact of assassination much less than do those in transition. A political system involved in some pattern of modernization is much more likely to be affected by all sorts of events than is that which is either in premodernization stages or which has already matured to some sophisticated level.

Whatever the degree of development, modernization, capability, or sophistication of a regime, it appears that the level of institutionalization of the political system (as contrasted to the level of personalism exercised) constitutes a key factor in determining the impact of a high-level assassination. In systems where institutions are strong, it is difficult to conceive catastrophic effects resulting from assassinations, except when one state uses assassination as an excuse to attack an-

---

development, Almond and Powell say, "*Development* results when the existing structure and culture of the political system is unable to cope with the problem or challenge which confronts it without further structural differentiation and cultural secularization. It should also be pointed out that a decline in the magnitude or a significant change in the content of the flow of inputs may result in 'development' in the negative or regressive sense. [We use the term *political decay;* see Samuel P. Huntington, *Political. Order in Changing Societies* (New Haven: Yale University Press, 1968) or his earlier article, 'Political Development and Political Decay,' *World Politics,* XVII, no. 3 (April, 1965), 386–430.] The capabilities of the political system may decline or be overloaded; roles and structures may atrophy; the culture may regress to a more traditional pattern of orientation" (p. 34).

other. The United States has weathered the assassinations of four presidents, one of which (Lincoln's) took place at a most crucial period. (Even Lincoln's death probably only intensified and expedited the move of the Radical Republicans for a harsher reconstruction policy, rather than caused this policy shift.) Changes to the system by these assassinations have been minimal. On the other hand, a personalized political system is more often subject to grave repercussions from the assassination of a chief of state. The removal of Trujillo of the Dominican Republic destroyed his regime and his family's political powers. We cannot push the argument too far, however, because the murder of Somoza in Nicaragua produced no important changes; our conclusion is that personalism may be a necessary, but not sufficient, condition for high impact.

In most political systems, institutions vary in degree of strength and substance. But even strong, relatively old states may be weakened by the presence of multinational or multireligious factions, socioeconomic unrest, and tribalism. Canada, which has almost no assassination, possesses disruptive potentialities in the French-Canadian (Catholic) minority concentrated in Quebec; Iraq has its Kurds; Malaysia its Chinese; the Sudan its blacks; Italy its South Tyroleans—all nonintegrable national minorities. India offers an example of an incredible religious, racial, and linguistic mixture. The existence of any heterogeneous mixture of this kind generates friction which may well on occasion not only produce assassination, but more importantly may react to assassination (when it occurs) by escalating factional strife.

The impact of assassination is also of course a function of the nature of the opposition within the state. The sophisticated acceptance of political opposition is generally restricted to advanced systems; the concept of *loyal opposition* is extremely difficult to comprehend in a political system undergoing substantial change or facing irreconcilable conflicts. Where opposition is forbidden, its parties outlawed, its leaders muzzled, its ideas sequestered—and this is not an unfair description of a great many political systems today—then a traumatic event like an assassination becomes the opportunity to force changes that would be otherwise impossible. There may be organized opposition even where it is outlawed, and if this opposition is prepared to act promptly in the aftermath of the assassination of an important figure, substantial changes can be brought about. Organized opposition groups may themselves resort to assassination; the Muslim Brotherhood in Egypt continues to be accused of fomenting assassination attempts against Nasser. In the 1930s Stalin constantly accused the Opposition of attempting to assassinate him and there may well have been a germ of truth in the accusation. On the other hand, mature political opposition, like that in the United States, by refusing to exploit a situation emanating from assassination, assists in reducing possible impact to the system.

The impact also depends upon the assassin and the conspiracy (if any) that has produced him. What kind of person was the assassin (a Bonnier for example)? What ties did he have with opposition groups? What political strengths did he possess? It is apparent here too that where a conspiracy does exist the choice of the actual assassin is of importance. He should be an individual with a knowledge of weapons, careless of his own life, strong-willed, and able to carry out a mission in the face of complications and hazards. (Such a man was von Stauffenberg.) It must be said that not all assassins are very competent. Many attempts are failures because the assassin loses his nerve or bungles his assignment. All of these considerations are pertinent to the success of the attempt and indirectly to the impact on the system.

An assassination isolated from other political acts—that of Verwoerd in South Africa or of President Kennedy in the United States—is rarely of significance. In stable systems, the assassin who seriously expects his act to bring about changes is courting disappointment. Of course, where his motive is vengeful or symbolic in character, systemic changes are irrelevant. The isolated assassin must accomplish his goals by the very act itself, and this is rarely possible in any but the most personal and psychological terms. Whenever more than the mere elimination of the victim is desired some kind of follow-up must be attempted. The planning of more than one individual is necessary for postassassination acts like attempting to seize power. John Wilkes Booth and his co-conspirators planned a number of assassinations, of which Lincoln's was the chief, and expected to be able to exploit the chaotic situation they anticipated. Moreover, the assassination itself may proceed much more smoothly from the collective effort of a group, as with the assassination of King Alexander. Since we know about some conspiracies, it is scarcely surprising that many persons imagine conspiracies to exist when in fact they do not. When John Kennedy was killed in Dallas in 1963, the first, and natural, thought of his successor, Johnson, was that the plot might still be unfolding and that he too was to be its victim. A half-dozen years later a determined district attorney in New Orleans, Jim Garrison, continued his crusade to demonstrate the existence of a conspiracy involving a number of individuals other than Oswald, but a jury decided quickly that he had failed to make his point. The guilty plea of James Earl Ray for the death of Martin Luther King, Jr., does not lessen speculation about a conspiracy in that case.[14]

If the assassin is a factor in determining impact, a much more obvious factor is the victim himself. All things being equal, the potential impact of an assassination is roughly proportional to the position occupied by the victim. The death of a mayor of a provincial town may well have a local impact of some magnitude, but it is unlikely that this will splash over into wider circles. National impact generally results from the death of a national leader. In addition to the position that he occupies, the role that the victim plays at the time of his death is important. If his role is purely ceremonial it is difficult to imagine any major impact from his death. The assassination of Queen Elizabeth II would produce enormous shock but would have, almost certainly, little measurable impact on the political system. Furthermore, is the victim near the beginning or the end of his political career? If toward the end, his departure as a political force may already have been discounted and consequently may evoke little impact response. If at the beginning, his political strengths are yet undeveloped and the impact of his removal may be relatively inconsequential.

The nature of the regime must also be considered in assessing impacts. We are not here speaking of the institutionalization of the political system, but rather of the nature of the congeries of political actors who occupy the chief positions in the system; in short, the regime. Is it cohesive, well-knit, likely to act decisively and in unison? Or is it divided within itself by petty quarrels, containing restless and ambitious men with conflicting claims of loyalties? What about the political heirs of the victim? Are they able, determined, and forceful? Contrast here the sons of Somoza in Nicaragua with the sons of Trujillo in the Dominican Republic; their respective abilities made a vast difference in the outcome.

Who commands the armed forces? How loyal are they to the regime? Do their leaders have independent ambitions? Are they willing to exploit political crises stemming from assassinations? What are the relations of the assassin and his victim to the armed forces? What control does the regime have over the modes of communication? How

14. See for example, the remarks of Judge W. Preston Battle as reported in the *New York Times*, March 17, 1969, p. 23.

effective is it in propaganda? Assassinations can sometimes even be disguised by a clever and powerful regime. The assassination of Beria in 1953 was certainly well stage-managed; the full facts have never been disclosed. (There were other, earlier, examples in the Soviet Union: Kuybyshev in January, 1935; Orzhonikidze in February, 1937; and Gorki in June 1936.)

Obviously, we have raised more questions than we have answered. It is impossible to present more than informed observations on many of these matters until a vast quantity of data is added to what we already have. We do believe, however, that our case studies throw much light on questions relating to the degree of impact of assassination on political systems and suggest explanations for the difference in degree among countries.

Of our ten case studies, the three with the lowest impact fall in countries with very different political systems—Nicaragua, South Africa, and the United States. At the time that these assassinations occurred, however, the three countries exhibited some vitally similar characteristics. Their political systems had the support of the vast majority of the politically active population, the political opposition to the regime in power was largely nonrevolutionary, and the potentially revolutionary elements were weak and fragmented. Second, the assassin (or assassins) was either deranged or deluded, and except in Nicaragua, made not even the slightest efforts to follow up the assassination with other kinds of political action. In Nicaragua the planning was ludicrous. As a result in all these cases the conspirators were quickly apprehended and brought to trial. Policy and political personnel shifts resulting from the assassinations were at most minor.

Half of our case studies (five) seem to involve moderate impact. These five cases are again from very different kinds of political systems—Mexico, Yugoslavia, the United States, France, and Egypt—but all the systems were undergoing relatively severe tensions and strains at the time the assassinations occurred. At the same time, the several societies and political systems were neither so badly fragmented nor so weakened as to collapse as a result of the removal of an important political figure. In the case of France, foreign occupation forces limited the degree of change permissible; continued army support probably propped up Farouk of Egypt and prevented wide-scale disorders when the government removed its leading opponent.

The two remaining case studies have resulted in substantial political changes. In both countries—the Congo and the Dominican Republic

—the political and social systems were badly fragmented and the removal of the national leader led to collapse. The assassin and those implicated in the assassination either were themselves important political personages or had connections with powerful leaders in their respective countries. Opposition groups were well formed, powerful, and revolutionary. The assassinations of Lumumba and Trujillo brought new persons and groups to power, resulted in major policy changes, and led to substantial alterations in the political systems themselves.

5

The Assassination
of Henrik F. Verwoerd
# of South Africa

The Assassination

On September 6, 1966, as the parliament of the Republic of South Africa was about to open its session for the day, a parliamentary messenger hurriedly approached the prime minister's desk. Dr. Henrik F. Verwoerd, the prime minister, calmly watched the man draw near and leaned forward as if to hear what the messenger had to report. At that point, the messenger lunged toward the prime minister, half jumped on his desk, and struck him with a long dagger. F. W. Waring, a member of the cabinet and a former athlete, sprang on the assassin and pulled him off. With the help of other members, he knocked the messenger to the floor. The attacker was disarmed and carried out. In the meantime, Dr. Verwoerd, ashen-faced, slumped forward on his desk. Four medical members of parliament rushed to aid him, one of them giving him mouth-to-mouth resuscitation. Within minutes stretcher-bearers carried Verwoerd to an awaiting ambulance, but the prime minister was dead on arrival at the hospital.

Profound shock was expressed by all elements of South African society, but the country remained quiet. After several days of negotiation with the majority National party, the minister of justice, J. B. Vorster, was selected to succeed as head of the party and prime minister. The transition was smooth and basic policies were continued. In the three years since the death of Prime Minister Verwoerd there has been no significant impact resulting from the assassination in terms of systemic policy, or even personnel changes.

The Life and Times of Henrik F. Verwoerd

The Republic of South Africa is a product of Dutch and later British colonization of the African cape area.[1] Subjugation of the native population and ultimate conquest by the British of the Dutch led to the creation in 1910 of the Union of South Africa as a self-governing member of the British Commonwealth. However, an important segment of the Boer (Dutch) leadership remained unreconciled to the British victory and sought first to regain control through political office, to deny political rights to all nonwhites, and finally to lead the country out of the Commonwealth. One of the prime architects of the final success and realization of these aims was Henrik F. Verwoerd.

Born in Amsterdam, the Netherlands, on September 8, 1901, Henrik Verwoerd was taken with his family to South Africa in 1903 by his father, a missionary of the Dutch Reformed Church.[2] After graduating from the University of Stellenbosch with a major in psychology, he took advanced work at the universities of Hamburg, Leipzig, and Berlin. At the age of twenty-six he returned to a professorship at Stellenbosch in applied psychology and during the next decade apparently developed certain theories about race and race relations that he was later to apply politically.

Verwoerd's political career dates from 1937 when he became editor of a Johannesburg newspaper, *Die Transvaaler*. In the ten years of his editorship he made the paper a leading organ of the then minority National party, which had been formed in 1934 by Daniel Malan as the political vehicle of Afrikaans nationalism to oppose British and British-Dutch political organizations. The party opposed South Africa's entry into the Second World War and throughout the war the Verwoerd newspaper was openly anti-British and thinly disguised pro-Nazi. Despite Allied victory in 1945, anti-British sentiments continued to grow and political conflict centered more and more around British and Afrikaans party affiliations. The election of 1948 marked the turning point. For the first time Daniel Malan's National party won a parliamentary majority and Malan became prime minister. Verwoerd

1. One of the best and most recent studies of South Africa is Alex Hepple, *South Africa: A Political and Economic History* (New York: Frederick A. Praeger, Inc., 1966).
2. Obituaries containing considerable biographical information of Verwoerd are to be found in *New York Times*, September 7, 1966, p. 16, and *Times* (London), September 7, 1966, p. 14.

lost his own race for office but was named a government senator and appointed to the cabinet as minister of native affairs. In this key post, which he held for eight years, Verwoerd became the architect of a policy of race separation known as apartheid. By a series of laws, apartheid came to mean the virtual disfranchisement of all nonwhites; their limitation in jobs, education, property ownership, movement, and places of residence; and the establishment of reserves for the blacks in which all tribal Africans would theoretically hold citizenship. Only one such reserve has ever been formed, and while its leaders have limited powers of internal government, all decisions can be reversed by the South African government.

In the meantime the National party was returned to power in 1958 for a third successive term, with an increased majority and this time with Verwoerd as prime minister. In 1959 he pushed through the Promotion of Bantu Self Government Act authorizing the tribal reserves, suppressed black agitation with bloodshed at Sharpeville in 1960, and, taking South Africa out of the Commonwealth, proclaimed it a republic in 1961. In the eight years of his premiership, Verwoerd was the unchallenged political leader of white South Africa. He led the country far down the road toward a police state, but he led willing followers who feared the black and Coloured majority of the population. Even the major opposition party did not object vigorously to most government policies. Although Verwoerd did not arouse affection in his political supporters, he inspired confidence as a "quiet almost gentle purveyor of extreme policies," advocating them "with sincerity and with the quiet avuncular air of a family lawyer." [3]

In his last years in office, Verwoerd further consolidated his political position with massive electoral majorities and a growing economy. Some observers see the Sharpeville incident as a turning point. The massacre of March, 1960, coupled with an unsuccessful attempt on Verwoerd's life in April and continuing black demonstrations, led the chamber of commerce of Johannesburg to urge the government to begin consultation with the blacks. Verwoerd, however, quickly recovered; the would-be assassin, a white man, had no relationship to the black demonstrations, and the black activists themselves were quickly overpowered. Soon thereafter the Congo went into crisis in the summer of 1960, and the other independent governments of black Africa developed severe problems that limited their threatened assault on South Africa. At the same time, the economy began to boom with

3. *Times* (London), September 7, 1966, p. 14.

the expansion of industry and increases in foreign investments. The closing of the Suez Canal in 1967 was a bonanza for South African ports, and the Middle East and other trouble spots even took United Nations' pressures off South African administration of the territory of Southwest Africa.[4] On the day of his death Verwoerd was at the height of his power in a country calm and prosperous for its white citizens, calm and poverty-stricken for its black subjects, and calm and bitter for its East Indians and Coloureds.

The Assassin

Despite its social and racial conflicts, South Africa has not witnessed many assassinations or assassination attempts, at least since the creation of the country in 1910. Some chieftains and other tribal leaders were murdered for collaborating with the Verwoerd government during black protests in the early 1960s against the apartheid policy.[5] In April, 1960, just after the Sharpeville incident, an English-born white farmer shot Verwoerd. The motivation for the attempted assassination was never made clear. There appeared to be no conspiracy and no relation to the racial strife of the time. The attacker was adjudged mentally incompetent and committed to an asylum.

The assassination was also the work of one man who was mentally unbalanced and it bore little relation to political events in the country. The assassin, Dimitrio Tsafendas, was born in Mozambique of a Greek father and a mother of mixed racial origin. One report noted that his father later married a Greek woman and that the family rejected Dimitrio. Forty-eight years old at the time of the attack, Tsafendas was also described as a bitter, frustrated man with few friends. His long history of mental disorder had been recorded by various countries as he wandered through many parts of the world. He seemed to be a drifter, often penniless, sometimes evicted from his rooms, occasionally jailed, and frequently treated for mental illness. The psychiatrists who testified at his trial described him as schizophrenic, mentally deranged, and unbalanced. According to this testimony, Tsafendas ascribed his misfortunes, and the murder of Verwoerd, to a huge tapeworm inside him, which he variously described as a demon, dragon, or snake. Although he could give no rational explanation for

4. Keith Irvine, "Southern Africa: The White Fortress," *Current History*, LIV (1968), 72–75.
5. Hepple, op. cit., p. 170.

his attack on the prime minister, one psychiatrist interpreted Tsafendas' action as a result of a general grudge against society; Prime Minister Verwoerd represented that society and thus became the target of that resentment. Apparently there was little premeditation for the attack. Tsafendas admitted that he had thought a great deal about killing many people, but denied that he had taken the job as a parliamentary messenger with the intent to kill. The fact that he had bought the dagger on the day of the murder seemed to bear out his story. Inasmuch as prosecution as well as defense witnesses agreed on Tsafendas' mental state, the judge halted the trial, declared the defendant insane, and committed him to an indefinite term.

The Impact of the Assassination

The assassination of Prime Minister Verwoerd had almost no effect on South African politics. The political system itself was unshaken, policy changes from the old to the new administration were more in terms of style than of substance, and personnel shifts were minimal. The impact of the assassination was negligible.

No disturbances followed the assassination. Despite racial tensions and strife and disputes over the authoritarian policies of the regime, no group made any attempt whatever to create an incident, much less touch off rebellion and violence. The country remained quiet and all groups—whites, Africans, Indians, and Coloureds—expressed shock at the murder. Within the ruling National party, quiet negotiations were carried on among party leaders with B. J. Vorster, minister of justice and police, emerging as the new prime minister.

In one of his first public addresses as prime minister, Vorster pledged to continue the general policy of apartheid and to continue Verwoerd's program of "separate development"—the resettlement of blacks in all-black tribal homelands or Bantustans. Although no new Bantustans were designated beyond the one established by Verwoerd, Vorster's government continued to push other aspects of apartheid such as evicting nonwhites from their homes in areas designated as white, outlawing multiracial political parties, and establishing a separate legislative assembly for Coloureds. In only one policy area did Vorster depart from his predecessor, and in fact the shift occurred as a result of a policy advanced by Verwoerd himself. Before his death Verwoerd had expressed the need for South Africa to live in peace and to establish economic relations with its neighboring black republics.

Vorster in his early statements reiterated Verwoerd's policy, speaking of the need for friendship with other African states and of mutual assistance on a "live-and-let-live" basis. Vorster particularly sought understanding with Lesotho, Botswana, and Swaziland, but in March, 1967, he signed a trade pact with Malawi, the first formal pact of this sort with a black African state since the National party came to power. Vorster also seemed to shift South African policy toward Rhodesia. While he continued Verwoerd's policy of doing nothing to help bring the Rhodesian government down, it soon appeared that he would do nothing overt to help shore it up. Similarly Vorster shifted South African policy on international sports. By the spring of 1967, the government opened the country to visiting multiracial teams for the Olympics. Despite these sports overtures South Africa was barred from the 1968 Olympics because of racial policies that still required segregation in domestic sports. Although the changes of policy by Vorster's government seemed slight, they were probably as far as the government could go without adverse reaction from the white population. Given the fact that racial extremism is still on the rise among South African whites, policy shifts in this area would have remained minimal no matter who was prime minister.

Few changes occurred in the seventeen-man South African cabinet in the transition from Verwoerd to Vorster. During his first year in office, Vorster shifted only four men, including himself. T. Dönges, the minister of finance, was elected president to succeed C. R. Swart, whose term had expired; Vorster shifted three ministers and named two new men to fill the vacancies created; no one was dropped from the Verwoerd cabinet. By contrast, Verwoerd had made seven shifts in his cabinet in his last year of office, including the replacement of two ministers with two new men. In other words, fewer personnel changes occurred at the top level of government in the transition from Verwoerd to Vorster than had occurred in Verwoerd's own cabinet after the elections of March, 1966.[6]

Conclusions

It appears that the assassination had little impact on South African politics because the assassin himself was nonpolitical, the opposition was fragmented, and the ruling groups were firmly entrenched, self-confident, and determined to maintain the regime despite foreign and

6. See the *Statesman's Yearbook* for 1965–66, 1966–67, and 1967–68.

domestic pressures to change. Tsafendas, the assassin, was mentally ill and unrelated to political groups of any sort in the country. His murdering of Verwoerd was the isolated, totally unpredictable act of a madman. There was no conspiracy, no planned coup, no contemplated revolution.

Despite the authoritarian nature of the regime and its racist policies, the majority opposition was fragmented and overawed, while the minority ruling elite was self-assured and determined. However unjust a regime may be perceived to be by the majority, there is little chance of rebellion until the opposition can organize, create competent leadership, and demonstrate a willingness to risk all, including life itself, to institute changes. This combination had not yet taken form within the South African opposition. The demonstrations of the early 1960s, culminating in the massacre at Sharpeville, indicated widespread unrest among nonwhites, but the firm suppression of the incipient revolt and the dogged determination of the whites to press on with apartheid broke up the resistance, destroyed much of its leadership, and prevented organized opposition from growing into a serious threat.

When Verwoerd was assassinated, no one was prepared to take advantage of the momentary confusion to incite demonstrations or rioting. In fact virtually all nonwhites exhibited shock at the murder, despite the fact that Verwoerd had been the principal architect of the discriminatory laws enforced against them. While the nonwhites were thus cowed, the white elite enjoyed supreme self-confidence. True, a few whites objected to the regime's basic policies, but these protest voices were drowned out by the extremist majority that demanded still more restrictive legislation. Even the major opposition party supported the political system as presently constituted. Violence can be expected only when the oppressed are better prepared, when the elite begins to lose confidence, and especially when the political leaders begin to make concessions to the reformers. In 1966 everything was against a violent outburst accompanying the assassination of Prime Minister Verwoerd.

## 6

The Assassination of Anastasio Somoza of Nicaragua

The Assassination

On September 21, 1956, late in the evening, a young Nicaraguan shot his president, Anastasio Somoza, Sr., at a dance at the Workers' House in the city of León. The assassin was knocked to the floor and almost instantly killed, as members of the president's guard pumped some twenty bullets into his body. Somoza himself, seriously wounded but still conscious, remonstrated with his men that they should have captured the assailant alive. Upon learning of the assault, officials of the United States government immediately offered assistance. Owing to the severity of his wounds, Somoza was taken to well-equipped Gorgas Hospital in the Canal Zone. At first it appeared that he might well recover, but he suffered a relapse and early Friday morning, September 29, he died.

In the meantime, Nicaragua remained calm, although the political atmosphere was somewhat tense. Governmental authority and political power passed smoothly into the hand of Somoza's eldest son Luis, supported by his younger brother, Anastasio, Jr., the commander of the National Guard. Luis, presiding officer of the congress and as such the heir to the office, was quickly inaugurated as interim president. The new president acted with dispatch. Within two days of the shooting, he declared a state of siege, arrested at least 200 opposition leaders and suspects, clamped a curfew on Managua, and ordered a full investigation.

The investigation itself moved ahead rapidly and efficiently. Except for some political exiles whom neighboring governments would not extradite, all the principal conspirators were rounded up within a few weeks, while most of those originally arrested were released. During January, 1957, twenty-two persons were brought to trial and sixteen found guilty. As a gesture of mildness to characterize the new regime, Luis saw to it that no sentences exceeded fifteen years and in February reduced some of the other terms.

With this ease of transition, Nicaragua seems to belie the commonly held belief that the sudden removal of a dictator will lead to some degree of political instability, possibly civil war. A dozen years after the assassination, the Somoza family remains as well entrenched as ever with Anastasio, Jr., the constitutionally elected president, the economy growing comfortably, and a minimum of overt or serious political or social unrest. Even should this pattern of stability crumble in the next few years, it would be difficult to attribute the change to the assassination. How then can we account for the peaceful transfer of power from an experienced and hard-bitten dictator to his untried sons? Seemingly three factors can offer us some reasonable explanations: the basic structure of the regime, the quality of the political opposition, and obviously, the nature of the conspiracy itself.

The Life and Times of Anastasio Somoza, Sr.

The twenty-year rule of Anastasio Somoza (1936–56) introduced the modern period of Nicaraguan history. Following independence in the 1840s, Nicaraguan political patterns fluctuated between periods of civil war and harsh authoritarianism and culminated in the occupation of the country by United States military forces for over twenty years (1912–33). The unrelenting civil strife had its roots primarily in the personal and family struggles for power within the tiny elite, but ideological, economic, and regional antagonisms also divided the country, Guerrilla warfare in the countryside and vendettas in the towns left the country in political turmoil and economic stagnation. Into this society Anastasio Somoza was born in 1896 of an upper-middle-class family of coffee planters. After receiving his *bachillerato* in Nicaragua, he traveled to the United States. Upon his return home he married into one of the leading Nicaraguan families and plunged into politics as a member of the Liberal party. Somoza was rewarded for his party work by a succession of political appointments and in 1932 was finally named commander of the Marine-trained National Guard. As head of the guard Somoza liquidated the last of the great guerrilla chieftains, Augusto Cesar Sandino. Following this coup Somoza prepared to contest the presidential elections of 1936. With the support of the majority faction of the Liberal party, some Conservatives, and the National Guard he effected a coup d'état in June, 1936. Under a provisional president elections were held in December; Somoza won handily, since most of the opposition refused to vote.[1]

Somoza's regime was characterized by authoritarianism and modest economic development. His rule was by no means an unrelieved tyranny. His blunt manner, his "machismo," and his gift of humor won him substantial support among the urban lower classes. His willingness to share patronage, political and economic, with his old opponents, and his obvious lack of revolutionary goals led "the upper class to endure his political style." [2] Even his reaction to public political opposition tended to be unpredictable. At times tolerant, on other occasions he permitted torture.

Somoza's primary instrument of control throughout his long rule remained the National Guard. He rewarded guard officers not only with salaries and military hardware, but also with fringe benefits, legal and illegal. But Somoza did not neglect the political needs of his administration. To satisfy "purists" among his entourage, he gave the Liberal party an honored position in his regime and more or less preserved the forms of democratic government. The Liberal party, as Anderson says, "also served to mobilize middle-class and mass support in favor of the regime, provided an agency which could to some extent screen for political purity in matters of patronage and lower level political recruitment, and gave an outlet for political activists to declare their unswerving adulation for the caudillo in the public forum, and thereby seek personal favor." [3]

Somoza's record of economic achievements is superficially impressive. Highways and roads increased from virtually zero to something over 2,000 miles, and the number of cars, tractors, and trucks in use also increased in spectacular fashion. Ports were improved, airports built, and a national merchant marine and airline were founded. Agricultural production was expanded and diversified and light industries flourished. Banking and credit facilities were vastly improved, taxes

1. Duncan E. Osborne, "The Assassination of Anastasio Somoza" (Austin: M. A. Thesis, University of Texas, 1968), chap. I.
2. Charles W. Anderson, "Nicaragua," in Martin C. Needler, ed., *Political Systems of Latin America* (Princeton: D. Van Nostrand Co., Inc., 1964), p. 100.
3. Ibid., p. 101.

were collected (and reduced), the budget balanced, and foreign investments encouraged. Some schools were built and the number of students attending increased.[4] The difficulty with these accomplishments is that the benefits derived from them accrued largely to the Somoza family and its close associates, and secondarily to the urban middle class. The majority of the population, the rural peasantry, profited hardly at all and the urban poor but little.

Despite the dictatorship and its retrogressive social policies, Nicaragua remained peaceful during most of Somoza's rule. A few exiles, for political or personal reasons, schemed the overthrow of the regime and in April, 1954, made a bungling attempt to kill Somoza. After the assassination of Sandino no important guerrilla or bandit groups troubled the administration. The peasantry remained apathetic and ignorant, the urban lower classes remained loyal to their caudillo, and the middle and upper classes on the whole acquiesced in a regime that brought them profit. It was in this political and social milieu that the assassination of Anastasio Somoza occurred and, at least temporarily, shook the complacency of the Nicaraguan elite.

The Assassin and the Conspiracy

Nicaraguan political exiles during Somoza's time tended to concentrate in El Salvador and Mexico.[5] The several groups communicated with each other and with disaffected persons within Nicaragua itself. It appears, however, that neither the internal opposition nor the exile communities ever seriously considered, much less organized, a revolutionary movement to overthrow the regime. However, the fortuitous appearance in the mid-1950s of a young man willing to sacrifice himself in an attempt to assassinate the dictator set in motion a plot to overthrow the government that in its chance circumstances and bungling methods suggests comic opera. This ill-conceived, ill-planned, and ill-executed conspiracy resulted in the deaths of victim and assassin and the imprisonment of local collaborators, but little else.

The assassin, Rigoberto López Pérez, from a lower-middle-class family, had sought to improve his lot by seeking employment in neighboring El Salvador. Religious-minded, sensitive, romantic, and idealistic, López Pérez dreamed of performing some great and ennobling

4. John D. Martz, *Central America: The Crisis and the Challenge* (Chapel Hill: The University of North Carolina Press, 1959), pp. 169–80.
5. The factual material for this section is taken primarily from Osborne, op. cit.

deed. In El Salvador he met Noel Bermúdez, an exiled former captain in the National Guard who apparently persuaded him to kill
Somoza. Returning to Nicaragua, López Pérez contacted other members of the conspiracy, who helped to train him and plan his course of
action.

From September 14 on López Pérez sought out opportunities to
shoot the president. The conspirators learned that on September 21
Somoza planned to attend a dance at the Workers' House in León. In
the festive crowd it might not be difficult to approach the dictator.
Beyond simple precautions, they do not appear to have developed any
definite plans to seize key strong points, open guerrilla warfare, neu-
tralize or subvert the guard, or in fact to do anything that would topple
the regime and install the conspirators in power. The assassin carried
out his part of the drama with nerve and perhaps with luck. He got by
the guards at the door with a gun tucked in his belt. He walked around
the hall, spotted Somoza, danced around to an advantageous spot, and
then coolly pumped four bullets into his victim. López Pérez himself
was pulled down and killed almost instantly. The remaining conspirators outside the hall at first hesitated, and after a few minutes, they all
fled into hiding.

Except for those in exile, the ringleaders of the plot and most of the
secondary figures (twenty-one in all) were rounded up quickly by
Nicaraguan security forces and brought to trial. Ten were charged
with rebellion against the government and of these, seven were also
charged with the assassination. The other eleven were charged with
prior knowledge of these crimes. All were found guilty, but none received the death sentence and most had their sentences later reduced.
The three principal leaders, however, were killed in 1960, allegedly in an
attempt to escape. Only a few of these men were prominent politically
or socially, but none had any wide political following or political or
military skills.

The Impact of the Assassination

In the thirteen years since the assassination of Anastasio Somoza,
Nicaragua has experienced a few changes but no substantial alteration
in its political system. The country has developed economically at a
rapid rate, it has entered the Central American Common Market, and
it has settled long-standing difficulties with its neighbor, Costa Rica.
Furthermore, in the first few years after the death of his father, Luis

Somoza, who succeeded to power, somewhat liberalized the harsher aspects of the dictatorship and amended the constitution to prohibit the succession to the presidency of any member of the Somoza family.

These reforms, however, never passed beyond their initial stages. The Somoza family and its associated clans have continued to dominate the country politically and economically. Their vast accumulations of wealth have not diminished and the Liberal party, under the domination of the dictator's sons, has continued as the vehicle for political rule and patronage. In 1963 at the termination of Luis's administration, the party nominated an old associate of the deceased dictator; he easily won. The new president, René Schick Gutiérrez showed some independence early in his regime but he fell ill and died before the end of his term. A provisional president served out the remaining months and held elections as scheduled in May, 1967. The extent of the continuity in Nicaraguan politics is well illustrated by the election to the presidency of Anastasio Somoza, Jr., a man who in his political style and personality much more closely resembles his father than his brother Luis. Although mellowed somewhat in the past few years, Anastasio is not likely to give up the reins of power easily, and it is probable that he will continue the rule of the Somoza family either through easily controlled puppets or by holding the office of president himself.

Conclusions

It might seem predictable in dictatorial and socially regressive regimes, particularly those in Latin America, that the death or sudden removal of the autarch will open the gates to violence and perhaps to social revolution. Obviously, neither occurred in Nicaragua—even the changes in personnel were of minimal importance.[6]

We may deduce any number of "causes" to explain the smooth transition of power from father to sons, ranging from the specific and fortuitous to the highly general and abstract. One student of the assassination has pointed to the span of eight days between the wounding and the death of Somoza, during which time the sons solidified their position while the opposition remained off balance, not knowing

6. In the immediate aftermath of the assassination five changes were made in cabinet positions and six more occurred within nine months of the assassination. "These changes, however, seemed to reflect infighting among members of the same group which held power when Somoza G. was alive." Paper by Ann Kerrey, University of Texas, 1969.

whether the dictator would survive. But this same observer doubts that the Somoza family would have been overthrown even if Anastasio, Sr. had died instantly.[7] One may also argue that Nicaragua had no past "golden age" in terms of either stability or prosperity, much less of democracy. The caudillo tradition was deeply imbedded in the political consciousness, and among the masses a leader with charisma had greater claims to political rule than one with an electoral majority. Undoubtedly, a vast number of events, both general and specific, contributed in some way to explain not only the lack of violence but even the absence of serious protest or demonstration in the continuance of the political system.

First and foremost was the nature and character of the dictator himself. Still vigorous and capable at sixty years of age, he remained on top of the political structure he created until the day he was shot. Always conscious of the necessity of keeping the guard loyal with generous perquisites, he was also careful to weed out potential challengers to his authority. As his sons came of age he prepared Anastasio, Jr., much like himself in temperament, to assume responsibility for assuring the continued armed support for the system. In a manner just as astute, he kept his political fences in good repair. He kept congress and the Liberal party viable political institutions, although of necessity they remained subordinate to his autocratic rule. He placed his elder son, who would be in the legal and practical position to succeed his father in an emergency, at the head of the congress. The elder Somoza also took care to keep his political support broad. His fateful attendance at the dance at a workingmen's convention hall is only one example of his contacts with the lower classes, particularly in the cities, where challenges to his regime might most likely occur. At the same time he kept the support of the middle and upper classes and neutralized his opponents by the economic opportunities he made possible. In fact, in terms of political stability and economic development, the Somoza era has been the only "golden age" that Nicaragua has ever enjoyed.

Closely related to the above conditions was the absence of a viable alternative to the Somozas. The traditional opposition, the Conservative party, concerned itself largely with philosophical discussions and issues long dead. While the Conservatives could draw support from some of the old families and their retainers, who were traditionally loyal to the party, they could engender no mass support. At the same

7. Osborne, op. cit., pp. 72–73, 120–21.

time, splinter groups from both the Liberal and Conservative parties that might have presented alternatives to the Somoza rule were seriously hampered not only by repressive measures of the regime, but more importantly by their failure to produce leaders who could popularize their programs and attract mass support. The most likely opposition leader, Pedro Chamorro, refused to become involved in the assassination plot, probably because he recognized its futility. The conspirators themselves, apart from the assassination, demonstrated no skill or imagination in attempting to overthrow the system. They apparently sought no mass support and prepared no hard core of guerrilla fighters. No Castro appeared. Ironically, the most charismatic leader to appear in the postassassination era is Anastasio, Jr., who promised to carry on his father's system with, at best, minor adjustments for economic modernization.

## 7

The Assassination
of Martin Luther King, Jr.

The Assassination

On April 4, 1968, Dr. Martin Luther King, Jr., was in Memphis, Tennessee to lend support to striking Negro garbage collectors.[1] At 6.00 P.M. he left his motel room to go to dinner before addressing a rally at a Memphis church. As he paused on the balcony, he was struck by a rifle bullet fired from a rooming house 200 feet away. The bullet severed his spinal cord and he was pronounced dead in a Memphis hospital a little more than an hour later.

The assassin quickly left the rooming house, dropped the rifle two doors away, and drove off in a white Mustang—all in the space of two minutes. Within nine minutes after this, police had discovered the discarded rifle, located the position from which the shot was fired, and obtained a description of the suspect and his vehicle. Nevertheless, the killer was able to get away in the heavy traffic of the evening rush hour. False radio calls and false leads sent the main police search into north Memphis while the killer actually fled south. In any event, he was almost certainly well into Mississippi within an hour after the shooting.

The FBI quickly assumed responsibility for the largest manhunt in American history. After initial confusion it became apparent that the wanted man was James Earl Ray, who left a trail of aliases in the United States, Canada, and Europe, where he fled in May. The story of his apprehension is well known. He was arrested in London on June 8.

1. A march a week earlier had been inadequately planned and controlled and young Negro militants had turned to vandalism and looting, leading to violence in which one was killed and sixty-two injured.

Ray did not fight extradition and was soon returned to the United States where he stood trial in Memphis for the murder of Martin Luther King. There were no astonishing revelations during the trial and even the trial judge, W. Preston Battle, later stated that a number of points about the case had not been cleared up. Ray himself ultimately pled guilty (and was sentenced to ninety-nine years in prison). Then, when placed in the Tennessee penitentiary, he repudiated his plea and demanded a fresh trial. He lost this request.

The immediate reaction to King's death was incredible shock, not alone among the black population in America. There was instant rioting in a number of major cities; lives were lost and much property was destroyed. One political result was the quick passage of the 1968 Civil Rights Act. There were, however, few other political results from King's death and it was almost without systemic impact.

The Life and Times of Martin Luther King, Jr.

Like many other great revolutionaries and leaders of social movements, Martin Luther King was the product of a relatively conventional background.[2] He was an American Negro, but he was never in his life a victim of severe economic privation. Although undoubtedly he suffered indignities and insults from time to time, these were far fewer for him than for most other American blacks. To begin with, he grew up in Atlanta, where a large and well-organized Negro community has existed for a long time and where the problems of black life were somewhat less severe than in many other areas. Also, his father, a prominent leader among Atlanta Negroes, was the pastor of a large Negro church with a relatively prosperous and stable congregation. Hence young Martin Luther King, born in 1929, could rely on a stable and comfortable family situation, family prestige within the black community, and a consistently satisfactory standard of living.

Martin Luther King attended the better Atlanta Negro schools and then Morehouse College. He was serious, relatively quiet, seemingly mature, and an excellent student. He moved on to Crozer Theological Seminary, a predominately white institution in Pennsylvania. He now became seriously aware for the first time of the major thinkers whose ideas he was to use later—Rauschenbusch, Hegel, Niebuhr, Heidegger, Marx, Sartre. He also learned of the life and teachings of Gandhi

2. The best biography of King is Lerone Bennett, Jr., *What Manner of Man* (Chicago: Johnson Publishing Co., 1968).

and began to perceive their relevance to the situation of the American Negro. After leaving Crozer as its outstanding student, King went on to graduate study in philosophy at Boston University.

King did well at Boston University. He took additional courses at Harvard before completing his dissertation. Although he intended to undertake an academic career and already had offers of university positions, he apparently decided that academic life ought to be preceded by a pastorate. In 1954 he became the pastor of the Dexter Avenue Baptist Church in Montgomery, with an upper-income congregation consisting largely of Negro professional people and faculty members at Alabama State College.

Many of King's admirers have argued that he was an intellectual and an original mind of great importance. In the sense that he was at home in the world of ideas, enjoyed the company of thinkers, and considered ideas vital tools in his work, he was certainly an intellectual. But he did not originate ideas.[3] Even the suggestion that the doctrine of nonviolent resistance might be applicable to the situation of the Negro in America was by no means original with King.[4] His true significance is to be found in the extraordinary effectiveness with which he selected and used the ideas of others and in the moral force through which he inspired people to act. America has had very few social leaders who have had such an impact in so short a time, and probably none of these started from such a limited base of power, influence, and prestige.

For more than a year after King moved to Montgomery he was not conspicuous outside his own church and the middle-class Negro population. Although he was a member of the NAACP and generally strongly supported its program, King avoided the occasions on which he might have become directly involved in calls for action. He also avoided commitments to any of the numerous political factions within the Negro community. But 1954 was also the year of Brown v. Board of Education.

The appropriate occasion for action came on December 1, 1955. A Negro seamstress named Rosa Parks, who had been sitting, as custom and law demanded, behind white bus passengers, refused to yield her seat to new white passengers who boarded at a later stop. Although

3. See Louis E. Lomax, *The Negro Revolt* (New York: Harper & Row, Publishers, 1962), pp. 89–90.
4. See, for example, Reinhold Niebuhr, *Moral Man and Immoral Society: A Study in Ethics and Politics* (New York: Charles Scribner's Sons, 1932), p. 254.

she was an active member and former officer of the local NAACP, her action was purely her own and appears to have been made strictly on the spur of the moment. In her own words, "My feet hurt." [5] Her arrest produced an immediate and feverish reaction within the politically sensitive part of the Negro population of Montgomery. King was one of those consulted before a hurriedly planned boycott was announced, but he was only one of a number of others involved. Only after the amazing success of the first morning of the boycott was attention given to the necessity of organizing a continuation of the protest effort. The ad hoc group formed for this purpose, the Montgomery Improvement Association, promptly elected King president, but King himself suggested that this was chiefly because of his newness in the community and his lack of identification with any of the feuding factions within the group.[6]

The remainder of the Montgomery story is well-known. Despite all the economic and legal pressure which the city government could muster, despite threats and actual violence from individual and organized lawless elements in the white population, and despite inevitable friction within the ranks of the Montgomery movement itself, the boycott persisted for a year with virtually complete success. It ended only when the Supreme Court affirmed a lower court decision holding state and local bus segregation laws unconstitutional. This, of course, was more than the Montgomery movement had initially set out to accomplish. But the failure of Montgomery's leadership to make any meaningful concessions to the first modest demands had long since driven the Negro population and its leaders to believe that only the end of segregation itself could assure their fair treatment. Ironically, although the direct action technique first attempted on a large scale at Montgomery was to become the most important tool for social change available to the Negro in the following decade, the successful end of the Montgomery boycott was itself dependent on the tried and tested device of litigation, a technique which the NAACP had been employing with conspicuous success for many years.

By the time the Montgomery struggle ended, Martin Luther King had become famous and popular far beyond the narrow Montgomery community of which he was a part. In 1957 the organization of the Southern Christian Leadership Conference gave him the institutional basis for moving outside the Montgomery setting. Speaking and writ-

5. Bennett, op. cit., p. 60.
6. Ibid., p. 65.

ing now occupied most of his time.[7] And Negroes in other cities, anxious to break out of confining patterns of race relations, sought to benefit from his leadership and inspiration.

The Nobel Peace Prize in 1964 was a final step in the public recognition of Martin Luther King as the dominant symbol of his race and his time. But the symbol by this time had long since parted company with the man. King himself had become aware of this even in the days of the Montgomery movement and he spoke from time to time of the way in which he was a prisoner of his reputation and of events, over most of which he could exercise only a little influence and no real control. He became increasingly troubled by the laudatory treatment he received from many who had little real understanding of his convictions, his goals, or his tactics. Well before his death, direct action had moved away from him and from many of his ideas, and while he was still by far the most popular Negro leader, much of the organized protest movement was paying only lip service to his leadership and some was no longer doing even that.

Nonviolence as a theoretical or philosophical commitment was deep and genuine in King and in some of his associates, but it never penetrated very deeply into most of the Negro population, any more than did Gandhi's philosophy into the Indian population. So long as it could be justified pragmatically, it would be an acceptable tactic. But let it cease to succeed, and it would be quickly abandoned. By the middle 1960s America's blacks were resorting more and more to direct action, but that action was less and less nonviolent.

The success of nonviolence in Montgomery and elsewhere had always been dependent on a proper environment. Thus nonviolence might work when a majority of the whites found granting the demands of Negroes less unpleasant than a continuation of an unsettled situation, disruption of public facilities, and economic boycotts. And in a wider environment nonviolence can work when a larger population elsewhere is brought to sympathize with the protesters and to support the accomplishment of their goals through legal action, economic pressure, or other techniques that the local white community cannot effectively resist. The second situation brought success in Montgomery and both were present to a considerable degree in Birmingham. But as the demands of the Negro population changed and the locus of protest

7. Five books by King were published between 1958 and 1968. Of particular value are *Stride Toward Freedom* (New York: Harper & Brothers, 1958) and *Where Do We Go From Here* (New York: Harper & Row, Publishers, 1967).

shifted from the deep South to the major metropolitan areas of other parts of the country, these conditions came to be met more rarely. The Watts riot dramatically demonstrated the irrelevance of those ideas to a significant part of the Negro population. And while much of that population might remain nonviolent out of prudence, it was apparent that the rioters had the sympathy of at least a large minority, and possibly a majority, of Northern urban Negroes.[8]

The struggle to retain a following for his ideas became a desperate one for King, as more and more Negroes, especially the young, began to perceive nonviolence as ineffective and "collaborationist." Although King's name remained a valuable asset in any racial effort, even in the SCLC itself other leaders were emerging who shared only a part of his commitment and to whom nonviolence was a tactic which should be employed when appropriate and abandoned for others when it was not. In the context of this struggle King was perhaps inevitably driven toward more emphasis on confrontation and less, at least in the short run, on the element of brotherhood which he had stressed so much in the past. To be sure, this apparent concession to the more radical young Negroes was never admitted at a theoretical level and was a reaction only to specific crisis situations, but its necessity was a severe blow to the whole mystique of nonviolence. This problem, and the need to achieve another major success for nonviolence, led King to his role in the Memphis garbage collectors' strike and to his assassination.

The Assassin

James Earl Ray was an obscure and rather unsuccessful professional criminal.[9] He came from western Illinois but was almost always thought of by his acquaintances as "hillbilly." His family was poor and unstable. He seemed of average intelligence but performed poorly in school. He was shy and never got along well with very many people. In the military he became a major disciplinary problem, and was later court-martialed and given a "general" discharge on grounds of "lack of adaptability to military service."

8. William Brink and Louis Harris, *Black and White* (New York: Simon and Schuster, Inc., 1967), pp. 264–67.

9. Ray and his background are described effectively in Clay Blair, Jr., *The Strange Case of James Earl Ray* (New York: Bantam Books, Inc., 1969).

and forgery. Much of his time was spent in jail. His crimes involved no serious violence; although he had carried guns and had used them in his robberies, he had never fired them. Nothing in his background or his history suggested that he was a potential murderer. To fellow criminals he was a small-timer of no particular significance.

In 1960 Ray was sentenced to twenty years in the Missouri State Penitentiary for a grocery store robbery in St. Louis. He made a number of efforts to escape, and the fourth of these, on April 23, 1967, was successful. For almost a year after his escape, Ray wandered around the United States, Mexico, and Canada. It has been suggested that Ray accumulated large funds while in prison, probably through participation in the drug traffic within the prison, and that he succeeded in smuggling this money out before his escape. Another possibility is that early in the period of his freedom he became party to a conspiracy, whether he was then aware of the object of that conspiracy or not, and that he was supported financially by his fellow conspirator(s).

Although there are various hints of collaborators with Ray, they remain shadowy, and the evidence for their existence is inconclusive. Yet there is the failure to explain satisfactorily the substantial funds spent by Ray before and after the assassination. To say that he *might* have obtained that money in ways not connected with the assassination is not quite enough when no evidence has been forthcoming to show that he *did*. It is obviously impossible without more evidence than has yet been brought to light to make a final judgment on the presence or absence of a conspiracy, but by a rather narrow margin the weight of the evidence appears to favor the conspiracy explanation in this case.

What was the nature of this conspiracy, and who besides Ray was involved in it? Evidence bearing on this is almost totally lacking. A plausible answer might be the Ku Klux Klan or one or more of its members. What is commonly called the Klan is actually a number of organizations. Some are loosely affiliated with each other, while some have no organizational ties with the rest. It is doubtful that the larger national Klan groups would have committed themselves officially to the assassination of a major figure in the civil rights movement, in part because their leaders are well aware of the extent to which their organizations have been infiltrated by the FBI, but it is much less certain that a small group of Klansmen would be similarly restrained. Violence, including assassination, has stemmed from this source in the past.[10] Other white supremacy groups might have been similarly motivated to remove King from the scene, but most have avoided forays into the realm of violence. However, it is obviously possible that an individual racist or a small group lacking formal organization might have constituted a conspiracy for such a purpose, and an ad hoc conspiracy of this sort would clearly be much more difficult to uncover.

A second possibility suggested at the time of the assassination was that it was the work of a local Memphis group, possibly part of the business community disturbed about the economic impact of the garbage strike. However, such evidence as we have seems to suggest that, if Ray was part of a conspiracy, it developed long before the Memphis troubles began. King's presence in Memphis provided the occasion for the assassination, according to this view, but it might just as readily have happened elsewhere. There is even evidence that it was planned earlier for Birmingham but that an appropriate opportunity failed to materialize. Furthermore, it is doubtful that very many Memphis businessmen would have considered King's murder economically beneficial, for the disturbances resulting from it would surely be more costly than the garbage strike and its attendant unrest. Indeed, after the murder, Memphis businessmen were active in promoting a settlement of the strike on terms more or less favorable to the strikers.

A third possible conspiracy would have involved one of the Negro groups committed to violence, revolutionary action, or separatism, and disgusted with King's nonviolence and his commitment to racial integration. There is evidence linking some of these groups to attempts on the lives of other leaders of moderate Negro organizations. An almost insuperable obstacle to this hypothesis, however, is the need to find a plausible link between Ray and such conspirators. Why would they have chosen such an instrument for their purpose? How could they even have developed a contact with such an individual? And why would he have agreed to carry out their aims? One cannot simultaneously make of Ray a Negro-baiting bigot and a willing agent of a violent black supremacy movement.

On the whole, the best judgment that can be made with the available evidence, is that James Earl Ray shot Martin Luther King, that he may have acted on his own but that he probably served as the

10. For accounts of violence connected with the Klan during the 1960s, see "Report of Task Force I," Vol. II, chap. IV, National Commission on the Causes and Prevention of Violence (Mimeographed, 1969).

agent of another individual or group, and that his fellow conspira-tor(s) were motivated primarily by antagonism to changing patterns of race relations in the United States and to the further changes in this area which King was demanding. If the other conspirators were part of a formal organization committed to white supremacy, they are more likely to have acted as an informal group within that organiza-tion than in response to any formal organizational decision at a high level.

The Impact of the Assassination

The immediate consequence of Martin Luther King's assassination was large-scale violence. It began within minutes after the word of his death reached the American public via radio and television. In Memphis itself, where a previous disturbance during the garbage dis-pute had caused one death, rioting and looting developed very quickly. But the scale of violence was far greater elsewhere. It affected a total of 125 cities, far more than any previous outbreak of simultaneous civil disorder in modern American history.[11] Many of these cities had never previously experienced racial violence. The four cities most critically affected were Chicago, Washington, Baltimore, and Kansas City, in all four of which the disturbances finally subsided only after several days and nights of looting, sniping, and arson. In Baltimore, Chicago, and Washington, 21,000 regular army troops had to be brought in to control the outbreaks, and 22,000 more were placed on alert ready to be employed in these and other centers of disorder, while 34,000 members of the National Guard were also used to deal with the violence. This constituted the largest military force ever put together to deal with civil disturbances in the United States (apart from the Civil War). The property destroyed was valued by in-surance companies at $45,000,000. There were forty-six violent deaths as a consequence of the riots. Forty-one of the dead were Negroes, and thirty-two were in the four cities previously noted. About 2,600 were injured, almost half of these in Washington alone, where the violence finally ended only when a sizable part of the Eighty-second Airborne Division was flown in to patrol the streets of the downtown business district and adjacent Negro residential areas. A total of 21,270 arrests were made.

In many cities the disorder developed spontaneously as soon as the

11. Data on the riots are from *New York Times,* April 14, 1968.

word of King's assassination spread. King's murder was the occasion of this, not its cause. But it is impossible to deny that there were many for whom another motivation was present—the psychological need to get back at the whites, who were blamed for the death of a hero and for the despair with which many Negroes regarded their situation and into which they were plunged even deeper by the manner of King's death. Where violence did not develop until a day or more after the death of King, it is possible to suspect some organized effort to foment disorder.

A second immediate consequence of the assassination of Martin Luther King was the passage of the Civil Rights Act of 1968. Prior to the murder there had been doubts that it could be passed without being substantially watered down. Political pressure within most of the white population for extension of further legal protection to members of minority groups had dwindled since 1964, and only an event of this sort could shock Congress into a major step along these lines.

King's death also contributed indirectly to an important shift of opinion against further governmental efforts to alleviate the problems of the Negro population, for the violent aftermath seems to have shocked and disturbed a majority of whites more than the assassination itself. As we have noted, King's death impelled Congress to pass within a few days the civil rights bill it had long been considering; it is doubtful that it would have been passed ten days or two weeks later, when strong public reaction within much of the white population had become obvious. That shift of opinion had been under way for quite a while—certainly since the Watts riot of 1965. But the riots following the death of King were a significant step in furthering this change. Following from this shift of attitude came a number of legislative actions designed to repress further racial violence (and often enough the nonviolent protest which was associated in the minds of many legislators with this problem). Most of these actions were taken at the state and local levels, but Congress was by no means immune. From April on the efforts of congressional liberals had to be devoted not to the passing of new legislation of benefit to members of ethnic minorities but to trying to stave off or water down actions aimed at retaliation against such groups.

In the electoral realm a major shift of support toward candidates perceived to be less sympathetic to the demands of ethnic minorities developed in 1968 and continued afterward. At the national level the most conspicuous result was the significant support received by George

Wallace—the most impressive showing for a third-party candidate in many decades. Given the narrowness of Nixon's victory, and given the rather obvious conclusion that a majority of the racially motivated white votes that did not go to Wallace did go to Nixon, the latter's success in reaching the White House must be attributed in part to the violence that produced the "white backlash." There might have been enough violence to produce that frightened reaction without King's death—but then again there might not have been. The changed pattern of voting behavior that led to Nixon's victory was even more impressive in state and local elections in 1968 and on into 1969—witness Yorty's election in Los Angeles and Lindsay's defeat in the Republican primary in New York. Even relatively conservative political figures who could be charged with appeasing violence-prone ethnic interests were defeated in large numbers. Only a small part of this was an indirect result of King's death, but the April riots surely had some effect.

The long-range consequences of the assassination are almost certainly less important in this case, for King, though still an important symbol, had lost before his death the capacity to control events or even his own movement. He had had to concentrate increasingly on avoiding the manipulation of his symbolism for purposes of which he disapproved, and he had not always succeeded. The militant part of the Negro population had lost the conviction that nonviolence, except as a tactical device in particular circumstances, was appropriate for their purposes. And Negro protest was focusing more and more on situations in which those circumstances were not present. The movement to which he had given inspiration had gone far beyond him. Most of what Martin Luther King could do for America and for American Negroes he had done well before his death, and that death, while it produced dramatic results in the short run, was of limited impact for the future.[12]

Conclusions

Martin Luther King, Jr., was one of the most honored and respected of Americans. He developed the technique of nonviolent civil disobedience into a massive weapon for the procurement and preservation of civil rights for blacks. He was most effective during the decade

12. Alternatively, some have argued that King's major service was yet to come and that the black community lost its one central leader and has floundered since.

ending in the middle sixties; by that time the civil rights movement had largely been captured by militants whose demands were less negotiable and whose methods did not exclude violence.

King died at the height of his prestige but after he had made his contribution and had lost much of his effectiveness. This statement alone may explain somewhat the enormous shock and the immediate large-scale violence that followed his death and the simultaneous lack of discernible systemic impact.

Although there seems little doubt that his assassin was James Earl Ray, there is considerable question about Ray's motives for the act and whether he acted alone or in conspiracy with others.

Although the deaths of King in April and Robert Kennedy in June were not without their political effects the systemic impacts proved negligible, illustrating the stability and capability of the American political system. The system was not disrupted or seriously altered—let alone destroyed—by the violent deaths of two very prominent and politically influential Americans. Undoubtedly a particular office (especially the presidency) may be of profound importance to the effective operation of a political system. Yet the survival of the office rarely depends upon the maintenance in that office of any particular individual. Few, if any, individuals are indispensable to the American political system, a system with strong institutional resources. The violent removal of an incumbent may be shocking but on the American scene at least it has never had any substantial systemic effects. Thus, if any assassin in the past has been motivated by the hope of accomplishing major political changes in the United States, his hopes were obviously frustrated.

8

The Assassination
of Huey P. Long
# of Louisiana

The Assassination

Returning to Baton Rouge in early September of 1935 for a special session of the state legislature, U.S. Senator Huey P. Long—the Louisiana "Kingfish" and virtual dictator—followed his usual practice of directing legislative activity in person. As the House of Representatives prepared to recess on the evening of Sunday, September 8, Long left the chamber, accompanied by five of his bodyguards. (Long had feared assassination since first assuming major office.) After a brief stop in the governor's office suite, Long stepped back into the Capitol corridor, took a few steps, and encountered Dr. Carl Weiss, a young Baton Rouge physician. Weiss advanced toward Long, holding a small automatic pistol, and without speaking, fired at him. The bodyguards immediately killed Weiss; altogether over sixty wounds were later counted in his body.[1]

1. Precisely what happened is far from clear, but the account related here is the official and most widely accepted version. It relies almost entirely on eyewitness reports by the bodyguards and close associates of the senator. Given the character of the available evidence, it is scarcely surprising that alternative versions have been advanced. One of these holds that Weiss shot Long only after some sort of altercation. Another suggests that Long was not killed at all by Weiss, but rather by his bodyguards, probably accidentally in the course of shooting Weiss. A mysterious cut on Long's lower lip, which appeared between his departure from the House and his arrival at the hospital, may support the contention that Weiss struck Long.

It is utterly impossible to reach a final judgment on what happened in that Louisiana Capitol corridor this long after the event. Two elaborately researched books published in the same year—Hermann B. Deutsch, *The Huey Long Murder Case* (Garden City, N.Y.: Doubleday & Co., Inc., 1963) and David H. Zinman,

The death of Huey P. Long was surely the most dramatic and probably the most significant American political killing since the assassination of President Abraham Lincoln. Long had achieved a position in national politics that far surpassed his nominal status as a backbench member of the United States Senate. Within the state of Louisiana he possessed political power exceeding that exercised by any other state political leader in American history. His career has attracted enormous attention; he has been the subject of novels, movies, and numerous works of scholarship. He has been variously described as dictator, demagogue, democrat, fascist, radical, and social reformer. For twenty-five years after his death Louisiana politics revolved around his family, his faction, and his memory. In the United States Senate his son Russell Long continues to play an influential role, narrowly losing a bid for majority whip in January, 1969, to the heir of another dynasty, Edward Kennedy.

The Life and Times of Huey P. Long

Huey Long was a product of the piney woods of northern Louisiana, still a relatively impoverished area. The Long family, by no means wealthy, was by local standards rather well off. Although Huey never obtained a high school diploma and attended law school for only one year, by prodigious effort he was able to pass the bar examination and within a few months begin his practice. He made his first money in the growing oil boom in northern Louisiana. The promise of greater wealth, however, appeared to be blocked through the tight control over oil marketing exercised by major petroleum firms, particularly by Standard Oil. To what extent his early antagonism to great wealth and large-scale economic power contributed to his political convictions is unclear. No doubt he was also influenced by the general poverty of the piney woods region. Whatever his original motives, he soon recognized that he was not alone in antagonism toward big business. He found that by articulating this general distrust and antagonism he had created a firm base for further political activity.

The Day Huey Long Was Shot, September 8, 1935 (New York: Ivan Obolensky, Inc., 1963)—reached diametrically opposite conclusions. Each supported its argument with plausible evidence. The direct evidence of the eyewitnesses may be discounted on the grounds of their own biases, especially if one assumes that one of them may have been, probably inadvertently, the actual killer of Senator Long. On the other hand, it is difficult to explain away the presence of Weiss, with a gun which was clearly his own property but which he was not in the habit of carrying on his person.

Long sought his first public office in 1918 by running for the Louisiana Railway Commission, the state regulatory body for utilities. He ran on a platform opposing corporate power (particularly Standard Oil) and demanding lower utility rates. By stumping the small towns and rural areas he won a surprising victory. Membership on the commission now gave him an opportunity to harass the major oil firms and to further his political ambitions by denouncing existing economic and political patterns in Louisiana. By 1924, when he ran for governor, he had attracted much more attention than usually accrues to a politician serving on a regulatory commission, a body often powerful but rarely newsworthy.

In spite of a hard-fought campaign, Long lost his first bid for the governorship in the Democratic primary, when he polled thirty-one per cent of the vote in a three-way race. Learning from his defeat, Long put together a winning coalition for the next gubernatorial contest in 1928. He demanded state-owned free bridges in the New Orleans area (in opposition to privately owned toll bridges) and made this the principal issue in his campaign. He also pushed for free textbooks, better schools, cheap natural gas for New Orleans, improved roads, and a shift of the tax burden from the lower-income population to large corporations. Long gained forty-four per cent of the votes in the first primary, and his leading opponent, who had been supported by only twenty-eight per cent, withdrew before the runoff.[2] But voter support for Long himself was not extended to other members of his ticket and both legislative houses contained large majorities that had opposed his election.

Patronage and other traditional political techniques, however, enabled Long to force most of his program through the legislature. Indeed his first months in office gave him a record of reasonably impressive accomplishments, although perhaps moderate by standards of other parts of the United States.

Long called a special session of the legislature in March, 1929, to consider a special tax on refined oil. This naturally stirred opposition from certain business quarters. New and old enemies now combined to demand Long's impeachment. To be sure, the impeachment charges were structured in terms of various illegal, unethical, or dishonest actions and he was certainly guilty of some of them. But many of the allegations, particularly those relating to the use of patronage, charged

2. Allan Sindler, *Huey Long's Louisiana: State Politics, 1920–1952.* (Baltimore: The Johns Hopkins Press, 1956), pp. 55–57.

Long with behavior that had traditionally been characteristic of Louisiana politics. It is clear that, while there might have been sound reasons for impeaching the governor, he was impeached not for those reasons but because of the fear and envy of those who stood to lose from his administration and his programs. But Long proved a better politician than his opponents. They managed the affair most ineptly, and when Long succeeded in persuading fifteen of the thirty-nine senators to sign a public statement that they would never vote to convict (conviction required a two-thirds vote in the Senate), the opposition quietly buried the proceedings. The impeachment only intensified Long's class-oriented antagonisms, his personal hatred for his political opponents, and his drive for greater political power.

The following legislative session resulted in an impasse between the governor and his opponents in the legislature. To break this deadlock, Long took his case to the people by running for the United States Senate. He promised that if elected he would remain in Louisiana to complete the remaining two years of his gubernatorial term. Long explained this unusual procedure on the grounds that he needed to fulfill his promises to the electorate. Politically, however, he sought to consolidate his organization and to forestall the lieutenant governor, who now opposed him. If defeated for the Senate, Long promised to resign immediately as governor. He won a more spectacular victory than he had in 1928. He gained a majority of the votes in fifty-three of the sixty-four parishes and trailed by less than 5,000 votes in New Orleans, where he had previously drawn very little support.

His victory in the senatorial primary brought an end to effective organized opposition. The remainder of Long's program passed through the legislature quickly: a greatly expanded highway and bridge program, a new state capitol, tax reforms, and the final dropping of the old impeachment charges. Within a short time, he maneuvered the lieutenant governor out of office and took his seat in the Senate. The 1932 election produced a solid victory for Long's slate. The next session of the legislature produced a host of new taxes, a substantial part of which continued to be aimed at large-scale business.

While he was continuing his efforts to provide economic benefits to lower-income Louisianians, Huey Long was also consolidating his own political organization, ruthlessly smashing such traces of opposition as still existed. The victory of his candidate in the 1932 senatorial election was tainted with large-scale election fraud, though the Long candidate, John Overton, would probably have won by a narrow margin with an honest count. The autonomy of local government was eliminated. The state government assumed control of local taxes and assessments, centered control of virtually all appointments in state officials, and took over control of local police forces. Hostile prosecuting attorneys lost the power to choose their own deputies, and hostile judges were gerrymandered out of office. The governor was empowered to call out the militia at his pleasure, and the State Bureau of Identification, which served as a state police force, was greatly enlarged.[3] Long himself returned to Baton Rouge to direct repeated special sessions of the legislature. With a careless disregard of parliamentary rules, the senator, holding no state office, took up bills his followers had introduced, offered brief explanations and justifications, and referred them for approval, which came in an automatic chorus. To be sure, there were occasional setbacks, both personal and political. But these episodes were exceptions to the prevalent pattern of Long's domination, not serious threats to his control.

At the national level, Long had devoted himself whole-heartedly to Franklin D. Roosevelt's nomination at the Chicago convention in 1932, but he broke with Roosevelt soon after the inauguration. Regardless of his reformist political views and programs, Roosevelt was too much the aristocrat to be tolerated. Long may have been genuinely angry at Roosevelt's failure to seize the opportunity offered by the Great Depression to produce a thorough social revolution, rather than a simple economic reform program, however far-reaching. And in any event, Long's own ambitions and egocentricity made it impossible for him to accept for any length of time the leadership of any other individual, even a Roosevelt. How seriously Long took his own prospects for the presidency is impossible to say. His closest associates assumed that the White House had been his goal for a long time.

Could Long have become president had he lived? Long's political magic was clearly not confined to his own state. He had campaigned impressively for Roosevelt in the Middle West in 1932, and in a fantastically successful week-long and almost single-handed effort that summer he had accomplished the reelection of Senator Hattie Caraway in Arkansas. At the same time, the areas which demonstrated his electoral prowess were all essentially rural, and Long had never

3. While the use of violence by the organization was rare, it was not unknown. See, for example, Stan Opotowsky, *The Longs of Louisiana* (New York: E. P. Dutton & Co., Inc., 1960), pp. 55–57.

managed to appeal to urban voters with the same success. In his own state he had carried New Orleans only when supported by the highly efficient city machine. But the United States by the middle 1930s was no longer a largely rural society. Long would have been opposed in a drive for national political power by still effective urban political machines and by a national administration which itself possessed a great deal of appeal to the urban masses. This is not to say that Long's possible candidacy in 1936 or 1940 would have been inconsequential. Roosevelt was obviously very much concerned about Long's ambitions and modified some of his programs and policies accordingly. But to argue that Long could have gained control of the Democratic party nationally or have won the presidency as a third-party candidate is to suggest that his capacity to work political miracles was far greater than he had ever demonstrated. The belief that only his death prevented Huey Long from becoming president is not supported by the available evidence.

The Assassin

Dr. Carl Austin Weiss was twenty-nine years old when he and Long died. He was born in Baton Rouge, and his father, a prominent physician, had been elected president of the Louisiana Medical Society in 1933. Young Weiss, having graduated from medical school at Tulane, undertook an internship at the American Hospital in Paris and then at Bellevue Hospital in New York. He was considered extremely able—probably brilliant. Weiss returned to Baton Rouge to go into practice with his father in 1932. A year later he married Yvonne Pavy, whose father, Judge Benjamin Pavy of Opelousas, was an annoying though not critically important political enemy of Huey Long.

Weiss himself had frequently expressed his disapproval of Long, but political matters did not appear to interest him very much or to be very important to him. His profession and his family absorbed most of his time and energies.

If Weiss was indeed an assassin, any of four possible motivations or a combination of them can be ascribed to him. He might have been the instrument of a conspiracy of anti-Long political leaders in Louisiana who had despaired of ridding the state of Long's control in any other fashion. He might on his own initiative have martyred himself for this purpose. He might have resented the gerrymander which Long was pushing through the legislature to deprive Judge Pavy of his place on the bench. Rumors that Long planned to accuse the Pavy family of being part-Negro as part of his campaign against the judge might have come to Weiss's attention.

In fact none of these motives is very convincing, and the lack of appropriate motivation is certainly one of the weaker aspects of the case against Weiss. The first two motives, strictly political in nature, are not in character for a man who had little to do with politics. He was disturbed about the gerrymander directed against his father-in-law, but Judge Pavy himself did not consider the matter critical, as he had held his post for twenty-six years and was nearing the age at which he had planned to retire anyway. If this was Weiss's motive, it is extraordinarily weak. The rumor of a Long-inspired racial slur against the Pavy family is more credible, for Long had employed such tactics on other occasions. But in this particular case neither Long's close associates nor the other members of the Weiss and Pavy families seem to have heard anything about the slander until after the shooting. Hence this explanation demands that Long's plan have come to the attention of Weiss before it reached any significant number of other people, including those who would have been most likely to know about it first. This is unlikely but not impossible, and in the absence of this motive, any effort to make of Weiss a deliberate, premeditated killer is not very plausible. Adding to the difficulties in this connection is Weiss's conduct during the day on which he died. He appeared relaxed and under no particular strain, and his last action before leaving the house that evening was to call the hospital to make sure all preparations for an operation he was to perform the next morning had been completed. This is strange behavior for an assassin who knew he was unlikely to survive the evening and that if he were still alive the next morning he would certainly be in jail.

If Weiss did not go to the Capitol with the intention of killing Long, the latter's death was not really an assassination at all but rather the outcome of an altercation with Weiss. In that event, the physician may have killed Long in a fit of temper. That is credible if Long seized the occasion to taunt Weiss with his plans for questioning the racial character of the Pavy family. Alternatively, Weiss may not have killed the senator at all, and one or more of the bodyguards, furious at a real or fancied affront to Long, or retaliating against a blow struck at Long, or believing Weiss an assassin, may have begun shooting at Weiss, killing Long accidentally with a poorly aimed bullet. Even if this is not a case of genuine assassination, it is worth considering for the purposes of this book. At the time, almost everyone perceived it as a political killing, and the impact can hence be examined as if it were such.

The Impact of the Assassination

If we accept the proposition that Long was not really destined for the presidency, the consequences at the national level of his assassination were limited. His influence in the Senate had never been great. He had too little respect for that body and for his party and its leaders to be fully accepted there. His importance lay in his capacity to mobilize and focus discontent within a substantial segment of the American population and thereby to cause the president to alter his political course in response to that discontent. In that respect Long's life and his death had consequences for American politics, but those consequences were indirect and of only moderate significance.

At the state level, however, his death led to developments of far greater importance. The Long machine had been a one-man organization. While Huey had had a number of close lieutenants, they were always subordinates rather than associates. Indeed, most of the major figures in the organization were not even very able men. When they erred in judgment, Long always covered for them. Only forty-two when he died and having no reason to anticipate a withdrawal from politics in the foreseeable future, he had made no effort to train a successor. Hence his death left the organization without leadership.

The immediate problem was to fill the vacancies in key positions. The most important post was the governorship, since the incumbent was ineligible to succeed himself. Much difficult and awkward negotiation was necessary before other aspirants stepped aside in favor of Richard Leche, a relatively unknown state judge. Leche, easily enough elected with the alleged posthumous blessing of Huey Long, ushered in an era of disaster for the organization. Graft, practiced on a small scale under Long, now got completely out of hand.[4] Within a short

4. Huey Long had not been endowed with saintly honesty, but money, though necessary in politics and desirable for its own sake, had always been second to political power for him. Hence he had always kept graft under control and had kept it subordinate to the task of maintaining the loyalty of the voters. What graft there was went chiefly to his subordinates and to the needs of the machine itself. Long died with an estate no larger than might be expected of any reasonably successful professional man. This may prove only that for an ambitious politician successful politics consumes funds as rapidly as efficient graft can produce them.

time the federal government began investigating charges of tax eva-
sion and mail fraud and even a few state prosecutions could no longer
be blocked. Leche himself, the president of Louisiana State University,
the state commissioner of conservation, and Seymour Weiss, once one
of Huey's closest allies, were among the leading figures jailed. The
total cost to the state of "the scandals" is estimated at $100,000,000.
Perhaps more important, the Long organization was temporarily
wrecked. Huey's brother Earl, who inherited the post of governor from
his backseat job as lieutenant governor, proved quite ineffective in
staving off disaster. And enough voters were alienated in the course
of the disclosures to defeat Earl by a narrow margin in his attempts to
gain the governorship on his own in 1940. For the first time in more
than a decade, the Longs were out of power.

But they were out of power only briefly. The hold of the anti-Longs
on the Louisiana electorate was never more than tenuous. No anti-
Long leader gained any deep hold on the affections of the electorate
and any political success at all was dependent on substantial gestures
toward continuation and extension of some of the Long programs. In
1948 the Longs returned in impressive fashion, with Earl winning the
governorship and Huey's son Russell gaining a seat in the United States
Senate. Through the 1950s the Long organization remained dominant,
though not free from challenge, in Louisiana politics. Even the apparent beginning of its breakup in the early 1960s and Earl Long's
tragic personal history toward the end of his last term as governor
left Russell Long as a member of the Senate and as majority whip of
that body through most of the decade.

One of the more enduring legacies of Huey Long was the development of a striking pattern of bifactionalism in Louisiana. From the late
1920s through the beginning of the 1960s Louisiana politics was
structured around two competing factional groups—Longs and anti-
Longs. These acted rather like competing political parties in areas of
competitive party politics and produced many of the consequences
of such competition.

In brief, the assassination of Huey Long destroyed his dictatorial
state regime. In the process, it led to changes in the personnel of
Louisiana state government and in the top echelons of the dominant
political faction in that state. It led to a loss of effective political
discipline within that faction, producing large-scale graft and temporary loss of political strength. This in turn led to its replacement in
power by the revived anti-Long organization and some moderately

significant changes in public policy (though the essentials of the Long policies proved politically unassailable). At the national level, it weakened the president's critics within the Democratic party who hoped to force Roosevelt into more vigorous reform positions on domestic economic and social issues. Hence Long's assassination produced virtually no systemic impact and had only moderate significance for American national policies. In Louisiana, needless to say, it was of greater importance in terms of personnel, policy, and systemic changes.

Conclusions

Why did Long's assassination have such a low impact on national politics and such a high impact on Louisiana state politics? What are the important factors that explain the political results of this murder?

On the national level the answer is fairly obvious. Long at the time of his death had not achieved such national stature, support, or position that his removal would bring substantial political changes. In a basically urban society, he was a rural-supported politician, and although many of his demands for reform struck responsive chords even in city folk, he was widely outbid by Franklin Roosevelt as a national leader for relief in economic distress and recovery from the Great Depression. Second, a state leader (even a dictator), no matter how powerful in his own bailiwick, can have little effect on broad-range national issues or the nature of the national political system. In fact the removal of a local dictator in a basically democratic country is likely to have a calming and consolidating effect on national politics.

For the same reason, the death of Long tended to have a high impact on Louisiana's political system. A state dictatorship in a federal democracy is an anomaly. Despite the popularity of his program, Long's rule was personal; he did not rule long enough to institutionalize his regime. A major factor in the demise of the system was Long's failure to provide an heir as capable of wielding power as himself. At the same time, the alleged assassin could not have seized control and had no political plans or ambitions. In some ways the Long family can be compared to the Somozas of Nicaragua. Despite the collapse of the dictatorship, the Longs remained powerful and for some of the same reasons. Both families had broad popular support, had instituted modern development programs, and faced a divided, outmoded opposition. In Nicaragua, however, the sons were clearly the heirs; in Louisiana no one had been designated by the dictator, and the factionalism within the ruling Long group nearly destroyed the organization. In Nicaragua the sons held together and sustained the system. On the other hand, Louisiana is not Nicaragua. Not only is it a part of a larger political system, but its political culture is different. However corrupt state politics may have been, open political competition, elections, and alternation in power had become deeply rooted. Huey Long was a unique political phenomenon and his removal opened the way for a return to competitive politics. His brother and son gained political office, but they could not reestablish Huey's political system.

9

The Assassination
of King Alexander
# of Yugoslavia

The Assassination

Late in the afternoon of October 9, 1934, Alexander of Yugoslavia was killed in Marseilles, France. The assassin was a hired killer of Bulgarian origin, Vlada Chernozemsky, in the pay of Ante Pavelich, a Croat separatist leader based in Italy.

Following the formalities marking his official welcome as a visiting head of state, Alexander joined Louis Barthou, the French foreign minister, and General Alfonse Georges (Alexander's personal guard of honor for the visit) in a parade through the streets of the city. As the entourage approached the Bourse, a powerfully built man dashed from the crowd lining the street, jumped on the running board of the limousine, and shot the king twice. Alexander died almost instantly. In the ensuing scuffle, Barthou was shot in the arm above the elbow and bled to death for lack of proper care. General Georges suffered four wounds, none fatal. Several bystanders were killed, and the assassin beaten to the ground was shot in the head. Chernozemsky died later in the day from the wound.

In Yugoslavia news of the assassination produced at first disbelief and then consternation. Prime Minister Nikola T. Uzunovich refused to credit the first reports, but when finally convinced, he ordered all theaters and movies closed, forbade newspapers to issue special editions, and ordered the police to disperse any crowds. In the meantime Prince Paul, the king's cousin, had also been informed of the tragedy. Paul proceeded at once to locate his cousin's final testament and insisted that the prime minister open it in the presence of military witnesses.[1] Paul, as he already knew, was named one of three regents for the young King Peter. Owing, however, to the relative unimportance of the other two, the prince assumed political control of the kingdom. No one questioned his authority and the country remained quiet for the transition of power.

The Yugoslav government and people could do little to avenge the death of the king, since the assassins and conspirators were all outside the boundaries of the country. At home Prince Paul had to address himself immediately to the pressing foreign and domestic problems that had plagued Alexander. Despite a strong sense of continuity Paul did not approach the problems of the country with the same perceptions as had Alexander. His government's personnel and policies differed in some important ways from the previous regime, but without changing the character of the political system. In his six-and-a-half years in power, Paul supported political leaders who sought to safeguard both Serb and Croat interests. He also removed the military from an active role in politics and tried to steer the country along the road to constitutional monarchy. He hoped to uphold the prerogatives of the crown, but without using the kind of force displayed by Alexander. In foreign policy he at first depended on the French alliance; but as that support appeared to weaken in the late 1930s, he attempted to come to terms at first with Italy and at the end with Germany. Paul's government was swept away in a military coup in April, 1941, ostensibly on the grounds that he had sold out to the Germans. Ironically, the monarchy itself disappeared in the maelstrom of the Second World War.

The Life and Times of King Alexander

Yugoslavia is an amalgam of heterogeneous territories created toward the end of the First World War. It was formed by the union of the kingdoms of Serbia and Montenegro, several parts of the former Austro-Hungarian empire (the most important of which was Croatia-Slavonia), and the Austrian-administered districts of Bosnia and Herzegovina. The critical factor in the viability of the new state was the acceptance of the union by the Croats under the Serbian royal house. On November 9, 1918, in Geneva, Serb and Croat delegations

1. This train of events is more fully described in Stephen Graham, *Alexander of Yugoslavia: The Story of the King Who Was Murdered at Marseilles* (New Haven: Yale University Press, 1939), pp. 242–58.

signed a declaration establishing the new state. On December 1, Prince Alexander, Regent of Serbia for his sickly and aged father, Peter I, proclaimed the Kingdom of the Serbs, the Croats, and the Slovenes.[2]

Despite these auspicious beginnings, Serbs and Croats soon fell to quarreling. The elections of November, 1920, for a constituent assembly resulted in a Serb-dominated coalition government. Thereupon, the Croat leader Stephen Radich and his followers withdrew. The resulting document, formally adopted on June 28, 1921, when the prince regent took the oath to support it, represented the strong centralizing tendencies of the Pan-Serbs.[3] For the next three years the Croats abstained from parliamentary participation, while the Serbs dominating the central government abolished "many institutions of local self-government that might have proved useful in maintaining the unity of the state." [4]

For a brief period in the mid-1920s Radich cooperated with the Serbs and on the special plea of Alexander again took his seat in parliament in 1928. There on June 20 Radich and other Croat leaders were assassinated. The shots that killed them destroyed the 1921 constitution. The Croats, withdrawing to Zagreb, formed an "anti-Parliament," and in January, 1929, Alexander, dismissing the Belgrade parliament and his council of ministers, set up what was in effect a personal dictatorship.

Alexander appeared at first to be particularly well suited to the task of uniting and governing this makeshift kingdom. His mother was a Montenegrin princess, and Alexander himself, educated in Geneva and St. Petersburg, seemed European rather than narrowly Serb in his views. Unfortunately, Serb nationalism and the attraction of military life conflicted with Alexander's broader political aspirations. His response to the crisis of 1928 was a military dictatorship and a further centralization of royal power, rather than a policy of conciliation among political enemies and concessions toward the federalism so fervently desired by the Croats. In a formal sense the dictatorship ended with the proclamation of a new constitution in 1931, but in effect Alexander remained the strong man of the kingdom. His dicta-

2. Stephen Clissold, ed., *A Short History of Yugoslavia: From Early Times to 1966* (Cambridge: The University Press, 1966), p. 164.

3. Upon leaving the parliament Alexander was the target of an assassination attempt. The bomb, however, hit some telegraph wires and was deflected.

4. Jacob B. Hoptner, *Yugoslavia in Crisis, 1934–41* (New York: Columbia University Press, 1962), p. 7.

torship, however, did not achieve his purposes. Not only did he fail in his efforts to weld national unity, but he atomized political life in the Serbian sector, the very sector that he had hoped to strengthen. At the time of his assassination Alexander was still plagued by the resistance of the Croats, the bickerings among Serb politicians, and the question of constitutional government. In addition he was faced by growing demands for social and economic reforms, emanating not only from the sufferings of the Great Depression but from the increasing political consciousness in all sectors of the population.

In foreign affairs, in contrast to domestic ones, Alexander's policies were generally consistent and, despite the severity of Yugoslavia's foreign problems, somewhat more successful. Hungary and Bulgaria desired the return of conquered territory; Albania and Rumania, with sizeable numbers of their people within Yugoslavia's frontiers, remained uncertain neighbors; and Italy, feeling cheated of territory promised by the Allies at the Treaty of London (1915), sought to disrupt the new state. In the early years Yugoslavia's first goal was "to secure the integrity of its frontiers."[5] In the longer run it sought to make a place for itself in the European state system and to form alliances to protect itself.

Over the years Hungary and Italy loomed as the major threats to Yugoslavia. To forestall Hungarian irredentism, Yugoslavia entered into a series of treaties with Czechoslovakia and Rumania to form the Little Entente. Alexander found Italy much more difficult to deal with. In the early postwar years the only possible counterweight to Italian pressure lay in France. That country, however, was far more concerned with resurgent German strength in central Europe than with aggressive Italian policy in the Balkans. At first France tried to play the role of mediator between Italy and Yugoslavia but finally signed a simple treaty of friendship with the latter in 1927. Alexander clearly understood that security for Yugoslavia required an understanding with Italy.[6]

To obtain a treaty with Mussolini, Alexander offered various guarantees and concessions to Italy. In return, Alexander wanted a guarantee of Austrian and Albanian independence and of Yugoslav territorial integrity. Mussolini at this time, however, was not willing to make such bargains. He still expected the eventual dissolution of Yugoslavia through Croat and other minority disaffections. Italo-Yugo-

5. Ibid., p. 9.
6. Ibid., p. 14.

slav negotiations ceased in May, 1934, six months before Alexander's assassination.[7] During these last six months of his reign, Alexander began informally approaching Germany for support against Italian aims.

The Assassin and the Conspiracy

Croatian disaffection manifested itself in forms more violent than party conflicts, parliamentary debates, and political abstention. Following the assassination of the Croat deputies in 1928, a number of Croat leaders had fled abroad. Among them was Ante Pavelich, who made his way to Bulgaria, where he recruited some Macedonian revolutionaries and professional assassins. Italy and Hungary provided support and protection for those Croat exile groups which in time became frankly separatist in goal and terrorist in means.[8] Pavelich himself established his headquarters in northern Italy.

Despite dissatisfaction with their political position, most Croatian leaders were resolved to settle their differences with the Serbs without resorting to revolutionary action. By 1933 Pavelich appears to have turned to the assassination of Alexander as a dramatic gesture that he hoped would spark a separatist movement in Croatia. In December, 1933, he sent an agent to Zagreb, the capital of Croatia, to bomb the king when he paraded through the streets. The would-be assassin seems to have been unnerved by the popular acclaim accorded the king and failed even to make the attempt. When Alexander announced his state visit to France, Pavelich began to lay more elaborate plans for his murder.

The chief agent selected was Vlada Chernozemsky, Pavelich's bodyguard and a professional killer from Bulgaria. In the event that Chernozemsky failed in his mission, Pavelich planned two other attempts—one in Versailles and the other at Lausanne.

Final preparations got under way in Italy in the late summer of 1934, and an agent, Pospishel, was sent to a Croat encampment in Hungary to recruit a second force. On September 26 a young woman, Maria Vudrasek, carrying bombs, pistols, and ammunition in her luggage,[9] and a high Croat official, probably Pavelich himself, took the train from Turin to Paris. The following day Eugene Kvaternik,

7. Ibid., pp. 19–21.
8. Clissold, op. cit., p. 179.
9. It was believed, and rightly so, that a pretty young woman would not be rigorously searched at a French customs station.

a trusted lieutenant of Pavelich, and Chernozemsky left Turin for Zurich, where they met the group coming from Hungary. The whole party then proceeded to Lausanne. The group crossed into France as tourists at an obscure customs station and went on to Paris.

Following conferences with Pavelich, two from the Hungarian group, Pospishel and Raich, took up their positions in Fontainebleau not far from Versailles, where the second attempt was to take place if the first failed. The other five then traveled south toward Marseilles and established headquarters in Aix-en-Provence. Chernozemsky and Kral, the third segment of the Hungarian group, received their final orders and took an early afternoon bus to Marseilles.

The plan was simple. Chernozemsky was to shoot the king and anyone who stood in his way; Kral was to throw one or more bombs into the crowd to distract attention from the assassin and allow them both to escape. As we have already noted, Chernozemsky carried out his primary mission swiftly and successfully. Kral, however, apparently lost his nerve and instead of throwing his bombs fled back into the crowd and made his way toward Fontainebleau. He was picked up by the French police on October 15. In the meantime, the police had also arrested Pospishel and Raich at the Swiss frontier. Pavelich and Kvaternik escaped to Italy.

Because of the international implications of the assassination, Yugoslavia brought charges before the League of Nations against Italy and Hungary. With the French and British unwilling to alienate Mussolini, the League resolution of December 11, 1934, said nothing of Italy and held Hungarian authorities responsible only for negligence.

Upon capture, the three conspirators talked extensively about their plans and organization, although they tried to shield Pavelich from direct implication. The captured conspirators were sentenced to life imprisonment at hard labor and the absent leaders to death sentences and confiscation of property.[10]

The Impact of the Assassination

The immediate impact of the assassination on political affairs in Yugoslavia was slight, but the long-run effects were at least "moderate" in terms of the changes in personnel and policies that occurred. On

10. A more detailed account of the conspiracy, assassination, and trial can be found in Graham, op. cit., pp. 1–78 and 289–307.

the other hand, in the international arena the immediate impact was fairly severe, while the long-run effects proved negligible.

Outside Yugoslavia the murder of Alexander caused some consternation in the various capitals of Europe. Yugoslavia's demands for action by the League of Nations put further stress on that unhappy body. The British and the French, however, prevailed upon the Yugoslav government to withdraw its demands for the censure of Italy and to be satisfied with a reprimand for Hungarian complicity in the affair. The crisis quickly passed, and Yugoslavia ceased trying to play any positive role in major European affairs. Thenceforward it could only react to Italian, and later German, pressures to preserve its independence as best it could.

Despite the smoothness of his accession as regent and the continuation, at least temporarily, of the prime minister and much of the cabinet, Prince Paul advocated and pursued policies somewhat at variance from those of the late king. While Alexander had been dynamic, dominant, and Serb in outlook, Paul was introspective and Yugoslav in attitude. His primary domestic policy was to dissolve the harsh features of the dictatorship and to solve the Serb-Croat dispute. On the other hand, regarding himself as a "caretaker," he proposed to carry out these changes within the terms of the 1931 constitution. Paul was confirmed in this position by the contradictory responses that he obtained from legal advisers concerning constitutional revision.[11]

Changes in domestic policies become apparent within six or seven months of the assassination. Their beginnings are marked by the parliamentary elections of May, 1935, and the appointment of Milan Stoyadinovich as prime minister in June; their culmination comes with the Serb-Croat agreement of August, 1939, which granted limited autonomy to Croatia in return for full Croat support for the national government. Between these two events, the regent gradually eliminated from the government the clique of officers and politicians surrounding General Petar Zivkovich, premier during part of Alexander's dictatorship. The regency also released most political prisoners and forced army officers to retire from active politics.

There was no dramatic shift from any of the policies established by Alexander and least of all in foreign policy. This continuity stemmed largely from the external environment. Italy had always posed the major problem, not only with her intrigues in Austria, Hungary,

11. Hoptner, op. cit., p. 32.

Albania, Bulgaria, and Croatia, but also with her designs on Yugoslavia itself. Because he could not count on his allies (including France) in any dispute with Italy, King Alexander had begun to make overtures to Germany. In the immediate aftermath of the assassination, Paul's government sought to refurbish its old ties with France, but the French failed to support Yugoslav charges against Italy. By the end of 1936, with German power clearly resurgent in Europe, with the German-Italian alliance threatening Yugoslavia with diplomatic isolation, and with the seeming weakening of French leadership and vigor in European affairs, Paul's Yugoslavia was forced to seek accommodation with the new order.

Prime Minister Stoyadinovich, in whom Prince Paul at first placed great trust, negotiated an economic agreement with Italy in September, 1936, and then moved to a political settlement of their long-standing differences. Stoyadinovich proved a hard negotiator. In the treaty that finally resulted in March, 1937, the Italians conceded some important points, including suppression of anti-Yugoslav political activities in Italy. Although the treaty with Italy did not mean that the Yugoslavs abrogated their understanding with France, particularly the treaty of 1927, it did mark a shift toward neutrality.

Stoyadinovich, not content with his diplomatic gains of 1937, began to imitate Mussolini in domestic politics, by transforming his political party into a fascist movement. As this trend developed in 1937 and 1938, Prince Paul became apprehensive of both a fascist dictatorship and the abandonment of neutrality for an out-and-out Italian and/or German alliance. Following general elections (in which Stoyadinovich's party lost strength) and a series of complicated political maneuvers, Prince Paul eased the prime minister out of office in February, 1939, and replaced him and his followers with ministers more attuned to Paul's own policies of constitutionalism and neutrality.

In its last two years the regency desperately pursued these same policies. Following the despoliation of Czechoslovakia in 1939 and the fall of France in 1940, Yugoslavia found its old alliance systems utterly destroyed and its neutrality policy in grave danger. Without hope of outside assistance, Prince Paul bargained as best he could to maintain his basic goals. Since he regarded military resistance as an invitation to destruction, he finally signed the Tripartite Pact in March, 1941, but only after he had extracted a pledge from the Germans. They agreed to respect the territorial integrity of Yugoslavia and to forego demands for Yugoslav military assistance, including transit rights for Axis troop movements.

Within a week the government fell to a military coup. The announcement of the signing of the pact provoked violent reaction among the Serbs in Belgrade. Opponents of the regent, particularly the military, misrepresented to the public the terms of the agreement and labeled Paul's action a "surrender" to the Axis. Despite the vehemence of their propaganda, the officers who led the coup used the treaty to win popular support to oust Paul because of their personal hatred for the regent rather than any outrage against the regime's foreign policy.[12]

The regency obviously failed to achieve its two interrelated goals of preserving the political system and of maintaining a neutral status in wartorn Europe. Events beyond its borders determined the fate of the Yugoslav monarchy, but the refusal of the old Serb leaders to accept coequal status with the other minorities of the kingdom must bear the primary responsibility for the downfall of Prince Paul, the regency, and the House of Karageorgevich.

Conclusions

The degree of political change that took place in Yugoslavia after the assassination of King Alexander may be explained largely in terms of the personality and outlook of the regent Prince Paul, the internal political situation, and the power alignments in Europe in the 1930s. In foreign policy Prince Paul assessed Yugoslavia's goals and policies in almost precisely the same terms as had Alexander. Paul was forced, however, to shift in 1937 from dependence on alliances to a position of neutrality, as France and the Little Entente proved unreliable. Even in signing the Tripartite Pact with the Axis in 1941, he was trying to maintain that precarious neutrality. In domestic affairs Paul scrapped Alexander's Pan-Serb, centralizing, and dictatorial policies. Perhaps these actions can be attributed to his love of Slovenia, his English education, and his nonmilitary career, all of which contrasted sharply with Alexander's *Weltanschauung*. Whatever the explanation, Paul not only believed that the moment was opportune but that the times demanded change. Although the whole country had been restive under the dictatorship, none of the various ethnic and linguistic mi-

12. Ibid., p. 250.

norities nor any of the opposition political groups showed the least inclination to revolt or even to rejoice at the assassination of the king. The country seemed united against Italy and Hungary for their involvement in the murder and became incensed at the League of Nations, and especially at France and Great Britain, for their failure to support Yugoslav accusations. Paul attempted to play upon these sentiments and bring about a reconciliation of Serbs and Croats and to mollify old-line Serb politicians whom Alexander had imprisoned. Although he eventually produced a Serb-Croat agreement, in the end he fell because too many Serb politicians failed to support him. Policies and especially personnel changed substantially under the regency, but basic problems remained unsolved, and Paul refused to alter the nature of the political system to try new approaches. He never fully democratized Yugoslavia, but on the other hand he forestalled a fascist putsch by Stoyadinovich.

That the assassination did not overthrow the political system in 1934 or 1935 seems to indicate that Pavelich misread not only the degree but the nature of Croat and other minority dissatisfactions. Most Croats appeared more fearful of Italian domination than Serb. Croat political leaders were fighting for autonomy within the kingdom rather than for independence. One indication of the monarchy's support was the rousing welcome given to Alexander in Zagreb in December, 1933, when a would-be assassin lost his nerve in the cheering crowds. Evidence of the weakness of revolutionary sentiment in Yugoslavia can also be found in the paucity of followers of Ante Pavelich in his Italian refuge. So short of men was he that he had to recruit paid agents among Bulgarians and Hungarians to serve as his bodyguards and agents. Furthermore Pavelich had been able to build almost no following inside Croatia. As a result, when the assassination took place no groups were prepared to carry out an armed uprising, and Pavelich had no troops with which to invade the country. Despite prior information, and some delay in the news of the king's death reaching Yugoslavia, the conspirators were in no position to influence the course of events within the realm itself. They could be spectators but not actors in the political development of Yugoslavia during the later 1930s.

Ironically Pavelich enjoyed a few years of power in Croatia under German auspices. When the Germans overran Yugoslavia in April, 1941, Pavelich proclaimed a separate state of Croatia and named himself *poglavnik* (leader). With the collapse of Germany in the spring of 1945, he fled at first to Austria and then to Argentina where he died in 1959. For Pavelich, the author of the assassination, the death of Alexander achieved practically nothing. It would be hard to argue that events affecting him would have been much different had Alexander lived.

10

The Assassination
of Hasan al-Banna
# of Egypt

The Assassination

In early February, 1949, the newspapers of Cairo, Egypt carried stories of "sensational plans to seize power by means of a march on Cairo, similar to Mussolini's march on Rome, and [to] declare Sheikh Hassan el Banna, Supreme Guide of the Moslem Brotherhood, as Caliph of the Moslems." [1] Whatever foundation the story had in fact, it was easily believed by many Cairenes who had endured at close hand the increasingly bitter and violent struggle between the Muslim Brotherhood and the Egyptian government for political control. In the previous December Nukrashy Pasha, the prime minister, had been assassinated by a Muslim Brother; there had been other victims as well, including Selim Zaky Pasha, the chief of the Cairo police.

The Muslim Brotherhood was an extremist, reactionary religious organization founded by Hasan al-Banna in 1928, organized into cells, with clandestine as well as open cadres; it was the most vital political movement in the Egypt of the late 1930s and 1940s. It originally preached the return of Muslims to the pure Islamic society of the Prophet's day (i.e., the seventh century), but as its strength among the people grew its leaders adopted objectives more political in character. Al-Banna himself, it was said, aspired to become caliph—the Muslim world had been without its caliph, or leader, since 1924—as well as prime minister of Egypt.

The postwar period saw the Brotherhood increasingly committed to violent means to obtain its objectives. Now each day brought new vio-

1. *Egyptian Gazette,* February 2, 1949, p. 5.

lence, accusations and counteraccusations, and the continued dete-
rioration of an already troubled atmosphere. The common thought in
early 1949 was that the Muslim Brotherhood was preparing for a coup
d'état.

On the night of February 12, around 8:30 P.M., Shaikh Hasan al-
Banna, accompanied by his brother-in-law, Abdul Karim, was fired
upon by a group of young men as he left the YMMA (Young Men's
Muslim Association) to enter a taxi. Al-Banna was struck five times
and was so gravely wounded that his condition was inoperable. He
died in the early hours of the next morning.

The assassins escaped by car but early police reports claimed descriptions were at hand. A servant whose identity card was found near
the scene of the assault was arrested but later released. The government suggested that the assassins were likely to have been malcontents from the Brotherhood itself and cited as evidence the fact that
al-Banna had allegedly denounced violence (saying that terrorists
were "neither brothers nor Moslems") and had offered to reveal the
secrets of the Brotherhood to the government.[2]

Al-Banna was quietly buried and the police just as quietly dropped
the investigation. With the Supreme Guide dead, the Brotherhood
had been struck a devastating blow. At the most critical moment of
its history its leadership was destroyed. The government did not lose
the opportunity to jail its leaders and harass its followers. Perhaps, as
Abdel-Malek has asserted, "The wave of terrorism unleashed by the
Moslem Brotherhood finally attained its objective: to provide the government with an excuse for suspending civil liberties and striking a
new blow at the national front [a shaky combination of leftists and
nationalists]." Abdel-Malek adds, "But the very excesses of the terrorists forced the government's hand: in order to protect itself, it had to
strike the clandestine organization as well."[3] Thus arose the suggestion that Hasan al-Banna had been struck down by the agents of the
political police, which is indeed the most likely explanation.

Egypt itself continued down the path of chaos that led to revolution
in July, 1952. But when the revolution came it was led not by the
Brotherhood, but by the army. The death of Hasan al-Banna rid the
monarchy of its most dangerous enemy and may have preserved it for
several years. In the immediate aftermath of al-Banna's assassination

2. *Egyptian Gazette,* February 13 and 14, 1949.
3. Anouar Abdel-Malek, *Egypt: Military Society,* trans. Charles Lam Markmann (New York: Vintage Books, 1968), pp. 27-28.

the Brotherhood was severely injured by his death. It enjoyed a brief period of prominence again with the events of early 1952 and the army coup in July of that year. After the eclipse in 1954 of General Neguib, who had been sympathetic to the Brotherhood, and the Brotherhood's ill-fated attempt to assassinate Nasser in October of that year, the organization was forced underground. And there it remains after fifteen years. Not without followers nor without latent strength, it is still but a pale shadow of a once powerful and significant religious and political movement.

The systemic impact of the assassination, though negative, was significant in that it forestalled, if not a coup d'état, extreme political turbulence. Of course the final collapse of the political system was only postponed for three years. But just as importantly, the death determined that the revolution in Egypt, when it came, would be one of the left (or at most the center) and not one of the right.

The Life and Times of Hasan al-Banna[4]

A number of powerful forces in Egypt in the period after the First World War profoundly affected the direction of its development and the nature of its political crises. The first of these was a turbulent religious reform which had its roots in the late nineteenth century. Jamal ad-Din al-Afghani, the Persian religious leader, swept much of the Middle East in the 1870s and 1880s with a fervent plea for the revolutionary revival of Islam.[5] The most prominent of his disciples in Egypt was Muhammad Abduh, whose contribution was an attempt to reconcile the truths of the Koran with the achievements of the modern age.[6] Although Abduh died in 1905, the essence of his message has continued to inspire ever larger numbers of Egyptians into the paths of liberal religious reforms.[7]

4. See Christina Phelps Harris, *Nationalism and Revolution in Egypt* (The Hague: Mouton and Co., 1964), and Ishak Musa Husaini, *The Moslem Brethren* (Beirut: Khayat's College Book Cooperative, 1956). The best work is Richard P. Mitchell, *The Society of the Muslim Brothers* (London: Oxford University Press, 1969). Mitchell's work became available only after the research for this volume had been completed.

5. See Charles C. Adams, *Islam and Modernism in Egypt* (London: Oxford University Press, 1933); see also Elie Kedourie, *Afghani and 'Abduh* (New York: The Humanities Press, 1966).

6. See Malcolm Kerr, *Islamic Reform* (Berkeley: University of California Press, 1966); see also Adams, op. cit.

7. Kerr, op. cit., passim.

Even if most Muslims could agree that the Muslim world was no longer so powerful or so very important in world affairs or that it did not possess a fair share of the world's material goods and inventions, they still did not agree as to the remedy for their misfortunes. Many, Hasan al-Banna among them, did not see a need so much to reconcile Islam with "science" as to return to the pure prescriptions of the Prophet. If the Islamic world was in the doldrums, it was because Muslims had departed from the true path and had attempted to imitate the alien philosophies of the West. To save Muslims and to save Islam it was necessary to return to the law of the Koran. This was to be the rallying cry of the Muslim Brotherhood.

But there were other things troubling Egypt besides religious controversy and uncertainty. The British had occupied the country in 1882 and had become a natural hate object for any Egyptian who felt insecure or exploited. One result of the occupation had been the development of Egyptian nationalism. Arabi Pasha (in 1882) had been its first hero, but Mustafa Kamil was its first philosopher.[8] Kamil's nationalism was purely Egyptian, not Arab or Ottoman or anything else. His early death (in 1910) preceded by only a few years the involvement of Egypt in the First World War, and it was out of this conflict that modern Egyptian nationalism finally emerged. At the end of the war a prominent Muslim, Mustafa Zaglul (later to be prime minister), dramatically but unsuccessfully demanded that Egypt be permitted to send a delegation (hence *Wafd*) to the Paris Peace Conference.[9] British intransigence merely spurred the Egyptian populace to white heat. Riots, demonstrations, and violence of almost every kind broke out sporadically during the next few years. In 1924, for example, Sir Lee Stack, the British commander of the Egyptian army, was assassinated and this act provoked harsh British retaliation. Undoubtedly Egyptian nationalism would have manifested itself in some way or another regardless of the British presence, but their occupation of Egypt furnished a perfect target for discontent and anger. In the midst of the turbulence of the twenties the Wafd Party constituted the great nationalist vehicle for reform and progress. In an Egypt charac-

8. For a discussion of Kamil's position in the ideological development of Egypt see Nadav Safran, *Egypt in Search of Political Community* (Cambridge: Harvard University Press, 1961).

9. Arab politicians have argued many times since that although a Zionist delegation, representing no state, was permitted a hearing in Paris, the Egyptians were not (at first), despite signal contributions to the Allied victory.

terized by religious turmoil and nationalist rumblings the British presence was a constant reminder of the low state of Egyptian politics.

The Egyptian economy was not prosperous and the socioeconomic
structure of Egypt was not merely traditional; it was archaic, exploi-
tative, and nonproductive. It was not that the peasants of Egypt were
about to rebel, for they have never rebelled, but rather that the top-
heavy, minority-dominated economy did not help win popular support for the government or the social structure. The system had many
defects; it limped along without revolution, but certainly not without
complaint, bitterness, and collective frustration.

Another factor that began to protrude in the 1920s seriously affected the fortunes of the Muslim Brotherhood. In 1917 Great Britain
had supported by the Balfour Declaration the establishment within
Palestine of a Jewish national home. After the war the British received
the League of Nations mandate for Palestine and set about implementing their earlier promise. Although the real influx of Jews into
Palestine did not come until the 1930s and reached its greatest figures
only after the end of the Second World War, there was a great deal
of political unrest and some violence in Palestine and among her immediate Arab neighbors over the efforts of Palestinian Jews to establish a national home. This was to become, by the 1940s, the great burning issue for Muslim Brethren, but even in the 1920s it contributed to
the frustrations and dissatisfactions of Egypt's Muslim Arab population.

It was in this milieu that Hasan al-Banna founded the Muslim
Brotherhood.[10] Al-Banna, born in the Egyptian delta in 1906, grew
up a deeply religious and sensitive boy who spent much of his time
in the mosques memorizing Koranic passages and conversing with the
religious teachers there.[11] As an adolescent he belonged to several
Islamic reform organizations, and his general notion, developed then
and never to be abandoned, was that "the sicknesses of Islamic society
could only be cured by a return to the regenerative springs" of the
Koran.[12] His early life was spent in a constant struggle to propagandize his views. A devoted nationalist, he could not be blind to the low
state to which Egypt had fallen; to a conditioned mind like al-Banna's,
political as well as religious salvation could lie only in a return to the

10. These paragraphs are based on Harris, op. cit., chap. IV.
11. His father was a Hanbalite, the most conservatively puritanical of the or-
thodox sects of Islam.
12. *The Encyclopedia of Islam,* new edition, I. 1018.

faith. He was educated to be a teacher and first taught in the town of Ismailia (north of Cairo on the Suez Canal). Here he witnessed even more vividly than before the stranglehold that foreigners had over his country and the helplessness of the central government (even that of the nationalist Wafd).

In 1928 he and a half-dozen like-minded young men founded a "religious revivalist" movement called the Muslim Brotherhood.[13] The idea itself was hardly unique; such small-scale movements were constantly going in and out of existence in the Egypt of the 1920s. The difference was Hasan al-Banna himself. "He had an extraordinary amount of personal charm and magnetism; he was a most eloquent speaker, with a degree of oratorical power that moved his audiences deeply; and he possessed an unusually good command of his native tongue." [14] He also possessed indefatigible energy, shrewd political acumen, and the highest of organizational talents. In more than superficial ways he must have resembled the Prophet himself in his religious fervor, his charisma, and his political and organizational bent.

The Brotherhood was organized as a complicated series of cells and tiers, so that although its membership steadily enlarged, there were not always many contacts among the rank and file. It was an authoritarian, clandestine organization with Hasan al-Banna its Supreme Guide. As with so many organizations of this type, its activities drifted along many tangents, with no control from below and sometimes only limited control from above.

Al-Banna was compelled to articulate the principles of the Brotherhood on many occasions. They are, en masse, an undigested congeries of theological beliefs, political slogans, and popular platitudes. Arab unity and of course the unity of Islam are praised; European exploitation is noted and a remedy suggested: "Moslems must prepare themselves and work in mutual support, united in throwing off their yoke; Islam will not be content with less than freedom and independence with national sovereignty and the declaration of Jihad [holy war], even though it costs blood, for death is better than a life of slavery and humiliation." [15] But most prominent, of course, was the hope for "religious government"; although the Brothers hastened to say that they did not seek this for themselves and that they would be "soldiers, supporters, and helpers" of any government dedicated to their prin-

13. A detailed description is to be found in Harris, op. cit., pp. 149 ff.
14. Ibid., p. 152.
15. Husaini, op. cit., p. 44.

ciples, they did not shrink from the possibility that they themselves might have to govern or that force might have to be used to attain their objective—"they will use force only where nothing else avails." Moreover they longed for a revival of the caliphate; it is scarcely surprising that many Brothers saw in their Supreme Guide the most eminent candidate for its reconstruction.[16]

The Brotherhood rapidly became the most potent politicoreligious force in the Arab and the Muslim world. It was undeniably popular and remains so today (1969), although its current status is a truncated one. Its Brothers came from every social stratum; neither the army nor the court was immune. Its wealth multiplied. Although suspicious of things modern, its leadership did not hesitate to purchase printing presses and the other paraphernalia of modern mass communication. Its appeals splashed beyond Egyptian boundaries and it had chapters virtually everywhere in the Arab world. As the years passed al-Banna himself assumed the heaviest responsibilities of leadership; whatever his original intentions, he could not escape being an Egyptian politician struggling for political ends within the Egyptian system of the day.

When the Second World War ended, Egypt was still saddled with the British occupation. Palestine was increasingly dominated by the Jews. Egyptian society was permeated by the corruption al-Banna detested—can any figure contrast more sharply with the ascetic al-Banna than hedonistic Farouk? It must have seemed in 1948 that the time was at last at hand to move, to save Egypt, the Arab world, Islam. Israel was proclaimed in May, 1948. An Egyptian army moved into Palestine and so did volunteers recruited by the Brotherhood for *jihad* against the Jews, but neither prospered. The same forces that in 1952 forced the army to intervene, in 1948 forced the Brotherhood to gamble on the early attainment of political control. Militant Brothers —there is some evidence of a split in leadership—were ready to use force, which meant assassination, arson, riots, and all the prerevolutionary acts that were to facilitate the final coup, if and when it came. It is possible that al-Banna, as many of his followers still claim, was personally aghast at the violence displayed by some of the Brothers and the retaliations from the government. But one can also note the brief summary of Anouar Abdel-Malek: "It [the Muslim Brotherhood] was the direct organizer of a series of murderous acts: the attempted assassinations of Mustafa el-Nahas (December 6, 1945; April 25, 1948;

16. Ibid., pp. 42–44.

then November, 1948); the assassination of Amin Osman by Hussein Tewfik (January 5, 1946); the dynamiting of the Metro film theater (May 6, 1947); the assassination of the deputy president of the Court of Appeals of Cairo, Ahmed el-Khazindar (March 22, 1948); the repeated dynamitings of Jewish businesses and residential quarters (Cicurel and Oreco, the Ades stores, in July, 1948; Benzion, Gattegno, the Me'adi Company, in August); but above all the dynamiting of Harat el-Yahud, the Jewish quarter in September (twenty dead, sixty-one injured); the explosion in Galal Street (November, 1948), and the discovery of a jeep loaded with explosives in Cairo (November 5, 1948)." [17]

There were arrests and jailings, killings and demonstrations, and a constant inflammatory oratory from all sides. The rules of the political game suddenly disintegrated and the stakes were raised. The Egyptian government was not necessarily out to destroy the Brotherhood, but it did want to insure its own survival. "The prime minister of the day, Nukrashy Pasha, recognized the danger. Fearful that the Muslim Brotherhood contemplated the overthrow of the government after their assassination in Cairo of the police chief Amin Zaki, he decided to move against them forthwith and to break the power of their organization." [18] He proceeded to do this by simply decreeing their dissolution and attempting to confiscate their properties and records. The Brotherhood promptly retaliated by murdering Nukrashi in December, 1948.

The Conspiracy

If the situation had been severe when Nukrashi was alive it was critical with him dead. Even the king was worried about his own survival. The organization of the Brotherhood was such as to make attempts to dissolve it ambiguous in their implications, if not meaningless. The Brotherhood could easily go underground; the best proof of this lies in its continued existence twenty years later. Hasan al-Banna —popular, ambitious, clever—was already a power in Egyptian politics. He was virtually immune to personal retaliation and as long as he survived, attempts at dissolution of the Brotherhood would lead to nothing.

Sometime in the early weeks of 1949 the government apparently

17. Abdel-Malek, op. cit., p. 27.
18. Harris, op. cit., p. 184.

decided to do the one desperate thing that might insure its survival. Hasan al-Banna would have to be killed, but this could not possibly be done openly through legal channels. On February 12 he was assassinated "by some supporters of the government who were not identified at the time." [19] As Harris has said, "it was later believed" that the king and prime minister conniving together ordered al-Banna's assassination.[20]

We are not likely ever to know the full details of the act. It was widely believed at the time that the political police were responsible for al-Banna's death and there is some evidence to support this. The government never really investigated al-Banna's death very energetically and it was easy for Egyptians to read things into this. Undoubtedly the government gained by the death of al-Banna. And, despite his popularity, his death unleashed no forces of destruction; there was no revolt, no coup.

But did the government actually do this deed? The prime minister, Ibrahim Abdel Hadi, was later tried by the revolutionary government (in 1953) and the crime of murdering al-Banna was one of the charges against him. But in 1953 the Young Officers were chiefly out to discredit the former regime. Not all that was said then can be believed. Also in 1953, the Brotherhood was enjoying a brief revival under the benign gaze of General Neguib.

It seems likely that the government used the one weapon that was quick and efficient. It is not likely that the conspiracy was very old. Nukrashy had thought that less severe methods would work. His death demonstrated that they would not. The actual assassins were never known.

For those to whom the evidence for a conspiracy does not seem sufficiently persuasive, the event can be left in terms of what we do know. Hasan al-Banna was assassinated. No official solution to his death was ever reached. No one profited more by his death than did the Egyptian government of the day.

The Impact of the Assassination

The assassination affected the government, the general political climate, and, of course, the fortunes of the Brotherhood.

The immediate popular reaction was one of shock. But al-Banna's

19. Ibid., p. 185.
20. Ibid.

funeral produced no furor and he was buried quietly. The government proceeded with its crackdown on the Brotherhood, with various arrests taking place. Ultimately, of course, a new Supreme Guide, Hasan al-Hodeiby, was selected. The Brotherhood moved into new phases of influence and disaster, but these are all beyond the scope of this study.

The most significant impact was the government's survival, in one form or another, for three more years. This is predicated on the likelihood that a Brotherhood coup would have occurred in 1949. We shall never know, of course, but the government expected a coup attempt. The assassination of two prime ministers might lend some credence to its concerns. If a coup led by the Brotherhood had occurred in 1949, the whole subsequent history of Egypt would have been incredibly different. The government bought time by an assassination and maintained a modicum of stability that otherwise would not have been achieved.

When the revolution did come it was to be a revolution of the left, not of the right, and the religious element was to be minimized.[21] The Young Officers contained only one strong adherent of the Brotherhood, Colonel Rashad Mehanna, and he was to be quickly shelved. There were revolutionary opportunities in 1952, after the July coup, but the leadership of the Brotherhood was too inept by this time to take advantage of them. This would hardly have been true had al-Banna still been its leader.

Conclusions

The Middle East was in extreme political turbulence in the half-dozen or so years following the Second World War. Overt colonialism in the Middle East was undoubtedly in extremis, but there were painful death agonies. Zionism was coming to full blossom and the failure of the Arabs to deal with it to their satisfaction produced overwhelming frustration. Delayed social revolution was also on the horizon. An incredible number of assassinations occurred. On the highest level these included King Abdullah (Jordan, 1951), Riad al-Solh (Jordan, 1951), Liaqat Ali Khan (Pakistan, 1951), Count Folke Bernadotte (Israel, 1948), a veritable chain of chief executives in Syria, beginning in 1949, and in Egypt, of course, a host of important political figures (including prime ministers). Among these was Hasan al-Banna.

21. Some Marxist writers, such as Anouar Abdel-Malek, like to insist that Nasser never was oriented to the left and ultimately sold out.

Al-Banna headed up a growing Muslim revivalist movement that was reactionary and increasingly violent. His religious ambitions also became political. The ultimate clash came in 1948 when the prime minister, Nukrashy Pasha, was assassinated by the Muslim Brotherhood. The challenge could hardly be neglected; it is also likely that the government welcomed the opportunity for general repressive measures against the leftist-liberal elements as well as against the Brotherhood. It is difficult to see how al-Banna could have been arrested and imprisoned without a great amount of continuing violence. The government chose instead to remove him by what might be called official assassination.

His death had considerable impact in that it severely dampened the likelihood of a coup, effectively destroyed the top leadership of the most dangerous political organization at the time, and deflected leftward the revolutionary pressures against the regime. The revolution was not long delayed in Egypt but when it came it was not under the auspices of the Muslim Brotherhood. The Brotherhood, indeed, has come to be (partly because it continues to be illegal) a negative sniping force which retains the power to damage extant political institutions but no longer has the ability to offer itself as a political substitute for any other regime.

## 11

The Assassination
of Alvaro Obregón
# of Mexico

The Assassination

On July 17, 1928, about noon, a young Mexican caricaturist shot President-elect Alvaro Obregón in Mexico City at a luncheon celebrating his recent election victory. Obregón died almost instantly. Arrested and held for trial, the assassin freely admitted his guilt and took full responsibility for the deed. His testimony, however, tended to implicate a Catholic nun as the "intellectual author" of the crime, and although both she and the assassin proclaimed her innocence, the nun as well as the assassin was found guilty.

The political impact of the assassination in the immediate aftermath was moderately high, in the short run of several years seemingly negligible, and in the long run of ten years substantial. This peculiar order of things stemmed from Mexico's political situation at the time. In 1928 the country was experiencing something of a "Thermidorean reaction" after the turmoil of revolution and civil war. Obregón and President Plutarco Elías Calles, closely allied politically and personally, planned to alternate the presidency between them, but their revoluntary followers were divided. Obregón's agrarian supporters immediately suspected some of Calles' henchmen; some even named Calles as the instigator of the assassination. Besides the immediate danger of renewed civil strife, Calles had to consider the question of the presidential succession, because at least one political slogan of the revolution was taken seriously by many people: "No reelection." He met the crisis squarely and astutely. He named Obregonistas to carry out the investigation of the murder, thus silencing accusations against him and his followers. He received assurance of the army's support, and, assembling the various political and military chieftains, prevailed upon them to accept his choice, an Obregonista, Emilio Portes Gil, for provisional president. The immediate crisis passed by mid-September.

For the next several years it appeared that Obregón's assassination had provoked few changes. Calles formed a loosely organized political party out of the major factions and continued to rule the country through hand-picked presidents. When one of these, Pascual Ortiz Rubio, did not serve his purposes, he dismissed him. Except for the emergence of new personalities and the absence of Obregón, in political terms Mexico appeared to be in 1934 approximately where it had been in 1928.

But appearances were deceptive in the early 1930s. The third of Calles' choices for the presidential office, Abelardo Rodríguez, was a capable politician and businessman. Interested in development as well as stability, he brought a group of younger men into the government and continued to carry out some of the revolutionary promises to both workers and peasants. Furthermore, the party that Calles had founded out of expediency became a permanent institution and channel for political advancement. Although Calles again picked the presidential candidate for the 1934 elections, the party played a prominent role in the campaign, and the new president, Lázaro Cárdenas, soon consolidated his position within the party and challenged his mentor. Following a national showdown in 1935 between the president and the Jefe Máximo, Calles left the country. At the end of his term in 1940, Cárdenas chose his successor but did not attempt to govern from behind the scenes. Cárdenas' successors have all represented compromises among the major interest groups of the country. Whatever the exact role of the party today, it has been an important part of the institutionalization process of the Mexican revolution, a process that began out of necessity with the assassination of Alvaro Obregón. Today the caudillo is an institution of the past; personal rule suffered a grievous blow with Obregón's passing. Calles could not retain personal control; Cárdenas did not try; no one today could, even if he desired to do so.

The Life and Times of Alvaro Obregón

Modern Mexico has its origins in the great revolution that began in 1910. Prior to that time the country had been ruled by dictators and plagued by civil wars. Despite some economic development in the late nineteenth century, political stability depended on the popularly charismatic or militarily competent leader; popular participation in political life was minimal; and the absence of strong personal leadership meant factional quarreling, regional rivalry, and sometimes bloodshed.

Alvaro Obregón was born in 1880 in the state of Sonora in northwestern Mexico of a large rural family of moderate means. After only a few years of schooling, he went to work on some of the haciendas in the area. Capable and imaginative, he made a local reputation for himself as a farmer. In 1912 he became an active participant in the revolution when, as mayor of Huatapambo, he mobilized several hundred farmers to defend the Madero government against the uprising of Pablo Orozco. When Madero was assassinated he joined Venustiano Carranza in his uprising against Huerta (who had overthrown and assassinated Madero). Without formal military training, Obregón nevertheless demonstrated natural talents for military leadership and operations. In time he became Carranza's commander-in-chief. He broke Villa's power at the bloody battle of Celaya (April, 1915), but lost his own right arm to a Villista grenade shortly afterward.

With Carranza firmly in power by the fall of 1915, Obregón became minister of war and held the post until early 1917, by which time his relations with Carranza had cooled. Although Carranza opposed his bid for the presidency in the 1920 election, Obregón announced his own candidacy in June, 1919, campaigned vigorously for some ten months, and then called for an uprising when the government attempted to arrest him. With labor and agrarian forces rallying to Obregón, President Carranza tried to flee the country but was ambushed and assassinated in May, 1920. Obregón was declared the winner of the September elections against token opposition.[1]

The Obregón administration (1920–24) was one of political consolidation, cautious implementation of some revolutionary doctrines, and efforts to achieve international settlements. Obregón was a mild sort of dictator, and eliminated his opponents with rewards if they accepted, and with assassination or legal execution where they proved recalcitrant. Not really a social revolutionary, he proceeded slowly with land reform, enforced anticlerical legislation only mildly, and

1. Fascinating details of this era are to be found in John W. F. Dulles, *Yesterday in Mexico: A Chronicle of the Revolution, 1919–1936* (Austin: University of Texas Press, 1961).

while supporting organized labor demands against business, kept the movement under political control. In international affairs Obregón finally restored diplomatic relations with the United States by settling the controversy over property rights, especially to oil-bearing lands.

As his term neared its end, Obregón announced his support for General Calles to succeed him. This choice of successor provoked widespread protest because of Calles' close association with organized labor, particularly with Luis Morones, Mexico's labor czar. Several military commanders revolted, but despite some tense moments, the rebellion was crushed within three months, and Calles was duly elected.

In most respects the Calles administration (1924–28) followed the same general policies as that of Obregón, although he identified himself more closely with the laborites than with the agrarians. In his relations with the United States, Calles threatened to undo the agreements reached with Obregón, but a new United States ambassador, Dwight Morrow, eased a difficult situation. Only on the Church question did Calles depart substantially from Obregón's policies. Where the latter had been willing to forego enforcement of much anticlerical legislation, Calles was determined to push forward. The bishops protested. Calles retaliated by expelling foreign priests, accusing the bishops of treason, closing convents and Catholic schools, and ordering the registration of all clergy. By July the bishops placed the whole country under interdict (to last for three years), and in the west revolutionists known as Cristeros raised the cry "Long live Christ the King." Fighting was still raging when Obregón was elected to the presidency for his second term in July, 1928.[2]

The Assassin and the Conspiracy

Several assassination plots and attempts against Alvaro Obregón occurred during 1927 and 1928. Seemingly none was planned against President Calles, even though the motivations in all cases stemmed from the church-state conflict.

The first assassination attempt took place on a Sunday afternoon in Chapultepec Park as Obregón and some friends were driving about prior to attending a bullfight. A car drove up alongside Obregón's automobile and the occupants hurled three bombs. Obregón was cut

2. See Howard F. Cline, *The United States and Mexico*, rev. ed. (New York: Atheneum, 1963) for a general history of the period.

by flying glass. Several of the attackers were captured and implicated others, including a Catholic priest. Four, including the priest, were executed without trial.

A second conspiracy against Obregón formed in Mexico City among a small group of admirers of María Concepción Acevedo de la Llata, a thirty-seven-year-old nun known familiarly as Madre Conchita. Madre Conchita apparently had no knowledge of plots against Obregón, but she was nevertheless a source of inspiration for them because of her staunch opposition to the government's Church policy. In April, 1928, three members of Madre Conchita's circle traveled to Celaya with a hypodermic needle containing poison, planning to inject it into Obregón. When they could not approach him closely enough to carry out their plan, they returned to Mexico City. One of these would-be poisoners belonged to a group that made bombs both for the Cristero rebellion and for attacks within Mexico City.[3]

In March, 1928, there had been introduced into this loosely-knit conspiratorial group José de León Toral, a young man of the lower middle class, born in the small town of Matehuala in the state of San Luis Potosí. Toral was something of an artist and caricaturist, and, like the other members of Madre Conchita's following, deeply religious and disturbed over the church-state conflict. Also he had been a friend of the persons involved in the first attempt against Obregón. According to his own testimony he at first disapproved of the attempted assassination, but the executions shocked him profoundly. By the end of 1927 he was no longer reluctant about killing the enemies of the Church and became determined to give his life for this cause. In early July he talked with Madre Conchita in general terms about how fortunate it would be for Mexico if God removed Calles and Obregón. She seemed to agree, remarking that God was testing them with these hardships. Shortly thereafter Toral made up his mind to kill Obregón. He borrowed a pistol and practiced with it. At the luncheon in honor of Obregón given by his political supporters from Guanajuato, Toral entered the banquet room with drawing pad and pencil and proceeded to make some sketches of the participants. He then approached the head table, showed his drawings to some of Obregón's top aides and then moved behind them, ostensibly to show them to Obregón. As Obregón turned to look, smiling at the artist, Toral shot him in the face and emptied the pistol into his body. Obregón fell forward on the

3. Dulles, op. cit., pp. 312–15, 362–64.

table and died almost instantly. Toral was taken into custody and questioned.

At first he refused to answer any questions even as to his identity. After he was tortured and identified, he still refused to say much except to request to see a friend. He then led the police to Madre Conchita's house, where he spoke to her about their conversation about God destroying Obregón and Calles. He said he had interpreted her answer as approval of Obregón's assassination. The police arrested Madre Conchita and some twenty other nuns. Within a few days all suspects were released except Toral and Madre Conchita.

At their trial in November both Toral and Madre Conchita proclaimed the latter's innocence. Toral insisted that she had had no idea he was planning the murder and that he had reached his decision before he met her. In explaining his own motives, Toral turned the tables somewhat and said that he regarded Obregón as the "intellectual author" of the persecution of the Catholic Church and Calles his instrument. He said that he expected the death of Obregón to create a popular uprising demanding the repeal of the laws against the Church. He denied that he had any plans to kill Calles but admitted that he would have assassinated the president if the opportunity had presented itself. Toral was found guilty of murder, sentenced to death, and executed. Madre Conchita was also found guilty as the "intellectual author" of the crime and sentenced to twenty years imprisonment.[4]

The Impact of the Assassination

The assassination of Obregón threw the major political elements in Mexico into temporary disarray. President Calles was left without a successor to whom he could entrust the presidency. Obregón's followers were left leaderless, and numerous aspirants to the presidency began jockeying for position. Personal and political animosities were exacerbated as the various groups tried to implicate one another in the murder. The fragile peace that Obregón and Calles had imposed on the nation threatened to disrupt into disorder, if not into renewed civil war.

Calles handled the crisis well and rode out the storm. To undercut any suspicion that he might have been involved in the assassination,

4. The best account of the conspiracy, assassination and trial is contained in the printed text of the trial itself: *El Jurado de Toral y la Madre Conchita* (Mexico, D.F.: n.p., n.d.).

Calles appointed Obregonistas to investigate the murder and prepare for the trial of the accused. He also accepted the resignation of Morones and two other labor leaders from high-level government positions. However, when these same Obregonistas demanded that formal charges be levied against Morones and his chief lieutenants and that all laborites be removed from government jobs, Calles demurred. He first assured himself of the support of his minister of war, General Joaquín Amaro, reassured the laborites that he was confident that they bore no responsibility for Obregón's death, and blamed "Catholic elements" for the assassination. By refusing to undertake precipitate action, by keeping firm control of the levers of power, and by making judicious compromises, Calles not only survived but seemingly enhanced his political position. By September the immediate crisis was over.

Although the threat of armed conflict had ended, Calles still faced the problem of the presidential succession. The revolutionary doctrine of "No reelection" had already been bent to permit reelection after an intervening term, as Obregón had proposed. Calles did not believe that he could repudiate the doctrine entirely. What he apparently planned was to elect a provisional president who was Obregonista in his affiliations but had no important power base. Second, Calles planned to create a national political party by fusing all the major regional and national factions, civilian and military, into one organization that he could control.[5] And finally, Calles expected to govern Mexico from behind the scenes by controlling nominations to political office, including the presidency.

For six years the Calles project worked reasonably well. In September, 1928, he succeeded in having the congress choose Emilio Portes Gil, an Obregonista, as provisional president for the period December 1, 1928, to February 5, 1930. Meanwhile on December 1, 1928, Calles and seven political associates named themselves an organizing committee for a new political party. At the March convention several candidates presented themselves, but the choice fell to Pascual Ortiz Rubio, a politician with even less political support than Portes Gil. He made a willing puppet for Calles, and basically agreed with the latter's call for a slowdown of revolutionary changes in land reforms and government support for labor demands. When Ortiz Rubio later op-

5. For the founding and development of the official party see Frank R. Brandenburg, "Mexico: An Experiment in One Party Democracy" (Ph.D. diss., University of Pennsylvania, 1955).

posed Calles, the Jefe Máximo withdrew his support and Ortiz Rubio had to resign. Congress, on Calles' orders, thereupon named Abelardo Rodríguez, a wealthy banker and businessman, to fill out the unexpired term for which Obregón had been elected.

Not all revolutionary leaders, however, had succumbed to Calles' blandishments of the good life for those who served faithfully. Younger men criticized the inadequacies of the school system, the land reform program, and the labor movement. Fortunately for them, Calles himself had provided a channel to propagandize their views and to organize for political action—the National Revolutionary Party, founded in March, 1929. Calles showed little concern for their voices of protest and named as the party's presidential candidate for the 1934 elections General Lázaro Cárdenas, a colorless but reputedly honest state leader in Michoacán. Cárdenas conducted a vigorous campaign to make himself known and was elected without difficulty.

Within a few months of his inauguration, however, President Cárdenas began to challenge the Jefe Máximo, and by the spring of 1935 had forced Calles into exile. Cárdenas had quietly lined up political support from party leaders, office holders, and interest groups. When the showdown came Cárdenas could present the greater show of force and Calles backed down. Cárdenas quickly consolidated his power by reorganizing the official party, by establishing a national peasant association, by reforming labor, and by making peace with the Church. He capped his various enterprises with his nationalization of the oil industry in 1938. When his term ended he hand-picked his successor but made no attempt to govern as Calles had done.

It may well be argued that the revolution would ultimately have been institutionalized even without the assassination of Obregón. However, it seems clear that his murder forced his partner to take some immediate action to consolidate his political position. That action was the creation of the National Revolutionary Party as a holding company for personal power to be exercised by Calles. But the party proved to be more than Calles could handle. He lost control of it, and his successors in power can no longer dominate the country in the personal way that Calles once did. Interest groups and political factions are solidly established both in and out of the party, and all political leaders must consult broadly on vital issues in order to gain and hold power.[6]

6. Robert E. Scott, *Mexican Government in Transition* (Urbana: University of Illinois Press, 1959).

Conclusions

Several major factors contribute to the explanation of why Mexico reacted as it did to the assassination of Obregón. That armed conflict did not occur despite deep tensions and antagonisms is owed primarily to the personality and political skills of President Calles. He proved flexible enough to give in to Obregonista demands to designate members of their group to investigate the murder and to dismiss labor leader Luis Morones and several of his top aides. At the same time Calles demonstrated his skill in limiting the agrarians' attack on labor, and in persuading labor to absorb some reverses without violent reaction. Calles was undoubtedly assisted materially in forcing such compromises (and thereby maintaining order) by the divisions within the agrarian-Obregonista ranks as well as within the labor unions and by the solid support of the regular military establishment.

The second result of the assassination, the creation of an official national political party, was dictated largely by the particular circumstances existing in 1928–29. By the late twenties, the revolution was already beginning to mature, although no new institutions were firmly established, whether political parties, labor unions, agrarian organizations, or a reorganized army. Obregón, before his death, spoke of the need for a new national party, but both he and Calles looked ahead to long years of tutelage for the Mexican people under their leadership. Both thought in terms of slow implementation of the socioeconomic promises of the revolution. With Obregón's death Calles had no choice but to establish some sort of organizational arrangement through which he could exercise power indirectly. He could not succeed himself legally or politically, and he could not turn power over to a strongly based potential rival without losing control. The party was his response to this crisis, and for a few years it worked as he had intended.

The final result of the assassination, the complete institutionalization of the revolution, and the concomitant disappearance of the strong man, appear in retrospect a normal outgrowth of Calles' founding of a political party that was national in scope and exclusive in the exercise of power and in the holding of political office. Partly through the party mechanism Calles himself was eliminated from power, and the changes that took place within the party as well as within the society at large during the latter years of the 1930s were responses to increasing demands for greater fulfillment of the revolution. That these responses were channeled as they were through an official party and through labor and agrarian organizations officially linked to the party was owed not alone to President Cárdenas who reorganized these institutions. They can also be credited to President Calles, who organized the party originally for his own purposes in direct response to the assassination of Alvaro Obregón. Obregón's murder did not "cause" the reforms of the 1930s or the institutionalization that set in strongly after 1940, but it did call into being certain political arrangements and alter certain political attitudes and actions, thereby influencing the timing and the mode by which these events were carried out.

12

The Assassination
of Admiral Jean Darlan
in Algeria

The Assassination

On Christmas Eve, 1942, about midafternoon, Admiral Jean Darlan, former commander of the French navy and high commissioner of French North Africa, and its chief administrator under the Allied occupation, was shot twice just outside his office in the Palais d'Été in Algiers. His aide grappled with the young assassin but was himself struck down. The assailant was quickly overpowered; Darlan was placed in a car and driven to a hospital. He died either on the way or subsequently on the operating table; the precise time has not been clearly established.[1]

Occurring only a month and a half after the Allied invasion of North Africa, Darlan's assassination proved important in several different ways. For Frenchmen in North Africa it reopened the problem of future national leadership. Many leading figures, especially those in the military, had considered Vichy the legitimate government until the German invasion of the previously unoccupied portion of France. The Free French leader, General Charles DeGaulle, had little prestige at the time and indeed was anathema to most high-level French administrative and military personnel in North Africa. DeGaulle, however, was gradually building support among many groups heretofore politically unimportant, especially among the young. Between these contending factions were the uncommitted (many of

1. The best description of the assassination and of the events immediately surrounding it is found in Peter Tompkins, *The Murder of Admiral Darlan* (New York: Simon & Schuster, 1965).

whom were professedly apolitical). Further complicating the political situation were the Communists, for the moment somewhat pro-De-Gaulle; monarchists, representing various competing claimants to the French throne; and avowed pro-German or pro-Nazi elements, now more or less underground.

The Allied commander, General Dwight Eisenhower, and the French military commander, General Henri Giraud, were hastily summoned from the Tunisian front by General Mark Clark, Eisenhower's deputy in Algiers, and Robert Murphy, the chief American diplomatic and civil affairs adviser. These officials attempted to keep Darlan's death secret for the moment. Given the undercurrent of unrest, they feared that the assassination might be the prelude to a coup d'état. In fact, no significant public disturbances occurred, and the situation remained outwardly calm. General Giraud, largely because of American pressure, became high commissioner, a post he retained for several months.

The Life and Times of Jean Darlan

Jean Darlan was born in 1881 into a solid middle-class family with good political connections. Embarking on a naval career, Darlan proved a highly competent but less than brilliant officer; he reached the position of commander of the French navy in 1939.[2] Although well respected within the naval service, his climb to the top had been aided more by political influence than by his service at sea; he was known primarily as a political admiral.[3]

Darlan harbored not only royalist but also authoritarian and strongly antidemocratic sentiments. Despite his contempt for parliamentary politics, politicians, and the Republic itself, he was forced to play the game of politics, both for his own benefit and for that of the navy. His attitude characterized that of many of the top officers of all the French armed services, but it was probably most widespread in the navy. Darlan was an Anglophobe as well, a sentiment that was to play an important role in his later political performance.

The nine months of active French participation at the beginning

2. George Mikes, *Darlan: A Study* (London: Constable & Co., 1943), pp. 16–19.
3. Alec de Montmorency, *The Enigma of Admiral Darlan* (New York: E. P. Dutton & Co., 1943), pp. 25–28. There is no satisfactory biography of Darlan in English and no good one in French. De Montmorency is reliable on the basic facts of Darlan's early life.

of the Second World War afforded little scope for action by the French navy and its commander. Darlan did argue for vigorous naval intervention at the time of the German invasion of Norway but the French cabinet, supported by the British government, overruled him. The defeat of the French army initially found Darlan reluctant to seek terms from the Germans. As late as June 14, 1940, with the front collapsing and the government fleeing first to Tours and then on to Bordeaux, Darlan threatened to depart from France with the fleet if an armistice were signed. On the following day, however, he reversed his position, throwing his support to Petain and Weygand, who were demanding an immediate request for an armistice. Whatever the reasons for Darlan's change of heart, his action was one of the decisive factors in the resignation of Reynaud and the assumption of power by Marshal Petain, who was committed to asking for an armistice.

In Petain's government Darlan became minister of marine and remained closely associated with the marshal for the remainder of his life. In February, 1941, he became head of the government and attempted to pursue a "moderate" policy. In effect Darlan attempted on the one hand to avoid provoking harsh German reprisals and on the other to avoid enthusiastic cooperation. Never contesting German demands in principle, he in fact yielded to few of them. While he sympathized with the authoritarian bias of the Vichy regime, he was far too concerned with practical affairs to pay much attention to the theoretical efforts at constitution-writing that occupied other Vichy politicians. Primarily, he was anxious to retain as much autonomy for France as possible in the clash between the Axis and the Allies.

Although Darlan's hatred of the British was exacerbated after the British attack on the French naval squadron at Mers-el-Kebir and the abortive Free French attack on Dakar, he remained steadfast in his determination to avoid active French participation in the war on Britain. Furthermore he was determined to scuttle the French fleet if necessary to avoid having it fall into German hands and to deny the Germans access to French North Africa. While prepared to negotiate with the Germans and to stress the close ties between France and Germany, Darlan refused to implement the most important German demands.[4] In the end, his delaying tactics proved intolerable to the Germans, and in April, 1942, they forced his removal. Still, he re-

4. The question of Darlan's motives remains extremely controversial. This analysis follows that of Robert Aron, *Histoire de Vichy* (Paris: Librairie Arthème Fayard, 1954), pp. 340–44. Cf. Mikes op. cit., pp. 28–35, 48–62.

tained his position as commander in chief of the armed services; in practical terms this gave him control of the fleet, the colonial possessions, and North Africa.

Darlan was in Algiers at the time of the British and American invasion of North Africa. Ostensibly, he was visiting his son, who was ill in an Algiers hospital. There is some evidence that Petain wanted Darlan to cooperate with the Americans, to facilitate joint efforts at further military action against the Germans, and to fend off any threats, presumably British, to French sovereignty in North Africa. In the meantime, Petain in Vichy could disavow his deputy, assure the Germans of continued French cooperation, and minimize the extent of German retaliation.[5] Whether planned or not, this is what happened.

French commanders in North Africa were under orders to resist any and all attacks on French African territory. Only high-level counterorders could have halted French military resistance to the Allied landings, and probably only Darlan possessed such authority. Prior to his appearance in North Africa, the American consul general in Algiers, Robert Murphy, had successfully subverted some second echelon French military and civil personnel. As a result, pro-Allied elements in Algiers were able to seize control of much of the city and to disorganize the military forces sufficiently to permit the Allied occupation to take place with little bloodshed. Darlan was the key figure in inducing the French authorities to accept the Anglo-American occupation.

General Giraud was the Allies' first choice for French commander in North Africa, but they discovered that he had little authority among the French leaders there, to whom the Vichy regime remained legitimate. Darlan became the channel through which this legitimacy was conferred. After the initial landings, his collaboration permitted the Allied armies to move directly against the Germans in Tunisia. Minimal forces were required for the maintenance of internal order and for the protection of communication lines through Algeria and Morocco. Although the cease-fire brought a prompt repudiation from Petain, Darlan received secret communications suggesting that his

5. Aron denies that Darlan had advance word of the North African invasion. See Aron, op. cit., p. 503. Eisenhower and Murphy share this denial in their memoirs, as does William L. Langer, *Our Vichy Gamble* (New York: Alfred A. Knopf, 1947), p. 345. But the contrary argument, developed by Tompkins, op. cit., pp. 57–66, is quite persuasive.

course was in fact approved by the marshal. The German invasion of unoccupied France enabled Darlan to argue that Petain was acting under German duress. Darlan was now firmly committed to the Allied cause, although he continued to cloak his actions in the mantle of Vichy authority.

Darlan thus became the de facto chief in North Africa and General Giraud the military commander. Darlan exercised his authority chiefly through loyal Vichy personnel. At the same time he attempted to control DeGaulle supporters and other "politically unreliable" elements, and to limit the scope of Giraud's authority. Many Gaullists were jailed, and some of those most active in the preinvasion efforts to aid the Allies were released only on direct command of General Eisenhower. Darlan's activities understandably led to turbulence behind the scenes in Algiers. When a key Gaullist, General François d'Astier de la Vigerie, arrived from London, Darlan ordered his arrest. Since the Algiers chief of police, Henri d'Astier de la Vigerie, was the general's brother, the job was "bungled." At the same time, followers of the young Count of Paris, pretender to the throne, were trying to revive the monarchist movement in Algiers. Darlan was not unaware of the activities of these groups nor of the dangers they generated. Indeed in a conversation with Robert Murphy shortly before his death he suggested that the American government should consider contingency plans in the event of his assassination.[6]

The Assassin

Darlan's killer was for a time unidentified. He possessed valid identity papers under the name of Morand. Within several hours, however, he was identified as Fernand Bonnier de la Chapelle, twenty years old, of mixed French and Italian parentage. He belonged to a youth group that had been mobilized to support the Allied landings the previous month. Questioned by police throughout the evening and night of December 24, Bonnier persisted in accepting sole responsibility for his act. A military court, meeting the following day, deliberated only briefly before finding him guilty. He was shot just after dawn on the 26th. Until shortly before his death, Bonnier appeared confident that he would not be executed.

Largely at American insistence General Giraud was named high

6. Robert Murphy, *Diplomat Among Warriors* (New York: Pyramid Books, 1965), p. 164.

commissioner. Darlan's supporters were reluctant to accept him, but they themselves were anxious to hush up the entire matter of the assassination lest the uproar further undermine their position. Nonetheless, evidence of a conspiracy mounted. Someone reported having sighted a parked car near the Palais d'Été at the time of the assassination, and speculation arose that it was a getaway vehicle. Various persons had attempted to save Bonnier (the very persons with whom he had tried to communicate from his cell), and these now came under suspicion as accomplices. And most crucially, it became known that Bonnier had made a detailed confession which had implicated a number of fellow conspirators, but which had been supressed by the police. As the plot unfolded (in one of its versions) it appeared that a coup had been planned to install the Count of Paris in power, at least nominally.

The direct instigator of Bonnier's action was reportedly the Abbé Cordier—a young Jesuit royalist. He had confessed Bonnier shortly before the murder and strenuously tried to save him from execution. Cordier, however, may have been only one of many urging Bonnier in this direction, since talk of removing Darlan had been current among his youthful associates for some weeks prior to his act.[7] The Algiers chief of police was also implicated in Bonnier's confession; in fact the appearance of his name persuaded the investigating officer to suppress that document. Behind the scenes loomed Alfred Pose, director-general for economic affairs in the Darlan administration; Pose had initiated the negotiations with the Count of Paris and was reguarded by some as the central figure in the conspiracy. Other alleged participants, some of them Gaullists, included Louis Joxe, chief of press relations for the administration; José Aboulker, son of the leader of the Algerian Radical Socialist party, and himself a leader of the insurgent groups that had aided the Allied invasion; Jacques Brunel, son of a former mayor of Algiers; René Achiary, a young police officer who had been a significant figure in the pro-Allied takeover of Algiers on the eve of the invasion.

Although highly placed Gaullists in Algiers were thus involved in the assassination, there is no direct evidence to connect DeGaulle himself with the decision to kill Darlan. At the same time, he made no effort after the fact to répudiate those responsible or to criticize

7. According to one story, Bonnier had actually volunteered formally for the assassin's role, after the drawing of straws had produced declinations from two of his peers.

their action. Many of those around Darlan insisted that the British secret service had instigated the murder in order to bring to power the British candidate, Charles DeGaulle.[8] Certainly, the British were reluctant to work with Darlan, and despite their problems with De-Gaulle, he was their choice for French leadership. There is, however, very little evidence of British complicity. Sufficient ingredients for the assassination can be found in French political factionalism without hypothesizing foreign intervention.

The Impact of the Assassination

The immediate consequence of the assassination was the assumption of authority by General Giraud. He already enjoyed relatively good relations with the Americans, having originally come to office with their support. He inspired much less enthusiasm in the British, but they were prepared for the time to accept him. To the Gaullists, he was a tolerable leader during a transition period. He had the virtue of being untainted with the sins of Vichy, and more importantly they believed that he was too naive politically to pose any permanent block to their road to power. To Darlan's close associates, Giraud seemed the best choice among those whom the Allies might approve. Their reactionary political views matched his, and like the Gaullists they regarded his innocence as a virtue. For the conspirators, Giraud proved something less than a blessing. As the facts of the conspiracy unfolded, the French administration moved quickly to search out and arrest those involved. Several remained imprisoned for many months, and only Allied intervention averted harsher treatment and additional death sentences.

In the short run the immediate plans of the conspirators came to naught, but in the long run they eventually achieved their major goal. Giraud blocked the plan to install the Count of Paris as a national symbolic leader. Although Giraud was a monarchist, he refused to support the pretender because of his political associations, particularly with DeGaulle. Giraud, however, was unable to provide effective leadership himself. Despite Roosevelt's later efforts at the Casablanca conference to establish the joint leadership of Giraud and DeGaulle, the rise of DeGaulle could not be checked. Six months after Darlan's assassination DeGaulle virtually controlled the entire French adminis-

8. Darlan himself had predicted his death for that reason.

tration in North Africa. By September the last of the conspirators had been freed and Giraud relieved of his military command. Royalist hopes remained a fleeting chimera. To many of the conspirators monarchism had been a means, never a primary or ultimate aim. Their primary goal was to provide a focus for the reunification of the French nation, and in this they proved successful.

In terms of broad motivation, the assassination of Darlan may well have been one of the more successful political murders. Darlan's removal facilitated the divorce from Vichy and made possible the establishment of a new French political system. Although these events might well have occurred in any case, Darlan's assassination made them certain. The assassination also carried in its wake changes in public policies. The persecution of democratic, anti-Nazi, and anti-Vichy elements in North Africa (which had resulted in the imprisonment of many of those who had most vigorously aided the Allies prior to the invasion) declined under Giraud and terminated altogether when DeGaulle gained power. Indeed a rather vigorous counter-persecution began, and many of the prominent figures of Vichy were subsequently imprisoned, some of them for several years. Insofar as both Darlan and DeGaulle were ardent nationalists, the consequences for French foreign policy proved negligible. Both Darlan and De-Gaulle desired to retain as much independence as possible for French action in the short run and to restore France to major power status in the future. DeGaulle had no more liking for the British than did Darlan, nor any more willingness to subordinate French to British interests.

Although transition from Darlan to Giraud saw few personnel changes, the subsequent transfer of power from Giraud to DeGaulle was accompanied by a removal of most of the important officials of the previous regime. Some were jailed; some merely lost political power. Some fled abroad, especially to Spain, where they could be relatively free from retribution. After his retirement, Giraud himself was seriously wounded in an assassination attempt, the motivation for which is not clear. Jacques Lemaigre-Dubreuil, Giraud's chief political adviser, fled to Spain when DeGaulle came to power. Ten years later he was himself assassinated in Morocco.

As for the conspirators, most of them ultimately occupied important positions in DeGaulle's government. Two, including a third d'Astier brother, served as cabinet members under DeGaulle. Louis Joxe became secretary-general of the committee for national liberation and served later as French ambassador to the Soviet Union. Brunel became chief of police for Algiers, with Aboulker as his deputy. Even poor Bonnier had his conviction posthumously quashed by the Algerian court of appeals, on the grounds that he had acted in behalf of the liberation of France.

Conclusions

How is the moderately high impact of Darlan's death on French politics to be explained? In the short run, the Vichyites in North Africa were demoted from political leadership to a position supporting Giraud, and when DeGaulle took over they were removed from political power altogether. There were some changes in public policies, though these were modified less than personnel. The political system itself underwent changes as well, but the Vichy regime would scarcely have survived an Allied victory in any event, and the Fourth Republic was not drastically different from the Third.

In retrospect DeGaulle's rise to power in postwar France may seem to have been inevitable, but this is to attribute to him an authority which was by no means unchallenged at the time. With effective leadership and favorable circumstances, anti-German moderates associated with Vichy might well have been able to negotiate arrangements whereby the Vichy government would itself have been dismantled, but would have been regarded as the legitimate government of France during the period of French defeat. Those elements would then have been able at least to share in the responsibility for building a new government for France. Darlan's presence, close to the highest military authorities of the Allies, would have been an important step in this direction. DeGaulle's road to power would have been far rougher had Darlan remained on the scene; we cannot be certain that he would have attained that power at all.

The lack of immediate disorder and uproar in North Africa is to be attributed to the entrenchment of French civil and military leaders with ties to Petain and Darlan, the lack of unity among the anti-Vichy elements in the area, and the military dominance of American and British troops. DeGaulle's prestige was not yet sufficient to permit him to unify the elements that were eventually to rally behind him. The British intended only to use him, and the Americans did not even want to do that. To most of the French military and administrative leaders in North Africa, he was a traitor. Hence it was only after some months of the transitional regime of the politically naive Giraud that DeGaulle could gain the authority he needed.

The British and Americans could probably have sidetracked De-Gaulle at any time before 1944. But to do so they needed an alternative leader or leaders and an alternative set of governmental institutions. Most of the old leaders of the Third Republic were either in France or in German jails or concentration camps. Giraud was the American candidate but he proved politically incompetent. Darlan, already possessing the loyalty of much of the French military and of the civil administration in North Africa and having the Allies already in his debt for terminating the resistance to their landings in North Africa, would have been a highly viable alternative. British objections to Darlan's past record could possibly have blocked his installation in a top position of formal authority on a permanent basis. But even had this occurred, a government excluding DeGaulle might still have been built with Darlan's help and approval around a mixture of anti-German Vichy personnel and resistance leaders with only loose connections to DeGaulle. Darlan's removal made DeGaulle's accession much more likely, if only because Roosevelt, Churchill, and Eisenhower had run out of other solutions to their French problem. Because of the very special circumstances in which it took place—the occupation of France by the Germans and hence the development of the postwar French government outside France, under the influence and subject to the veto of other governments and their armed forces —Darlan's assassination is the rare case of a political killing unconnected with any very well formulated plans for a revolution or coup which nevertheless produces significant consequences for a political system.

13

The Assassination
of Patrice Lumumba
of the Congo

The Assassination

We will probably never be certain of the exact details of the death of Patrice Lumumba, the first prime minister of the independent Republic of the Congo. The Congo received its independence on June 30, 1960, amid threats of disorder and violence and throughout the remainder of that chaotic and troubled summer Lumumba precariously clung to the premiership. In early September, however, he was dismissed by his political rival, President Joseph Kasavubu, who was in turn "dismissed" by Lumumba. Faced with the potential disintegration of the state, Colonel Joseph Mobutu (now, nine years later, the president and strongman of the Congo), commanding the remnants of the army, assumed control and virtually suspended the operations of the regular government. Lumumba sought the protection of the United Nations' forces then in the Congo, but he was in effect under house arrest (in Leopoldville) until November 27, when he escaped in an attempt to reach his supporters in Stanleyville. Captured on December 1,[1] he was subjected to considerable brutality[2] before being flown under somewhat mysterious circumstances on January 17 to Elisabethville.

Under the leadership of Moise Tshombé, Elisabethville, the capital

1. The actual date is somewhat uncertain.
2. According to reports received by the United Nations, "he was brutally manhandled and struck with rifle butts" by Congolese soldiers (*Security Council Official Records,* Supplement for October, November, and December, 1961, [United Nations, 1963], p. 81, paragraph 52). Lumumba was also "beaten up" on the flight to Elisabethville.

of Katanga province, was the center of revolt against the national government. Here occurred a dramatic confrontation between Lumumba, the nationalist expremier, and Tshombé, the pro-Belgian secessionist.[3] With Lumumba were Senate Vice-President Joseph Okito and Minister of Youth Maurice Mpolo; both were to share his fate. Most records agree that the appearance of the three prisoners upon their arrival suggested that they had already undergone extreme physical brutality, and that they were then dragged from the plane and beaten by soldiers. But from this point on the many accounts diverge.[4]

3. "Mr. Tshombé had also stated that he had personally seen Mr. Lumumba and his companions on the evening of 17 January, and that as a result of the beating and ill-treatment which they had received on the airplane they were 'in a sad state,' and that Mr. Lumumba, whose face was all puffed up, had appealed to him, somewhat piteously, for his protection" (Security Council Official Records, op. cit., p. 91).

4. The conclusions of the U.N. Commission of Investigation were as follows: "(1) The weight of evidence is against the official version of the government of Katanga province that Mr. Lumumba, Mr. Okito, and Mr. Mpolo were killed by certain tribesmen on 12 February 1961. (2) On the contrary, the Commission accepts as substantially true the evidence indicating that the prisoners were killed on 17 January 1961 after their arrival in a villa not far from Elisabethville and in all probability in the presence of high officials of the government of Katanga province, namely, Mr. Tshombé, Mr. Munongo, and Mr. Kibwe, and that the escape story was staged. (3) A great deal of suspicion is cast on a certain Colonel Huyghe, a Belgian mercenary, as being the actual perpetrator of Mr. Lumumba's murder which was committed in accordance with a prearranged plan and that a certain Captain Gat, also a Belgian mercenary, was at all times an accessory to the crime. . . . (5) The Commission wishes to put on record its view that President Kasa-Vubu and his aides, on the one hand, and the provincial government of Katanga headed by Mr. Tshombé on the other, should not escape responsibility for the death of Mr. Lumumba. . . . For Mr. Kasa-Vubu and his aides had handed over Mr. Lumumba and his colleagues to the Katangan authorities knowing full well, in doing so, that they were throwing them into the hands of their bitterest political enemies. The government of the province of Katanga in turn not only failed to safeguard the lives of the three prisoners but also had, by its action, contributed, directly or indirectly, to the murder of the prisoners. (6) The record of the Commission's work bristles with evidence indicative of the extensive role played by Mr. Munongo, the Katanga minister of the interior, in the entire plot leading to the murder of Mr. Lumumba . . ." (Security Council Official Records, op. cit., pp. 117–18).

One other explanation of Lumumba's death may be mentioned. Jacques de Launay wrote in Le Figaro in 1966 ("How Lumumba Really Died," Atlas, XII, no. 4 [1966], 16–19) that Lumumba and his colleagues were so badly beaten on the aircraft taking them to Elisabethville that they were already mortally injured when they were landed. He quotes Tshombé that the Belgians and others had decided, in August, 1960, to eliminate Lumumba politically and that it was not until Lumumba was under house arrest that the first thoughts of murdering him occurred to anyone. According to de Launay, Mobutu "had no part in hatching the plot," and Munongo was hardly so guilty as he is generally made out to be.

Apparently, although agreement on details may always elude us, Lumumba, Okito, and Mpolo were quickly shot in the presence of one of the Katangan ministers—possibly Munongo, the minister of the interior—and very probably by one of the Belgian mercenaries. Their bodies were quickly disposed of.[5] Certainly the government of Tshombé and his Katangan secessionists connived at the assassination, and Mobutu, Kasavubu, and others in Leopoldville winked at it.[6] Officially the Katangan government announced on February 10, 1961, that their prisoners had escaped; several days later it disclosed their deaths at the hands of Katangan villagers. Tshombé and the Katangan government then sat tight to face the inevitable reaction from within and the almost universal condemnation from abroad.

The central government of the Congo was able to contain the domestic violence that ensued from Lumumba's murder. Tshombé, with Katanga returning to the federation, ultimately (1964) became the premier. He overreached himself, however, in his struggle with Mobutu and was eventually forced into exile. Ironically, while conspiring to return, he was captured by the Algerians and died under questionable circumstances in the summer of 1969. Mobutu thus emerged the victor; his contemporary Congo, although suffering from most of the defects of the newly emergent African nations, is one of considerable order and stability and, appropriate to its mineral riches, one possessed of a measure of prosperity. But it is a Congo withdrawn into itself, politically autarkic and seemingly unambitious for African renovations. In short it is not a Congo that could be said to be Lumumbist.

What, then, was the impact of Patrice Lumumba's death? The short-run effect was intense, but it was more shock and disbelief than anything else. The medium- to long-run impact is more difficult to discern in detail, but there is no doubt that had Lumumba lived the Congo and possibly Africa would be much different from what they

---

Kasavubu was largely instrumental in the event; he "knew he was signing Lumumba's death warrant by sending him to South Kasai," where other political enemies (Kalonji) awaited him. The plane that arrived at Elisabethville was allegedly on its way to South Kasai. De Launay argues that Tshombé received a telephone call, only moments before the plane's arrival, from Kasavubu, who said that he was sending Tshombé "three packages"—Lumumba, Okito, and Mpolo.

5. The bodies were never produced by the Katangan government.

6. Tshombé argued that Kasavubu had asked for Katangan detention of Lumumba at least two months previously. Was Lumumba deliberately sent to Elisabethville, or was it simply accidental that the plane carrying him was unable to land elsewhere?

are today. Lumumba was a pan-Africanist, intensely nationalistic, but in no narrow-gauge sense; he was a leader with political magic at his fingertips. His death abruptly altered the direction of development of the Congo and its place in the black African system.

The Life and Times of Patrice Lumumba

The 1920s, the years of Lumumba's childhood, witnessed the Belgian effort to reinvigorate the Congo through European civilization and economic development. The traditional administrative structure of society was reorganized and Belgium assumed direct responsibility for many local activities. The missionaries were active, Protestant as well as Catholic. Partly because of their presence, education of the blacks progressed.[7] By 1938 there were over one million students (with a population in the Congo of 10,300,000), "a ratio which was much better than that in any other African territory." [8] The 1920s saw the beginnings of the mining and industrial enterprise that was to give the Congo its ultimate impressive prosperity. The Belgians saw to it that the blacks benefited from this as well as themselves, although there was always to be a discriminatory differential between the wages of one and the other. On balance, however, when the year of independence arrived in 1960, the Congolese had one of the highest standards of living in Black Africa.

Like the Portuguese, who contrived the delightful distinction between the *uncivilized* and the *civilized* (those who had learned Portuguese), the Belgians spoke of the *évolués*, those blacks who had learned French and some of the attributes of European civilization, in short, those who had evolved. Although the process of granting privileges to the *évolués* was itself to be evolutionary, ultimately in the forties and fifties measures were taken to insure that *évolués* would be subject to European courts, that they would be able to buy real property more readily, and, in theory at least, that they would be able to attend European restaurants and buy alcohol with minimum restrictions.[9] Patrice Lumumba was an *évolué*.

In spite of Belgian efforts to improve their lot (and partly, perhaps, because of it), the blacks in the Congo harbored resentments which

7. See Roger Anstey, *King Leopold's Legacy* (London: Oxford University Press, 1966), p. 58.
8. Ibid., p. 90.
9. Ibid., p. 208.

manifested themselves in protests and chiliastic movements. In retrospect we can discern a fantastic Belgian insecurity, a predilection for seeing in every protest the harbingers of revolution. Paradoxically, at the same time the Belgians mesmerized themselves into believing that "their" blacks were happy and grateful for the largess of their colonial masters. The Belgians reconciled these two feelings by insisting that the discontented were not representative, but were in fact individual troublemakers who had to be eliminated for the general welfare of all.

It is not possible to detail the political development of the Congo through all the years of depression, war, and reconstruction. Inevitably more and more blacks flooded to the cities; and the kinds of jobs they found were such as to increase gradually their leverage in economic and, later, political life. Education, of course, facilitated this process; it is significant that the first black "political parties" were outgrowths of what were, in effect, secondary school alumni associations. The early postwar period saw the establishment of Congo branches of Belgian labor unions. Although their practical effects remained minimal, they contributed in a small way to growing realization among the *évolués* that they possessed some (perhaps still inchoate, but nevertheless real) political power.

In 1957 the Belgians instituted trial elections in Leopoldville, Elisabethville, and Jadotville. It was to be Pandora's box. African political parties multiplied, often on ethnic lines. Frightened Belgian industrialists attempted to maintain some semblance of control by bribes, by contributions to all political factions, and by a suddenly awakened display of concern for the black and his condition. Then came the Leopoldville riots of January 1959 with over-reaction by the Belgians "which had the ironic effect of politicizing the back country. . . ."[10]

What then occurred was a mad rush toward independence. In January, 1959, the Belgian government hastily promised independence —and without delay. Eighteen months later, with only a modicum of planning by either the Belgians or the Congolese, independence came. With it came Patrice Lumumba's brief quest for the sun.

Patrice Lumumba was born on July 2, 1925, in Kasai Province, where he received a primary education in a Catholic mission.[11] As a

10. Crawford Young, *Politics in the Congo* (Princeton: Princeton University Press, 1965), pp. 152–53.
11. The excellent account of Lumumba's life in chap. 9 of René Lemarchand, *Political Awakening in the Belgian Congo* (Berkeley: University of California Press, 1964) has been of great value here.

young man, he obtained employment as a postal clerk in Stanleyville. Despite his meager education,[12] he entered upon an energetic literary career, becoming the editor of one magazine (*L'Echo Postal*) and a contributor to many others. He became active in the Association des Évolués de Stanleyville, and built its membership from 162 in 1951 to more than 1,000 in 1956.[13] He gained leadership posts in a number of other organizations, with the intent of using his contacts as a political base against the colonial authorities.[14] His arrest and imprisonment by the Belgians in 1956 for embezzling about $2,500 from the post office served only to enhance his charisma and further publicize his leadership qualities. He spent his year in prison in writing[15] and in nursing grievances. Ultimately he "rejuvenated the MNC [Mouvement National Congolais] and gave a fresh élan to its cause." [16]

In 1958–59 Lumumba visited Belgium, Ghana, and the Ivory Coast and rapidly acquired an international reputation as *the* Congolese leader. After the Belgians committed themselves to independence, Lumumba became (for them) increasingly difficult, demanding every concession and seemingly offering little in return. He was adamant that independence not be delayed.

Although the most influential leader of the MNC and perhaps the best-known political leader in the Congo, Lumumba was not able to hold his party together for the elections in the spring, 1960. It split into several wings, with Lumumba holding firm control over only the most radical. Moreover, Congo politics outside the MNC was utterly fragmented. The 137 members of the National Assembly, elected in May, 1960, were divided among twenty-six "parties." With Lumumba's MNC by far the largest with thirty-three seats, no one doubted that Lumumba was the chief national leader of the divided Congo and would be its first prime minister.

The Congo became free on June 30, 1960. Within hours of independence the *Force Publique* mutineed, and various secessionist forces began to raise their banners (notably in the Katanga). Public order vanished. A few Europeans were killed, and a larger number at-

12. He was not permitted to enter Lovanium University (the university for the blacks) because he had been married.
13. Lemarchand, op. cit., pp. 198–99.
14. Lemarchand, op. cit., pp. 198–99. Paraphrased and adapted.
15. Among other things he wrote his book, *Congo, My Country,* published in the United States by Frederick A. Praeger in 1962.
16. Lemarchand, op. cit., p. 201.

tacked or otherwise harassed. Communications broke down. The Belgians sent paratroops in to protect their nationals. Lumumba appealed to various sources: Nkrumah sent support of sorts, the Soviet Union remained on the periphery, Tshombé sat proudly on the Congo's wealth in the Katanga, and the United Nations finally flew troops in to restore order. Before the chaos ended, the Congo's ill-fated "democratic" government was in utter ruins, a military dictatorship had been established, its first prime minister murdered, and his murderer himself exiled. Among a potpourri of tragic events the UN itself planned and carried out an attempted coup d'état, and lost its secretary general, Dag Hammarskjold, in his flight to the Congo.

The important point is that Lumumba never enjoyed an instant's respite to act as the prime minister of a stable, functioning state. From the time of his formal accession to power until his deposition by Kasavubu and imprisonment by Mobutu, he had no opportunity to do anything but struggle for sheer survival, for both himself and the Congo. He failed, but it was a failure born of events beyond his control. It is well to remember in assessing subsequent events that the Congo did not slowly deteriorate from some well-established and carefully supported political equilibrium. It simply collapsed, largely because neither the Belgians nor the Congolese had made any realistic preparations for the transfer of power. The Belgians had never faced up to independence for the Congo, and when they finally were forced to concede its occurrence, they had neither the will nor the time to facilitate the transition. As for the Congolese, how could they be expected to develop a political sophistication that few other emergent peoples have shown? All they could contemplate was the expulsion of Belgian authority. They never doubted that they were quite adequate to deal with the "problems" of government.[17]

The Assassin and the Conspiracy

In one major sense there was no assassin or conspiracy in the death of Patrice Lumumba. His death was simply a by-product of the widespread and senseless slaughter that characterized the Congo in the summer and fall of 1960. There is little direct evidence that Mobutu, Tshombé, Kasavubu, or any other Congolese leader directly planned

17. Yet at the time of independence only a handful of Congolese were "university" graduates.

the sequence of events that led to his death. But this was not to say that none of these men (or the Belgian mercenaries in Katanga) was above an act of this kind or did not profit from it.

When Lumumba lost political support in September, 1960, enabling Kasavubu to dismiss him, for a moment no one could claim legitimate authority in the Congo. Lumumba's response, dismissing Kasavubu in turn, was a bold move, but he could not carry off his gamble. This was the crucial moment of Lumumba's failure. It permitted Mobutu to move to restore order. A second opportunity came when Lumumba escaped from house arrest and tried to flee to Stanleyville. Stanleyville was his bailiwick, and there is little doubt that he could have used it as a continuing political base. But with his recapture he became a mere pawn.

Was Mobutu clever in permitting his prisoner to be sent for safekeeping to a man who seemed likely to kill him? Was Tshombé too a pawn here, in doing the dirty work for Mobutu? Or was Mobutu truly innocent in this pageant of murder? Was Kasavubu the real culprit? There are those who say he was. Mobutu on the other hand was never blamed very seriously for what happened to Lumumba.

It seems unnecessary to say very much about the background of Mobutu, Tshombé, and Kasavubu, the "assassins" in this venture. Joseph Mobutu was a noncommissioned officer in the army of the old Belgian Congo. Independence meant instant promotions for whatever officer material there was at hand. Moise Tshombé, the son of one of the few native entrepreneurs the Congo produced, grew up in prosperous circumstances. Shrewd and able, but with no national following, perhaps of necessity he opted for friendship with the Belgians in his attempt to sever Katanga from the Congo. Joseph Kasavubu was born in obscure circumstances—his ancestry was partly Chinese—sometime before 1920. His early training was for the priesthood, but he ultimately became a clerk in the colonial bureaucracy. His rise to prominence was in many ways similar to Lumumba's, through the politicizing of tribal cultural associations in which he held significant positions.

Did Tshombé kill Lumumba? Hardly with his own hand. Very likely, if lifting a hand might have prevented it. Tshombé certainly recognized how much he had to gain from the destruction of the strongest of his political enemies.

Lumumba's death then, it seems, was less the product of a detailed conspiracy and more the result of accidental circumstances that per-

mitted ruthless enemies in a time of bloodshed and chaos to eliminate
their rival.

The Impact of the Assassination

Whatever the exact nature of the events that led up to the assassination of Patrice Lumumba, there is surely less controversy about
the impact that it had on the Congolese political system. This impact
can be structured in the following way: (1) the immediate political
shock within the Congo itself and in the international community;
(2) the long-run effect on the direction of Congolese political affairs
and on the role of the Congo in African affairs.

Lumumba was the only Congolese political figure with the *national* following necessary for political integration in any but a military sense. Even if not in power, his presence (in Stanleyville, for
example) would have been an impossible impediment to such integration by anyone else, including even a military man like Mobutu.
While living he would either have been the Congo's leader or he
would have made it impossible for anyone else to rule.

Lumumba was clearly identified with revolutionary reform. He
resembled Nkrumah, Ben Bella, Touré, and Nasser far more than he
did Houphouët-Boigny, Tubman, Ironsi, or Kenyatta, and certainly
more than Tshombé or Mobutu. This was why he was not "safe" (as
was Tshombé) in western eyes. His death slowed down social reform and the bold and perhaps even wild programs that he was
already advocating. Moreover, he was strongly *African,* like Nkrumah,
and never envisioned his mission to be restricted solely to the Congo.
He wanted African federation; he wanted to fight the vestiges of European colonialism everywhere they were to be found, e.g., in An-
gola immediately to the south of the Congo.[18]

The immediate shock of his death of course passed, as did the
propaganda repercussions throughout Africa and Asia. Gradually
the secessionists were compelled to acknowledge the supremacy of the
Leopoldville government. Ironically Tshombé later assumed the prime
ministry, but neither he nor Kasavubu was a match for Mobutu and
the army. Mobutu took over and gave the Congo a stable, if rather
severe and puritanical, regime.

18. Colin Legum, foreword in Patrice Lumumba, *Congo, My Country* (New
York: Frederick A. Praeger, 1962), p. xxvii.

Conclusions

Patrice Lumumba was a product of the humanitarian side of Belgium's mission in the Congo, of their attempts to bring the advantages of European civilization to the blacks in the Congo River basin. Lumumba received a mission education at the very time when expansion of this kind of activity was at its height. Intelligent, perceptive, dynamic, he would not be just a postal clerk in a period which gave promise to a new social and political order for Black Africans. He quickly rose to prominence as the most popular and exciting of the young Congolese leaders, and when independence came suddenly to the Congo in June, 1960, there was no question that he was to be its national leader.

But independence had come too suddenly. Wild chaos describes the summer of 1960 only too accurately; Lumumba was not able to maintain control over the country without the support of an army whose leaders had ambitions of their own. The army facilitated the handing over of the prime minister to the worst of his political enemies, who permitted his murder out of hand.

The death of Lumumba removed a strong, and perhaps able, political leader whose ambitions and ideologies were such as to be termed radical at the time. His death came at the birth of the political system, when the future political tendencies of the state were being formed. It was an assassination of relatively high impact.

## 14

The Assassination
of Rafael Leonidas Trujillo Molina
of the Dominican Republic

The Assassination

On May 30, 1961, sometime after 10:00 P.M., a group of assassins, some of prominence and high rank in national life, shot and killed Rafael Trujillo, Sr., dictator of the Dominican Republic since 1930. The conspirators apparently had mixed motives of revenge, power, and patriotism. Following the death of Trujillo, they attempted to carry out a coup with the aid and support of the minister of armed forces, but their plans miscarried. Rafael Trujillo, Jr., a general in the military, flew home from Paris, assumed command of the military and police, and together with President Joaquín Balaguer, an old and widely respected associate of the Trujillo family, supervised an investigation of the murder of his father. Thousands were reportedly arrested, and within a few days a conspiracy was uncovered. Some of the plotters were killed immediately; others were captured and killed later. Only two survived.[1]

Despite the vigor of the investigation and the firm control of Balaguer and young Trujillo in the first days after the assassination, it soon became apparent that the political system could not remain unchanged. Balaguer had neither the support nor the inclination to assume dictatorial powers, and Rafael, Jr., did not seem to have the stomach for running a regime in the image of his father. It seems that his ultimate goal was to preserve the family fortune and social

1. Various detailed reports of the assassination have been published. Two of the best are Robert D. Crassweller, *Trujillo, The Life and Times of a Caribbean Dictator* (New York: The Macmillan Co., 1966) and John B. Martin, *Overtaken by Events; the Dominican Crisis from the Fall of Trujillo to the Civil War* (New York: Doubleday, 1966).

position in the republic without having to assume his father's political responsibilities.[2]

These expectations were not fulfilled. When he and Balaguer opened the political system to the exiles and to the opposition at home, political parties hostile to the old regime began to organize and they soon demanded the dismantlement of the dictatorship and the ouster of the Trujillo family. By the end of 1961 the entire family was in exile and part of its fortune had been nationalized. Early in 1962 Balaguer himself stepped down from the presidency and the new regime made plans to hold elections in the hope of establishing some semblance of a democratic system. Although the Dominican Republic to the present time has not succeeded in creating a viable democracy, and although the economic and social patterns of the Trujillo years are still much in evidence, the political system of the dictatorship has disappeared.

The Life and Times of Rafael Trujillo

The long rule of Rafael Trujillo ushered in the modern period of the Dominican Republic in terms of social and political change as well as economic development. His death found the process of modernization far from completed, but the changes that he had wrought were striking.

After gaining its independence from Haiti in 1844, the Dominican Republic was wracked by conflicts among rival personalities, political factions, and regional *caciques*. In 1861 Spain reannexed the country as a colony, but Spanish officials soon provoked revolt. After the expulsion of the Spanish in 1865 Dominican politics returned to its former ways of oppressive rule and rebellious response. By the end of the century, however, the United States, as its investments increased and as its political interests became paramount in the Caribbean, had come to be vitally interested in Dominican disorders. By 1910 bandits terrorized the countryside, and several European powers were threatening intervention.[3]

Trujillo was born in 1891 in the village of San Cristobal, about fifteen miles west of the capital city. The family was rather well off by village standards, and young Rafael was sent to the village school for

2. Thomas P. Whitney, "In the Wake of Trujillo," *The New Republic*, CXLV (December 11, 1961), 7.

3. Sumner Welles, *Naboth's Vineyard. The Dominican Republic, 1844–1924*, 2 vols. (New York: Payson and Clarke Ltd., 1928), is the standard history.

a few years. Trujillo became moderately literate but his formal education was very limited. For about six years during his young manhood
he turned to petty crime, but in 1916 he took a job at a sugar mill first
as a weigher and then as a guard.[4]

In the meantime, the United States had intervened in the Dominican Republic, and after 1917, attempted to create a new Dominican
National Guard. Enlisted men signed up readily, but men with sufficient education and status to serve as officers refused to cooperate
with the detested occupation forces. In this situation, Rafael Trujillo
saw his opportunity, applied for and received a commission, and rose
rapidly in rank with the enthusiastic support of his foreign superiors.
In 1925, the year after the marines departed, he became colonel-com-
mandant of the guards. Later he married into a socially prominent
family, having divorced his first wife. Early in 1930 he overthrew
the government, had himself elected president in May, and consolidated his position by his able handling of the rescue and reconstruction operations following a disastrous hurricane that same year.

During his long reign Trujillo permitted no more than token political opposition, and for many years not even that. Until 1938 he held
the presidency himself, then turned it over to trusted subordinates for
four years and resumed office from 1942 to 1952. He had his brother
elected chief executive for the next two terms but forced him to resign
in favor of vice-president Joaquín Balaguer in 1960 when the regime
began to falter. The "Era of Trujillo," as his rule has come to be
known, was based on force and violence. Assassination of political opponents marked the opening of his regime and a virtual reign of terror marked its closing. He hated the oligarchy and the upper class
in general and went out of his way to embarrass and humiliate them.
Trujillo was no social revolutionary, however. Although he developed
the cities through public works, industry, and social welfare projects,
and encouraged the increase of sugar production, he left the rural
areas undisturbed socially and made no effort to radicalize the urban
working class. Whatever his motives, however, Trujillo's actions produced urban growth and its consequences: middle-class professionals,
skilled workers, and proletariat.

Until the late 1950s Trujillo managed to rule his country with a
combination of cruelty and showmanship. Efficient to the point of
fanaticism, with little sense of humor, he controlled the nation's
political apparatus by generous rewards to his family and collabora-

4. Crassweller, op. cit., pp. 26–37.

tors and ruthless suppression of dissenters. Some difficulties developed about 1955 when the economy began to slow down, and serious troubles arose in 1959 when Trujillo engaged in senseless persecutions and merciless vengeance against real and alleged participants in a June invasion from Cuba. Opposition groups, until then at odds among themselves, began to coalesce into an underground movement centered primarily in the capital. The leadership of the opposition came from the upper middle class and included professionals and students. The greater the opposition, the more determined Trujillo became to destroy his enemies. In a completely irrational mood, Trujillo attempted to assassinate his old rival and personal enemy, Romulo Betancourt, president of Venezuela. The Venezuelan government lodged an official protest before the Organization of American States (OAS), and at a meeting of foreign ministers, the majority voted for a severance of diplomatic and commercial relations with the Dominican Republic. The most damaging blow of this action was the withdrawal of the preferential price for Dominican sugar in the United States.

Despite his difficulties, Trujillo still had a substantial number of supporters in important political sectors. The bulk of the officer corps, though perhaps not dedicated to him, was basically loyal. So too were most politicians and many businessmen who profited from the stability the regime had provided. The Church, though critical by 1960, was hardly revolutionary, and the lower classes, both urban and rural, when not apathetic, probably supported the dictator out of a habit of obedience to authority, or from gratitude for social progress and spectacles, or from a sense of personal attachment. On the other hand, the conspirators and the underground groups included important members of the governing class. By 1960 Dominican society was badly fragmented and the Trujillo family was thoroughly hated by a great number of important families.[5]

The Assassin and the Conspiracy

The details of the death of Rafael Trujillo remain in some dispute, but the principal actors and events in the drama are clear.[6] In late

5. A rather good brief account of the Trujillo regime is given by A. Terry Rambo, "The Dominican Republic," in Martin C. Needler, ed., *Political Systems of Latin America* (Princeton: D. Van Nostrand Company, Inc., 1964), pp. 165–68 and 172–76.

6. Crassweller, op. cit., pp. 433–47, is the account basically followed here.

1960 a plot to kill the dictator was formulated by a group of Dominicans, some of whom were themselves prominent or had high connections in economic, political, and military circles.[7] By February,
1961, the conspiracy had become operational.

Initially the conspiracy worked smoothly. By prearrangement Lieutenant Amado García, who held a post in the national palace, was
to alert his colleagues when Trujillo announced plans to visit his
Estancia Fundación, located on the road to San Cristobal. Such visits
were of rather frequent occurrence. On the evening of May 30, at
about 7:00 o'clock, García made his fateful call, and although the
plotters were not fully prepared and coordinated, they had taken up
their positions on the highway an hour later. Two cars were to block
Trujillo's automobile while a third would follow him out of the city.
At about 9:45 P.M. Trujillo's chauffeur picked him up, drove him first
to his daughter's home for a short visit, and then set out for Fundación. By 10:00 P.M. they neared the city's outskirts, and the waiting assassins began to tail them. Several miles out one of the cars
swung out to pass Trujillo and, as it did so, its occupants poured
a fusillade into Trujillo's car, wounding him. Trujillo ordered the
driver to stop and fight. The assassins turned their car around,
shining its headlights at the Trujillo car. Everyone jumped out of
their cars except Trujillo's chauffeur, who continued to fire his
weapons from within. In the ensuing gun battle, Trujillo was killed
and his chauffeur seriously wounded and left for dead, and at least
one of the attackers was badly shot up.

To this point all had gone well, but now bad luck and ineptitude
took over. General Arturo Espaillat, one of Trujillo's most trusted
agents, heard the shooting from a nearby bar and restaurant, investigated and verified what had happened, and immediately called on
General Román Fernández, the Secretary of State for the Armed
Forces; together they went to Ozama Fortress to alert the police and
troops. When the conspirators returned to the city with Trujillo's
body in the trunk of one of the cars, they parked the car in a garage
and scattered.

Several other events also played into the hands of the authorities.
The wounded chauffeur recognized the voice of Lieutenant García
during the battle, and the conspirator Pedro Cedeño, who had been

7. Howard J. Wiarda, *Dictatorship and Development: The Methods of Control
in Trujillo's Dominican Republic* (Gainesville: University of Florida Press, 1968),
pp. 170–71.

taken to a local hospital to be treated for his wounds, was reported to the authorities and taken into custody. Cedeño implicated General Román Fernández. Apparently information came to the authorities from other sources as well, for within a week all of the conspirators were known and several had been killed or captured. García was machine-gunned to death on June 2, and two others on June 4 in the heart of the capital. On June 8 General Román was dismissed from his post, in July sentenced to thirty years imprisonment, and in November killed. All the other major conspirators who were captured were eventually killed. Only Luis Amiama Tío, a wealthy businessman, and General Antonio Imbert escaped and today are important figures in Dominican life.

The Impact of the Assassination

Seven months after the assassination of the dictator his political system of over thirty years' duration collapsed. After the initial investigation of the murder had uncovered the conspiracy and the suspects had been arrested, the regime, supported by the younger Trujillo, announced that the elections scheduled for 1962 would be held as planned. Furthermore, political exiles were invited to return and were assured that all political parties would be permitted to operate freely. The only restriction was that the opposition parties not advocate or resort to violence. At the same time the government attempted (not always successfully) to restrain the police from attacking the political opposition. It also began to nationalize some of the vast holdings of the Trujillo family and disbanded some of the private armies of the interior, at least one of which was commanded by the dictator's brother José Arismendi.

On the whole, the process of transition from a dictatorship toward a more open political system proceeded surprisingly well during the summer and early fall of 1961. Both government and opposition demonstrated remarkable restraint, given the many provocations, the lack of experience in democratic political practices, and the political and personal animosities that had built up over the years. Some clashes occurred between government forces and opposition groups, but perhaps the most serious struggle ensued within the regime itself. Rafael, Jr., and Balaguer seemed perfectly willing by midsummer to surrender power to their opponents through orderly processes, but the dead dictator's two brothers, Hector and José Arismendi, attempted to hold the line on political change. Late in October Hector and José did leave the country, but they suddenly reappeared on the island on November 15. Balaguer and Rafael, Jr., opposed their power play, and the United States threatened to intervene. In the confusion Rafael, Jr., resigned his position and went into exile, and within a few days the two brothers followed him. In the meantime, virtually the entire Trujillo family left the country.

Balaguer now faced a stronger and more threatening opposition. When he failed to meet opposition demands for a provisional government, a general strike gripped the nation for several weeks in November and December. When the government overcame the strike, Balaguer announced his own plan for a provisional regime. On January 1, 1962, a new council of state took office with Balaguer as temporary president, but composed of a majority of opposition members, including Imbert Barreras and Amiama Tío, the two surviving members of the conspiracy group. In mid-January the chief of the armed forces attempted to overthrow the council of state, but the majority of the officer corps refused to support him. The council regained its authority but President Balaguer resigned. With the removal of Balaguer from office, the last vestiges of the Trujillo political machine were gone, and what has occurred since—open elections, coups, civil war, foreign intervention—has resulted only indirectly from the Trujillo years; such occurrences are a common legacy of other Caribbean countries.

Conclusions

While the Somoza regime has lasted well over a decade since the assassination of Anastasio, Sr., with few changes in personnel and minimal changes in policies, the Trujillo political system was swept away within eight months of the killing of Rafael, Sr. The Trujillo family has been completely removed from political life, and although some of Trujillo's associates still occupy positions of leadership, they act in a completely changed political environment and support domestic and foreign policies greatly at variance with those of the years of the dictatorship. What factors account for these basic political shifts in the Dominican Republic?

The primary factor seems to be the character of the dictator and the nature of the regime that he established. Coming as he did from a provincial middle-class family with a minimum of education, Rafael

Trujillo was never accepted socially by the old Dominican aristocracy. He retaliated by punishing and/or humiliating many of its members, thereby engendering smouldering hatreds under the façade of unity during his long rule. Moreover, Trujillo had a penchant for asserting his superiority even over his close associates by ridiculing them in public, thus extending the area of animosity and desire for revenge. In these respects Trujillo's character contrasts sharply with that of Somoza, who remained on good terms with all who would meet him at least halfway. Where Somoza was jovial, outgoing, "hail-fellow-well-met," Trujillo was taciturn, humorless, and aloof. Somoza made some enemies, but they were far fewer and certainly less highly placed and less vengeful than those of Trujillo. Exacerbating these basic divisions in the Dominican ruling elite was Trujillo's fearful vengeance on real and alleged conspirators involved in a June, 1959, invasion by Dominican exiles. When this was capped by his assassination attempt against Betancourt of Venezuela, resulting in the OAS retaliation against the Dominican Republic, a number of high-ranking Dominicans decided that Trujillo had to be removed and a small group determined upon assassination.

A second important factor was the nature of the conspiracy. The assassination group in the Dominican Republic was far more highly placed in national life than that in Nicaragua. Many of the conspirators were themselves key men or had associates in key positions who were willing to take advantage of the death of the dictator to topple the regime. The conspiratorial group in Nicaragua was composed either of exiles or of persons without status or connections. Several individuals and families of consequence in Nicaragua seemingly knew of the assassination plans but refused to become involved. No one in the government took part. The Nicaraguan effort was amateurish and apparently no political follow-up was even planned. The Dominican assassination was much more professional and coup plans were well-laid. Unfortunately for the conspirators these efforts failed. Despite this setback, undercover supporters of the conspiracy began to demand political changes within two weeks of the assassination, and by the beginning of 1962 the two surviving members of the assassination team emerged on the new council of state as members of the major opposition party to the Trujillo regime.

Third, the immediate heirs of the two regimes were vastly different. Each dictator had two sons who might succeed to political leadership.

In Nicaragua these men were both serious-minded, well-educated, and politically astute. Both were also well-placed politically, one as the legal successor to the president and the other as second in command to his father in the National Guard. Both were on hand when their father died and smoothly took over their respective functions without challenge and without rivalry between them. By contrast, the two sons of the Dominican dictator were totally unequipped for their responsibilities. The younger suffered a virtual breakdown upon his father's death, while the older was on one of his customary sprees in Paris. Although he returned home immediately and assumed control of the armed forces, he quickly made it clear that he had no desire to take over his father's position. That attitude, combined with the demands of the political opposition, opened the way to the dismantling of the dictatorship. The only threat to a peaceful transition came from the two uncles of Rafael, Jr., but they had little organized support. Whatever hope they and their followers had of maintaining the Trujillo rule in the country was dashed by the threat of United States intervention.

Finally, in the Dominican case, foreign influences must at least be mentioned, although they appear to be of secondary importance. Some observers have suggested that the Balaguer regime may have been motivated in opening the political arena by a desire to reestablish normal relations with the other American states. The theory seems unlikely. The regime had economic difficulties, but it was not desperate. Would-be dictators seldom let such circumstances determine their actions. Furthermore, Balaguer and Rafael, Jr., apparently foresaw that free elections would sweep them from office, and that if they desired to retain political power, they would have to suppress the opposition. Foreign relations appear to have been at best a secondary consideration. The same is true of the second departure of the dead dictator's brothers. Certainly the United States threatened intervention if they seized power, but it is clear that they could have rallied little support in any case. The old Trujillo forces had been demoralized not only by the assassination and by the vehemence of the opposition, but also by policies of Balaguer and Rafael, Jr., in their moves to introduce a considerable degree of political freedom and to tolerate political opposition and criticism of the old regime. In summary the old regimes in Nicaragua and the Dominican Republic seemed to have much in common, but the similarities were more superficial than basic. Beneath the surface, the political systems, the bonds holding them together, the forces of tension and conflict, and the provisions for continuity (and therefore the reaction to assassination) were substantially different.

Terrorism and Assassination

The Linkages

In the five years since the original edition of this book was published assassination of major and minor figures has continued unabated. At the same time these past years have demonstrated that assassination has been increasingly linked to the broader spectrum of terrorism. There is one significant distinction in general between assassination and terrorism, however, and that is with respect to motivation. Terrorism seems much more specific-issue or specific-grievance oriented than assassination.

Like many concepts in the social sciences, *terrorism* and *terror* are not easily delineated. However difficult it is for us to be precise and unambiguous, and at the same time, conceptualize these terms in a useful and operational way, most of us on a very practical level are convinced that we know what the phenomena are. Terrorism is not simply violence or the threat of violence. It is not coercion, even on a grand scale. Indeed, terror may result from no act at all but from a perception. Inescapably we recognize the psychological nature of terror and terroristic acts. Experiencing terror is something quite different from experiencing violence or brutality. Some individuals are so insecure that they exhibit terror as a reaction to all sorts of ordinary events. A person may experience a paroxism of terror over receiving a notice from the IRS, or in the days when it was possible, a draft notice. Yet whatever else the IRS and the Selective Service wanted to achieve, it was not terror.

But what then is terrorism? For our purposes it is a series of acts, politically motivated and usually violent and dramatic, that is designed to produce in potential targets (victims may be individuals or groups) a psychological state of anguish, fright, uncertainty, desperation, or despair—or some combination of these. Second, the activities, carried out randomly in terms of timing and targets, are meant to affect not only a narrow group of designated enemies but a broader base within the general populace. Third, the acts are planned to have a cumulative effect, in that while immediate objectives such as the freeing of compatriots from prison, accumulation of guns and money, or the removal of a particular enemy by assassination, may be sought in the short run, more fundamental goals of basic political and economic and social systemic change are pursued in the long run. The latter can be achieved only when large sectors of the populace come to believe that resistance is dangerous and futile—and that belief can be produced only by the cumulative effect of terroristic acts over time, not by a single deed. Fourth, it should be pointed out that while we have usually associated terroristic acts with opposition political groups, they have frequently been utilized by governments to destroy their critics and opponents.[1] And finally, whether carried out by governments or their opponents, terrorist acts are signs of weakness and insecurity on the part of the perpetrators. They mean that the government lacks the normal institutional means of asserting its authority and that the opposition lacks the strength to displace the ruling powers by constitutional means or by armed uprising.

Terror is the psychological reaction often produced in individuals subject to such stimuli: severe, irrational, and unrational fright, perhaps ultimately a state that can be described as anguished despair. These strong words are not carelessly chosen. Terror results from not knowing the dangers one faces, of knowing at the same time that one is a likely target of attack by virtue of one's uniform, nationality, race, or some other non-personal characteristic. The Zebra killings of whites in the San Francisco area in 1974 produced terror among many who otherwise would have walked the streets in some assurance of safety. Of course, a terrorized community will possess individuals of all

1. In Latin America well known terrorist groups supported by or in alliance with regime personnel include the Halcones (Hawks) of Mexico, the Mano Blanca (White Hand) of Guatemala, and the Argentine Anti-Communist Alliance.

shades of behavior patterns. Not all people react the same way to the same stimuli, but some, "terrorized" by what they perceive to be "threats" to themselves, may become frenzied and utterly unpredictable in their behavior.

In May 1975 two American airforce colonels, on active duty as part of the American military mission in Iran, were killed by Iranian terrorists, who were opponents of the Shah's regime. There was no special antipathy to these particular individuals; they were chosen at random as representative of a class of targets. It is likely that both of these individuals had seen active service in Vietnam and had bravely faced death in combat on numerous occasions. Their families had grown enured to the possibility of death in war. Yet the immediate and unquestioned response of a large part of the American military community in Iran and other similar areas where military missions are located was and remains a modicum of terror. Facing death in combat is a very different thing from facing the uncertainty of life or death as the random target of groups who have no personal interest in the victim except that killing him can be convenient and useful. For such a military community of course various actions may be taken by officers who view that uncertainty seriously. They become more alert. They abandon habitual times and paths of going to their offices or of returning. They arm themselves. They organize special defenses, which may result in some cases in the creation of sizeable security "armies." They send their families home. They themselves hole up in the American compounds and go out on the country as little as possible. They may ask for reassignment and eventually may depart before their tour of duty has expired. At best they are more suspicious of the "natives," less accommodating and less eager to do their job. Their morale has been lowered. The above things will not all apply to every individual but the picture is not an inaccurate one.

The significant thing is that all of these responses are very acceptable to the terrorists themselves. At relatively low cost and risk to themselves—assassinating two field grade officers is not a remarkable achievement—they have exerted a substantial terroristic leverage over the attitudes of American military personnel and have embarrassed the Shah's government. The return on their investment has been manyfold.

To an outside observer much of this fear appears "irrational." We

say irrational because even with the terrorism of today in its world
context, the chances of an American ambassador being kidnapped or
murdered, or of an American military officer being killed, are not very
high. But one who becomes a possible target knows that he might
become the next victim, however low those chances are. With a
minimum investment of time or money the perpetrators of these acts
can achieve a gigantic response of concern on the part of those whom
they have chosen as targets. This is the nature of terrorism and is
the reason why it has been so widespread in space and time. Perhaps
because in the 1970s we are all subject to the mass media and their
tendency to emphasize the bizarre and the spectacular, we exaggerate
the amount of terrorism there is in the world. Like assassination, however, it is a rare phenomenon when the sizes of the world and its
population are taken into account.

The perpetrators of these activities (the terrorists) normally have
grievances that have remained unredressed; these may be real or
imagined. Terrorists may work in cooperation with other similarly
minded individuals or, less frequently, they may work alone. They
may be involved in overthrowing a regime (the British in Ulster),
destroying a state (Israel), or expelling an alien power (the United
States in Vietnam). Is there, however, a common thread that ties these
types together? Can we construct a profile of a terrorist? One observer
says that we can. The terrorist tends to be young, male, middle class,
and economically marginal. He is dedicated to his cause, believes in
its fundamental rightness, and is willing to take life and give his own
for its successful outcome. He is often a part-time revolutionary, holding a job in society that serves as a cover for his unconventional life.
And finally the terrorist tends to be poorly formed ideologically; his
commitment is to the deed, not to the idea or even to the final results
of his acts.[2]

What is the nature of the terrorist act and what "threats" do terrorists employ? Although people can become terrified from a wide range
of events and activities, modern terrorism can be somewhat more
narrowly delineated. Public buildings are bombed, aircraft hijacked,
and explosive devices are used to kill or destroy. People are kidnapped

2. Irving Louis Horowitz, *Political Terrorism and Personal Deviance*, External
Research Study, Department of State, Washington, D.C., (XR/RNAS-5), Feb. 15,
1973, pp. 2–5.

and held for political or monetary ransom. On a minor key, mysterious telephone calls, threatening letters, and nuisance acts all fall within the rubric. In a more serious vein, hostages are taken in forays against the enemy and are on occasion murdered. And finally public—and sometimes, not so public—officials are "executed."[3] Such executions are of course forms of assassinations; they support our contention that the more general study of terrorism must accompany the study of assassination.

Whatever the motivations or intentions of assassins there seems little question about the symbolic quality of most terroristic action. A hostage is rarely killed because of *his* qualities or lack of them; he is killed because some hostage must be killed. When the British were in their last phase of trying to hold Palestine after the Second World War, a three-pronged terroristic struggle was going on among the Jews, the Arabs, and the British themselves. Typically news accounts would report that the body of a British sergeant or sometimes that of an officer would have been found dangling from a tree. He had been "executed." No particular hatred had been directed at him personally; he had merely been conveniently found, and killed.

Victims like these are enormously difficult to protect. Not every British soldier in Northern Ireland can be given the kind of protection he needs from those who are willing to kill him merely to remind Irishmen that all is not yet well, and Englishmen that they must continue to pay a heavy price for their intransigence. Constant news accounts of one or two deaths or maimings a week for week after week are emotionally difficult for most people to bear. Governments find their support sometimes eroding not because of the final cost in dead and wounded but because of the constantness and never-endingness of it.

Terrorism is apt to be more highly organized than are single acts of assassination and is similarly more likely to be the result of ideological or nationalist urgings than assassination, which can be pro-

3. Two of the most publicized examples recently were the Olympic Games massacre of Israeli competitors (see Serge Groussard *The Blood of Israel: The Massacre of the Israeli Athletes, 1972* [New York: William Morrow and Co., 1975]) in 1972 and the murder of American diplomats in Khartoum in 1973. These deaths were by terrorism but, in contrast, the death of the American ambassador in Cyprus in the disturbances there in 1974 was not.

duced by individual grievances and perversities. Although we found in our original study no clear-cut nexus between political turbulence and the assassination of high-level political figures this connection is considerably more apparent with respect to terrorism. Political turbulence breeds ideological tension. National struggles for independence, or what passes for them,[4] are even more likely to create the conditions for terrorism, because terrorism is the one weapon that such movements, often small and poor in their initial stages, can afford.

In the United States, the Vietnam •War alienated a generation of youth—or if the explanation is not so simple, certainly that war contributed heavily to the alienation—and led frustrated students and sympathizers into attacking the "system" by any means that could come to hand.[5] It is difficult to read an account of the SDS—that by Alan Adelson comes to mind[6]—without recognizing the seeds of terrorist extremism, the Weatherman in this case, in the more normal activities of the SDS itself. Probably the great bulk of the SDS would, quite properly, object to the identification of their organization or of their methods with those of the Weatherman. Yet the anomic, chaotic atmosphere that they themselves engendered and encouraged laid the foundations for those who found exhilaration from nihilism itself.

At the more modest end of the terroristic spectrum, a terroristic act can be performed with almost no effort at all. A telephone call, from

4. This phrase is not intended to ridicule the genuine struggle for independence of a people from, say, a colonial regime. Yet no struggle of this kind has the support of all people. After all, there were Tories during the American revolutionary period. Some "struggles for independence" are so small and illusory that to treat them seriously is difficult. There is little to stop a very small group from beginning terroristic operations in the name of the "people" when their support is almost vanishingly small. The French Canadian nationalists in Quebec might fall into this category; certainly the Puerto Rican nationalists do.

5. See Lewis S. Feuer *The Conflict of Generations: The Character and Significance of Student Movements* (New York: Basic Books, Inc., Publishers, 1969). On June 9, 1975 Susan Edith Saxe, a student "radical" of the late 1960s, pleaded guilty to "bank robbery and theft from a Federal arsenal and said she did not regret those 1970 crimes." In a "defiant statement" before the judge she said, "That armed struggle against the American state was a valid and necessary escalation of the politics of the sixties." (*The New York Times,* June 10, 1975) See also Susan Stern *With the Weatherman: The Personal Journal of a Revolutionary Woman* (New York: Doubleday & Co., 1975).

6. Alan Adelson *SDS* (New York: Charles Scribner's Sons, 1972).

a pay phone, that warns that the state capitol contains a bomb, often empties its chambers. Usually there is no bomb, but there have been a few in the past and buildings have been destroyed and lives lost. So the warning is taken seriously and people are inconvenienced. They have perceived the threat. A little publicity can often be obtained afterward by an anonymous letter to a newspaper editor. Sometimes an "amateur" group of malcontents can generate publicity by taking credit for all bad incidents, even those that have happened without other apparent cause, e.g. an accidental derailing of a subway train. The result in this last example is that some people may not ride subway trains for a time. Even escalating terroristic activities is at first not expensive. Bombing a building takes more effort than merely threatening to bomb it but not a great deal more. The most complicated thing is making the bomb itself, but knowledge is widespread and the ingredients for bombs are commonplace and cheap. So a bomb is made, planted in an appropriate building and ignited. It is heady work. Assaults and robberies can also be "pulled off" without a great deal of effort. Each success inspires the group to bigger and more grandiose things. Perhaps a killing, an assassination, is planned and carried out. A business man, a school superintendent, a public official or perhaps some inconsequential individual is chosen as the target. It is not difficult to kill such a person if he has had no warning. A kidnapping is more complicated, and takes advance planning and a modicum of sensible organization. But kidnappings have become very commonplace; a goodly percentage of them is carried out to satisfactory (for the terrorists) conclusions. Organizing guerilla raids across borders—we are thinking of Palestinian terrorists here—requires even more planning and a great deal of derring-do. It takes dedication and a willingness to cast one's own life away.

At little cost in time and manpower, terrorist groups can win enormous successes instilling fear and anxiety in the enemy, and strengthening conviction of ultimate victory in their supporters. They have no budgets that run into billions of dollars—or rubles or rials—and they do not have fleets of planes and millions of troops. They may possess merely a few dozen dedicated followers, a few bombs and sub-machine guns and a mimeograph machine. They are do-it-yourself warriors and their success is often, but not always, out of all proportion to their numbers. The Symbionese Liberation Army in the United States certainly is an example.[7] Probably never numbering more than a few individuals in the San Francisco area and indeed never carrying out very many terroristic acts, it has gotten enormous publicity. It "first achieved notoriety by claiming responsibility for the murder of Oakland's Superintendent of Schools, Dr. Marcus Foster, and the serious wounding of deputy superintendent, Robert Blackburn, in an ambush on the night of November 6, 1973. On November 10, the Oakland Tribune, San Francisco Chronicle and radio station KPFA-FM, a part of the Pacifica network, each received a photocopied letter from the Western Regional Youth Unit of the Symbionese Liberation Army taking credit for the shootings."[8] Since then several suspects have been apprehended, charged and convicted for this act; since then too a number of SLA members have been killed in a shootout with the police in Los Angeles. The killing of an Oakland school superintendent was attention getting and the SLA got all of the publicity that it wanted. But it pulled its greatest coup in the kidnapping of Patricia Hearst in February 1974. Hearst's father was a famous and wealthy publisher of newspapers and magazines. The event was bound to get the maximum amount of publicity. The result was a food giveaway program demanded of the Hearst family, a robbery of a bank with Patricia Hearst as an alleged accomplice, and finally a statement by Patricia Hearst that she had decided to become a member of the group that had kidnapped her. Despite an unprecedented effort by police and the FBI Patricia Hearst was not apprehended until September 1975, nineteen months after the kidnapping. All of this attention has been given to the SLA to illustrate the principle that it often costs little for a terrorist gang to achieve enormous publicity. A killing or two, a kidnapping, a robbery more or less—although personally tragic to the individuals concerned, the sum total was and is not that great in a nation that generates much crime and much bloodshed. Nevertheless this modest amount of violence against cleverly chosen targets, and

7. See *Terrorism*, A Staff Study of the Committee on Internal Security of the United States House of Representatives (93rd Congress, Second Session), (Washington: U.S. Government Printing Office, 1974) for some details on the SLA. It includes a summary of its activity as well as selected documents and newspaper clippings about its organization and demands. A recent book about the SLA and Joseph Remiro, one of its members, is John Bryan *This Soldier Still at War* (New York: Harcourt Brace Jovanovich, 1975).
8. *Ibid.*, p. 135.

a flair for publicity, have given the SLA far more attention than its members could ever have expected.

The conclusion to be drawn from examples like this one is that a terrorist campaign is cheap and easily put together. Almost any small group can do it. If it has small goals they can often be achieved. And in any case it is easy to get attention, and some of it sympathetic. Put more succinctly, *terrorism often pays off*.

Although the SLA campaign was of little significance to the United States or to the world, other terroristic campaigns have achieved important results with international implications. There is no room for a detailed resumé of the history of such terrorism, even in the 20th century, but several examples can be offered. Three not unrepresentative examples are Cyprus, Palestine, and Ireland (including both the Irish Republic and Ulster).

Without being concerned here with the long and troubled history of Cyprus, the island in the eastern Mediterranean, its record since the mid-1930s has been one of violence, revolution, terrorism and civil war. Conquered by the Turks in 1511, it came under British control in the late 19th century. Its population is approximately 80 percent ethnic Greek and 20 percent Turkish. At first Greeks and Turks were moderately in agreement that they would prefer their own government, whatever it might be, to that of the British. Many of the Greeks, however, wanted *enosis*, or reunion with mainland Greece. A terrorist campaign against the British went a long way to driving the British out by 1960. But an independent Cypriote government under Archbishop Makarios could not gain legitimacy in the eyes of the most rabid of Greek nationalists; their terrorist campaign in later years did much to undermine Makarios' authority; finally their attempt at a coup brought in the Turkish government in an attempt to protect the interests of the Turkish minority. Today (1975) a de facto partition of the island into Greek and Turkish enclaves has occurred, the worst solution by Greek Cypriote standards. Had terrorism not been used, largely by Greeks against the British and the Turks (and against each other), almost certainly the current political situation would have been different. The British would not have left when they did, and when they did leave, they would have probably left a more viable successor regime behind them. The agony between Greece and Turkey, as well as between Cypriote Greeks and Turks, would not have been so acute. Probably there would not have been any partition of the island. It is not that this partition is bad or even that the above analysis is necessarily correct in detail, but that without terrorism the final result would have been different in important ways. Terrorism was a cheap but effective way for the Greeks to fight the Turks and the British. It resulted in substantial change.

The word "Palestine" is chosen here deliberately rather than Israel to emphasize the Palestinian nature of the major contemporary terrorist struggle going on in the Middle East. The British were in control in Palestine from the First World War to 1948, when Israel declared its independence. During much of that time there was Arab and Jewish terrorism against each other and against the British. The British left in May 1948 largely because they no longer could control the situation; simply stated, they no longer could maintain order.[9] After the establishment of Israel, that government faced, and has subsequently faced repeatedly, war with its Arab neighbors. In general it has defended itself successfully against this kind of threat and also against the old fedayeen raids of Nasser's day—the launching across the Israeli borders of small raiding parties, ostensibly of Palestinian character, and with the connivance and encouragement of Egyptian authorities. But after the June War (1967) when the Israelis made shambles of the Jordanian, Syrian and Egyptian armed forces, a totally new kind of terrorism has come into being. In effect both Palestinian refugee groups *and* neighboring Arab governments recognized that there was little to hope for in early reliance on conventional military encounters with the Israelis. If Palestine was to be regained it would have to be done by the Palestinians themselves. Of course, few Palestinian leaders were naive enough to believe that they would be able to liberate Palestine from the Israelis with their own efforts alone. But they did believe that they could, with support, raise such an *international* ruckus by systematic terrorism against Israel not only within her borders but also in other parts of the world, and also against sympathetic targets, as to cause serious political problems for the Israelis. They also believed that at least they would be able to get financial support in large amounts from the oil rich Arab states as well as staging areas from,

9. Appropriate chapters in Edwin Samuel *A Lifetime in Jerusalem* (New York: Abelard-Schuman, 1970) are useful for their descriptions of the collapse of the British mandate in Palestine.

Syria, Iraq and, if reluctantly, from Lebanon. Although they did not publicize these aspirations much in the early stages of their activities, they believed that they could embarrass those Arab governments that were lukewarm in their support of the Palestinian cause and make it impossible for them to find accommodation with the Israelis.

Although there developed a number of Palestinian liberation groups of various shades of ideology and extremism, the most famous one has undoubtedly been *Al Fatah*, with its leader, Yasir Arafat (technically today, Chairman of the Palestine Liberation Organization). Arafat has almost always eschewed terrorism in his public statements, but little is known of the internal arrangements through which violence has been unloosed. Arafat is also the leader respectable enough to head an independent Palestinian state should one emerge, and acceptable enough even now to address the United Nations (November 13, 1974)—his message was that he had an olive-branch and a gun and would be willing to depend upon either.

In the last half-dozen or so years just about every terrorist act imaginable has been carried out by one or another of the extremist groups. In 1973, about 1250 "military operations" were ostensibly carried out inside Israel proper.[10] In 1974 terrorist acts also occurred in such far flung places as Singapore, Kuwait, and Pakistan. In May, 100 Israeli children were captured in Galilee; a number of them died in the melee that followed. In other years there have been repeated hijackings of aircraft, including the destruction by bombs of several that had been flown to the Middle East. Ambassadors (the latest example being the Egyptian ambassador in Spain) and others of lesser rank have been kidnapped and in some cases murdered. Plastic bombs have been mailed to worldwide addresses of "enemies." The result has been a great deal of success. This success can be summed up as follows: (1) The Palestinian cause has received more publicity, including more that has been favorable, in the last half-dozen years than for all the other years going back to 1948. (2) The Israelis themselves have been forced to accept the need for some consultation with the Palestinians, although of course none of this has taken place yet. (3) The Palestine Liberation Organization has achieved international status. (4) It has become increasingly difficult for Arab

10. Figure taken from John K. Cooley, "New Attention Focuses on the PLO," *The Americana Annual, 1975* (New York: Grolier, Incorporated, 1975), p. 46.

governments to negotiate any agreement with Israel without some attention being given to Palestinian needs.

There can be no question that these things would not have occurred if there had not been terrorism. No Palestinian "army" could be strong enough to contest anything with an Israeli army! But not much of an organization is required to hijack an international airliner and blow it up if need be. Such a hijacking commands instant world attention. A world audience asks itself, not merely for an explanation of the horror of the event itself but something about the people who feel so desperate as to use terrorism in this way. The moment the story of the Palestinians is told, it elicits some sympathy among a portion of its recipients. This is natural and understandable. To that very degree, then, terrorism has paid off for a people too weak to contest their political needs by more conventional ways. And by that degree the Israelis, in this case, are weakened.

We turn to the seemingly never-ending problem of Ireland. Again there is an agonizing history that goes back for centuries. All students of British history know of the "Irish question" and its impact upon a long succession of British governments. For our purposes it is necessary merely to point out the long struggle of the Irish nationalists (never all of the Irish, of course) for independence from Great Britain, at least before the First World War.

Throughout the First World War, which Ireland proper did not enter, the British had extreme difficulty in maintaining the simplest rudiments of order. The problem had gone beyond the normal efforts at political persuasion. The police were augmented by British troops. Irish terrorist tactics—which ran the usual gamut of assaults, kidnappings, murders and bombings—were met by counterforce. Stringent regulations, including curfews, were promulgated. Terrorists when found were tried for their crimes and sometimes executed. Each execution catalyzed Irish opinion still more strongly against the London government and offered an occasion for a terrorist "execution," usually some kidnapped British soldier. The toll of life was heavy, and not all because of terrorist action. The British too used terrorism —counter-terrorism—but ultimately they abandoned not only these tactics but Ireland as well. It was the only "solution" that finally seemed possible, that is, abandonment. This had been, of course, the precise goal of the terrorist organizations. Terrorism as a device had worked against a major power. Great Britain had participated successfully in the military defeat of Germany in the First World War but she had neither the skills nor the determination to defeat the Irish nationalists.

Northern Ireland (with Belfast), sometimes called Ulster, sometimes the Northern Irish Counties, is different from the Irish Republic (with Dublin). In Northern Ireland a majority of the Irish are Protestant rather than Roman Catholic; Ulster is also somewhat more urbanized and industrialized than the Republic.

It is in Northern Ireland that violence and terrorism have once again broken out over the "Irish" question.[11] But the contemporary situation in Northern Ireland is much more complicated than was the old problem in the Ireland to the South. Many of the Catholic Irish have sought union with the Republic. This has been fought by the Protestant Irish who view themselves as an expendable minority in any such arrangement. Both elements demanded support from the British. Ultimately, both factions resorted to terrorism, Protestants against the Catholics, Catholics against the Protestants, both against the British, and on occasion Protestants in Northern Ireland against the Republic—thus the bombings in Dublin in May, 1974. The division is not entirely religious. Northern Ireland has suffered economically, currently from inflation as well, and the struggle, although carried out with the symbols of religion and nationalism, often has been inspired by the economic realities. No "solution" seems compelling, since the Protestant-Catholic antagonism would remain, independently of whether the British no longer had control or indeed whether some amalgamation of the Northern Counties with the Republic was consummated. The most likely direction for progress might seem through some agreement between the Republic and Great Britain. Such a preliminary agreement was made in late 1973 but a general strike by Protestant labor made a shambles of this prospect. And so terrorism, if sometimes muted, continues as each side, unable to move to its goals by legitimate methods, resorts to the most violent of alternatives.

The Republic of Ireland was freed from British rule by politics, leavened with terrorism. Northern Ireland may very well be abandoned by Britain too, when the cost of maintaining order there be-

11. See David E. Schmitt *Violence in Northern Ireland: Ethnic Conflict and Radicalization in an International Setting* (Morristown, N.J.: General Learning Press, 1974).

comes too high. But violence will continue in Northern Ireland, and could conceivably entangle the Republic, which would feel some responsibility for the Catholic Irish in the North. Either the forces of terrorism will simply die down, which is not impossible, or terrorism will continue until some government in the Northern Counties is politically powerful enough to stamp it out. Although the most recent example of Irish terrorism cannot be said to have succeeded—partly because much of the terrorism is between different groups of terrorists —one can say that without that terrorism, few of the political issues, whose solutions are now actively sought, would have been given much attention.

Summarizing from the available materials, we can say the following: Terrorism has existed in one form or another for all of the centuries that we have records of human existence. There is much of it today, in every area of the world. There is also international terrorism, inspired in one country but taking place in another. It seems likely that terrorism will increase as private groups, weak in resources, and governments, conscious of its uses, will all succumb to the need for employing it. It could become a war surrogate. Certainly terrorism is and has been a very effective political weapon. It is much more effective than isolated acts of assassination can be. It will increasingly come to characterize the world in which we live. As it does so, our attitudes toward it and the response mechanisms that as individuals we put up against it will develop new characteristics of their own.

A Summary of Findings

At the very beginning of this work we defined assassination generally as the killing of public officials for political rather than for personal reasons. Very few political systems have not had to endure assassination and very few public officials, at the highest level at any rate, have not had to be concerned about attacks against their persons. It might be added that apparently few governments have not contemplated at one time or another the use of assassination as a political weapon against foreign enemies. The climate for this type of microviolence continues to be favorable in the last quarter of the 20th century. The spin-offs in the United States from the Watergate investigations have revealed that the CIA apparently at least *contemplated* the use of assassination against such figures as Fidel Castro of Cuba, Salvador Allende of Chile, and Rafael Trujillo of the Dominican Republic. At the moment of writing we have no direct evidence of this, although the indirect evidence is substantial. Apparently the Rockefeller Commission Report was shortened at the last minute to exclude certain statements about such assassinations. In fact, the Report deals with assassination only insofar as it attempts to scotch the rumors involved in the Kennedy assassination in the United States.

There has been no end to the speculations about whether the *whole* story has been told about the death of John Kennedy. Murky innuendos about the role of the CIA in this death have frequently surfaced. Speculations about the impact of high level assassinations have continued as well. For example, the murder of King Faisal of Saudi Arabia in early 1975 produced the usual concerns of whether the succession would be orderly and whether the new regime would prove stable.

Originally our chief concern in this book was the political impact of the act of assassination. We also wanted to know the degree to which political change could flow from assassinations. The distribution of assassination over space and time was similarly a relevant concern.

Our conclusions continue to be valid: Assassination seems to be essentially a random process, at least with respect to the distribution over time of the deaths of chief executives. Some of the more turbulent periods in history seem more conducive to assassination, but the assassination of a chief executive is a rare event with a constant, though low, probability of occurrence. The distribution of assassination by region and country is, however, not so random as that in time. There is more assassination in the Middle East than in Western Europe, more in Syria than in Iceland. Some researchers (e.g., the Feierabends[12]) have attempted to correlate various characteristics of political

12. The Feierabends (Ivo K. and Rosalind L.) have produced an impressive body of research in their efforts to quantify relations between violence and socio-economic variables. Some of the flavor of this research can be found in Ivo K. Feierabend, Rosalind L. Feierabend and Ted Robert Gurr (eds.) *Anger, Violence, and Politics: Theories and Research* (Englewood Cliffs: Prentice-Hall, Inc., 1972). Their article (with two other authors), "Political Violence and Assassination: A Cross-National Assessment" [William J. Crotty (ed.) *Assassinations and the Political Order* (New York: Harper and Row, Publishers, 1971), pp. 54–140] is also interesting.

systems with the incidence of assassination, but we have not found this kind of work very revealing. And for those to whom causal models are important, it is evident that causal linkages between assassinatory activity and economic indicators are fairly tenuous.

Although it is not possible here to investigate empirically the distribution of terrorist activities, it seems that terrorism is even more widely distributed spatially than is assassination; in time, its random character seems evident, although there also seem to be fashions in terroristic activity, not only as to the degree of its existence but also as to the forms it takes and the demands made in its name. Although terrorism is very widespread, there are several great pockets in which it seems especially concentrated. These are primarily Latin America and the Middle East, and to a lesser extent Africa. African terrorism, however, appears to be assuming greater importance—the kidnapping of American students in Tanzania in May (1975) represents almost the classic example of terrorism. In the Middle East it is the issue of Palestine and the Israelis that produces the great bulk of terrorism, but it is a terrorism that also spreads beyond the physical dimensions of the area. That is, some Middle East terrorism occurs in Europe and elsewhere.

Whereas the terrorism in the Middle East, Africa, and Northern Ireland results largely from colonialist vestiges of an earlier age (and therefore has serious international implications), terrorism in the Americas centers primarily around domestic policies and politics. In the United States the terrorists may denounce the foreign policies of their government, but their actions are directed against their own, not foreign, authorities. The Weatherman, the Black Panthers, the Symbionese Liberation Army have protested racism, poverty, war, oppression, and the quality of life in this country and have used terrorism to make their points—but their acts are directed against U.S. citizens and U.S. officials. Terrorism in Latin America follows the same general path. The various "armed liberation" or "national liberation" movements confine their activities largely to a single nation, although some cooperation among the groups transcends national boundaries. The Tupamaros of Uruguay have contacts with the youthful Peronist terrorists in Argentina, and individual terrorists have at times sought refuge in neighboring countries. Furthermore, some of the terrorist acts have been directed against foreign officials, primarily U.S. but also some

Europeans. Terrorist propaganda has often assailed "foreign economic imperialism," but the actions themselves have been launched far more often against local people and officials than against foreign nationals.

Terrorist activities have been intense in several countries of Latin America since the Second World War. Some 300,000 persons lost their lives in combined guerilla war, terrorist attacks, and assassinations in Colombia from the late 1940s to the mid-1960s. An estimated 3000 persons were killed in Guatemala from the mid-1960s to the mid-1970s, and scores were killed in Venezuela in the 1960s. Presently Argentina is the scene of the most spirited action. Sporadic assassinations and terrorist attacks have plagued the country since the fall of the populist dictator Juan Peron in 1955. These intensified as successor regimes failed to unite the country politically and to strengthen it economically. For a brief time after Peron's return in 1973, it appeared that he might restore peace. The old leader, however, was never able fully to unify his fractious followers, and when he died in mid-1974, the killings, kidnappings, and attacks were renewed with unprecedented fury by groups of left-wing and right-wing extremists. One Buenos Aires newspaper counted over 500 individual political deaths from Peron's demise in July 1974 to May 1975. British observers believe this is an underestimate by half.[13]

The Tupamaro terrorists of Uruguay offer an excellent illustration of success and frustration, much like we found in some assassinations: the offending target was removed but the aims of the attackers were not fulfilled. Angered with the economic stagnation, social rigidity, and political immobilism of their country, some young professionals and students in Uruguay launched a series of Robin Hood attacks against banks and wealthy individuals during the 1960s. Usually careful not to hurt or kill, and distributing much of their booty to the needy, they attracted a growing following in the country, especially in the capital, Montevideo. In the late 1960s, however, they began more direct attacks on government officials including the police. Some of their support eroded, and when the political coalition they entered for the election of 1971 dented but did not overturn the old party system, they

13. *Latin America*, Vol. IX (June 6, 1975) No 22, p. 172. An A.P. dispatch in June 1975 reported the largest ransom ever paid to terrorist groups: $60,000,000 to the Argentine Montoneros for the release of the Born brothers, Jorge and Juan, heirs of a huge grain fortune.

launched out once more into fullscale terrorist attacks. This time the army moved in, but the outcome was curious. Documents seized by the Tupamaros and captured by the army, convinced the officers of the truth of the terrorist charges of corruption against the old-line politicians. Slowly the military assumed greater control over the political system. Working with an authoritarian-minded president, the military forced the closing of the legislature, the dissolution of the political parties, and the suspension of civil rights. Simultaneously the military directed fullscale attacks on the Tupamaros, virtually destroying them as an effective organization. Uruguay, once a model of democratic parliamentary government with a civilian controlled military, has resulted today in an authoritarian, militarily-controlled state. Terror produced change, but not quite the change terrorists contemplated.

The ten case studies of assassination included in this work were chosen as illustrating different degrees of impact in various types of political systems since the end of the First World War. The examples range from the assassination of Verwoerd in South Africa, which we labeled as a very low-impact case, to the assassination of Trujillo in the Dominican Republic, whose impact seems to be the greatest of any modern example that we have found. It is difficult to imagine the assassination of a prime minister in any place and time that would have less impact on the system than did that of Verwoerd. The clue may lie in the ambiguity of the political motivation in this case; one can argue, as we do several paragraphs below, that a killing may be only partially an assassination. Verwoerd's case seems to illustrate this well. In the case of Trujillo, all the superficial evidence points to a very significant impact. The system underwent rather severe alterations. Yet Trujillo's case is as exceptional as is Verwoerd's and is subject to alternative interpretations.

It is perhaps useful to touch briefly upon the very recent case of the assassination of King Faisal. Faisal was a strong and powerful ruler of a nation struggling to achieve modernity in an area rich with uncertainty and turbulence. Saudi Arabia has enormous deposits of oil although it is underpopulated for its size and wealth. But it lies in an intense political environment. Thus across the Persian Gulf lies Iran, powerful and ambitious. There had been speculation for years as to what would happen when Faisal died. No one in the royal family seemed his equal. Several of his brothers were ambitious yet none seemed to command the necessary support to make the transition smoothly. The crown prince, Khalid, was a brother without much ambition. It was assumed by some that there would be a struggle for power among the leading figures of the family. Although it is too soon to know fully, this has not come about. Khalid assumed the kingship with little fanfare and has seemingly been accepted not only by the royal family, but by the army and the bureaucracy, though it must be remembered that the royal family permeates the bureaucracy. Institutional arrangements that had been made by Faisal are being continued by Khalid. The impact here upon the system, the immediate impact at least, has been minimal. Long-run changes are not precluded, but one could hardly have precluded them had Faisal lived. The assassin, it turned out, was an allegedly deranged nephew of the king; few political aspects of his deed have been revealed.[14]

Close examination of the case studies as well as of the corpus of modern assassination, as exhibited in this book, indicates that *the impact of an assassination on the political system tends to be low.* What appears to be clear impact rarely holds up under close scrutiny. Difficulties of analysis sometimes complicate the problem beyond measure. We should be interested primarily in one variable only, the impact of assassination (I_a), which is not identical with the impact of death (I_d) or the shock of death or assassination.[15] Nor is it always

14. The assassin, Prince Faisal ibn Musaed, was executed by beheading on June 18, 1975. An Associated Press dispatch of June 19 quoted at length commentary from his former girlfriend, with whom he lived as a student in the United States, Christine Surma

   predicted her former boyfriend would one day be recognized as the liberator of his country's people.

   "The way I feel about it is that if he did it—and I still want to emphasize the 'if'—he did it for the good of mankind," she said.

   Miss Surma spoke of the major changes in Saudi Arabia that have begun since Faisal's death, including what she said were modernization of customs and the country's proclaimed interest in achieving peace with Israel.

   "My friend, who was a humanitarian—kind and gentle and just—if he did the job, his purpose for doing it was realized. There are many avenues open for peace that were not open with the previous ruler."

The analysis is not convincing.

15. Crotty's book mentioned in the preceding footnote 12 deals to some degree with what we are discussing here. Part III is entitled "Public Reactions to Assassinations"; Part IV, "The Political Implications of Assassinations." Chapter 5 (Murray Edelman and Rita James Simon, "Presidential Assassinations: Their Meaning and Impact on American Society") and Chapter 6 (Dwaine Marvick and Elizabeth Wirth Marvick, "The Political Consequences of Assassination") of Part IV are of particular interest.

useful (without many methodological safeguards) to try to guess what history would have been like had the victim's life continued.[16] In the Trujillo case, much of the impact may have come about not because Trujillo had been assassinated, but simply because he was no longer there. Had he died a natural death, some similar changes would have occurred. Symbolically we can assert that I (the total impact) $= I_d + I_a$, and that I_a tends to be low, although not usually vanishingly low. When I_d is low as well we have a case like that of Verwoerd. If we had a method of quantifying these terms the ratio I_a/I_d would be of interest. (It perhaps should be emphasized that we mean impact to be equivalent to "systemic impact." To be very precise we do not even mean "policy impact" on the grounds that policy is not always causally connected with system. Certainly we do not refer to shock or emotional responses.)

If, as seems likely, I_d is the major source of variance, then the broader question of the impact of death of any kind becomes the pertinent one. The total impact is difficult enough to measure, and we have no operational way of separately measuring I_d and I_a. However, the evidence of our work indicates that I_a is low. In the case of Faisal, I_a seems very low indeed.

16. Even less proper is the assumption that if some "evil" individual had been removed in the past the subsequent "evil history" would have been necessarily erased. Nicholas Katzenbach, former attorney-general, has been quoted as saying, for example, "If somebody had knocked off Hitler in 1936 or 1937, I think it would have been a big help." (Clifton Daniel, "The Assassination-Plot Rumors," datelined Washington, June 5, 1975, *The New York Times*.) (A few days later CIA Director William Colby said, that although he opposed assassination, he would have volunteered to have killed Hitler.) Was Katzenbach implying that Castro was as evil as Hitler? With respect to Hitler those who once were in a position to do so now find it apparently necessary to apologize for not having committed the deed; one should note the following paragraph from Lucy S. Dawidowicz *The War Against the Jews, 1933–1945* (New York: Holt, Rinehart and Winston, 1975), p. 4.

" 'A raw-vegetable Genghis Khan,' wrote Friedrich Percyval Reck-Malleczewen, observing Hitler without his usual bodyguard in a Munich restaurant in 1932. It would have been easy then, in the almost deserted restaurant, to shoot Hitler. 'If I had had an inkling of the role this piece of filth was to play, and of the years of suffering he was to make us endure, I would have done it without a second thought. But I took him for a character out of a comic strip, and did not shoot.' " The unfortunate thing about such apologetic advice is that it encourages those odd characters, of whom every society has its share, to hazard guesses about the future suffering that our public officials will cause us, and perhaps be impelled to become assassins.

I_a is especially low when the assassin is a loner, perhaps mentally deranged, without the backing of a conspiratorial organization. In such cases there are no forces ready to take advantage of the hiatus of leadership during the chaotic period of shock that follows the death of some political leader. Where there are forces in the wings ready to move in some ways, however inefficiently and stupidly, there is greater probability of some impact (I_a). Probably in the case of Somoza in Nicaragua I_a approximated o. Had Somoza simply died of a heart attack the results would likely have been strikingly similar.

Impact tends to be low when there are competent heirs or successors to support the regime or when political inertia maintains the regime in the post-assassination period. When the heirs are incompetent or suspect, higher impact from the death of the victim may develop. However, the assassin can take full advantage of a situation of this sort only when he acts for a group that is big enough and rich enough in political resources to alter the regime. Such occurrences are relatively rare.

Another major point that our research reveals is that the unadulterated case of pure assassination—the phrase is awkward—is perhaps more rare than we thought. Most assassinations are really "partial" assassinations. Only a fraction of the political figures who are assassinated are killed for motives that are purely political. To turn the idea about, many assassinations seem to be only tangentially political. Assassination is often directed against political figures as symbols of authority and not always focused on specific political issues or against specific political systems. It is not surprising that in most cases of this kind systemic impact stemming from the assassination tends to be low.

What about the aims of the assassin? It is apparent that the assassin succeeds completely only when his objective is the simplest possible, nothing more than the removal of the victim. Perhaps there is still a simpler aim, that illustrated by the act of Puerto Rican nationalists against President Truman in 1950. Here the object was not *necessarily* to kill, but merely to attract attention by the act. (Was this Squeaky Fromme's intention in her threat to President Ford?) In the late spring of 1975 the prime minister of Turkey was beaten by an assailant, again without any apparent intention to kill. Strictly speaking no assassination was intended by the attackers in either of these examples, but nevertheless attacks were made, attacks that could have led to deaths.

These deaths would have been assassinations. Such motivation is very common to terrorists, who are eager to gain attention and who do not necessarily expect systemic alterations to flow from their acts. In any event, only simple goals like these can have any real expectation of success. Attempts to achieve more complicated objectives are very likely to go astray.

In most cases, looking at it from the perspective of the assassin, success is at best incomplete. No changes at all may take place, either in institutions or in policy. Or if changes do occur, they may be the very opposite of what the assassin desired. Indeed one can say that on most occasions assassinations result in utter failure as far as the political aims of the conspirators are concerned. There is simply little political profit in assassination for the assassins themselves or their supporters.

There is one other type of assassination that was discussed a great deal in the late spring of 1975. The Rockefeller Commission Report on the CIA was reported originally to have devoted almost disproportionate attention to the interest that the agency allegedly took in the possible assassination of foreign figures. This material was apparently deleted from the published report. Fidel Castro is commonly mentioned as an intended target in the early 1960s. It is not necessary here to go into all the accusations and counter-accusations, or the possible political motivations in some of the current discussions and charges. Whether or not any of these charges are true, several points seem immediately pertinent. It is highly unlikely that the CIA would engage in any activity of this kind without clearance from the "highest authority," that is from the president himself. It is also obvious that that clearance would be given only if it could be assumed that the United States would derive some major political advantage from the deed. The fact that the existence of preliminary discussions on possible assassinations has surfaced indicates that someone felt that that advantage was evident. How does this mesh with our earlier statement that assassinations rarely benefitted the assassins or their followers? The general statement remains true, we believe. Systemic impact is likely to remain low regardless of the nature or identity of the assassins. Government assassins are no more likely to attain the objectives of their sponsors than any other assassins, with the following exception. The objectives of a government cover perhaps a broader spectrum of advantageous possibilities. Simple removal of a political leader is hardly a very significant objective for an individual or a group within the system itself. But removal of a *foreign* leader may be perceived to be a very important thing for another government. Would the removal of Castro in 1962 have resulted in a better political situation for the United States in the Caribbean? It might be added that the removal of Diem in Vietnam in 1963 hardly resulted in long-run advantage to the United States, although his removal was perceived as advantageous by American government officials.

One additional argument must be met here. It is sometimes said that criminal gangs, which certainly can be viewed as political organisms, are heavily involved in "political" murder. If there are practical payoffs to these low level "assassinations" why isn't the same thing true in larger organizations, in political systems? We think the answer evident. The smaller the organization the more personal is the leadership and the network of political relations that emanate from that leadership. Killing the leader of a small gang may well destroy it as a viable organism; it would be equivalent surely to a devastating defeat in war for a larger political system. The larger the system the more institutional arrangements are in existence and the less effect the loss of any particular individual has. Of course in gang killings a particular act may be intended symbolically as conveying a message of contempt, or anger. In that sense the same thing can be true of assassination at a national level. Here, however, no one talks of systemic change.

Many times it is simply not possible to discern any motive for the assassin. This is especially true when he acts alone, which is often the case when he is truly mentally disturbed. The assassin of Henrik Verwoerd apparently attacked his victim as a symbolic act against all authority. The assailant had a long history of mental instability; it is tempting to ascribe his act to insanity.[17] In the case of an important victim the community conjures up no end of explanations, exposés, hypotheses and theories as to who did what and why, which again points up the extreme difficulty of assessing motive objectively. Perhaps attempts to determine motives are irrelevant, for once the act has

17. Although largely a criminal case, the well publicized murder of two Mormon missionaries in Texas in 1974, apparently as a symbolic slap at the Mormon Church for its "injustices," is of similar nature to the Verwoerd slaying. These murders were surely partial assassinations.

been committed the public manufactures its own motive in harmony with its own political predilections. Thus a dozen years after the death of President Kennedy speculations about the identity of the assassins (sic!) continue with undiminished fervor. There has been no end to the imaginative creation of conspiracies, plots and intrigues which allegedly culminated in the death of the president. The authors of this work have no reason to believe that any of the major conclusions of the Warren Commission Report were in error. But of course our possessing these views neither makes them correct nor stills the suspicions of others. As long as President Kennedy's assassination is of interest to people, so long will they speculate as to why and how it occurred.

As far as the individual assassin is concerned, even when some of his aims are achieved by his act, his own personal fate is frequently oblivion. Most assassins of important political personages—although not always all the conspirators—are caught; many are killed on the spot or quickly executed. The chances of successfully killing a prominent political individual and escaping are small, and those of gaining political power as the result of such action are virtually nil. The assassin of Somoza in Nicaragua seems to have been motivated by little more than the desire to remove his victim; certainly he made no effort to escape his own death, even though his associates had devised some ineffectual plans to overthrow the regime. What this means is that such assassins have to be so emotionally and politically "turned on" that they willingly cast their lives away in the accomplishing of their ends.

The Mexican and Yugoslav assassinations were utter failures as far as the motivations and goals of the assassins were concerned. If the physician who murdered Senator Long sought only personal revenge, he obtained it; but he lost his own life. The Egyptian government bought itself some time by removing Hasan al-Banna; but it fell to other revolutionary forces a few years later. The Darlan assassination in Algeria appears to have been rather successful. The immediate assassin lost his life, but some of the "intellectual authors" of the deed succeeded in restoring French authority in world politics and in bringing Charles DeGaulle to power in a reborn France. The question remains: Could it not have been done without the assassination of Darlan? In the Congo and the Dominican Republic, the assassins saw the overthrow of political systems that they opposed. They and their associates in the deed included important political personages and others who had connections with powerful opposition leaders in their respective countries. And yet we must again raise some questions: How much of the change, substantial though it was, can be attributed to the assassination and how much to other political variables? Would these changes have come about ultimately in any case, even though the assassination had not taken place? Although we ask such questions we do not mean to suggest that the effects of assassinations on political systems are always vanishingly small.

What did we learn from our original study, and have we learned anything more since the initial version of this was published? As we stated it then, we were "dismayed by the high incidence of assassination." Today we are no longer certain that we know what constitutes a "high incidence" of assassination or of terrorism. What is the irreducible minimum of such things in the world that is ours, tightly bound together with communication and technology? Whatever it is, that minimum may be greater than we originally thought. Automobile accidents are an inescapable aspect of motor transportation; political violence seems equally connected with the political process. We were also impressed, several years ago, with the modesty of impact of single acts of assassination. Nothing that has happened since 1970 has caused us to alter this conclusion. But the very opposite is often true of terrorism, especially with respect to policy; this is true even though terrorism may contain acts of assassination.

The general conclusions we reached about assassination still hold true. Although assassination seems to be random in character, there are great variations in its rates over time and within individual countries. There is some connection between assassination and other "big" disturbances, such as revolution and guerrilla warfare. Assassins usually fail to achieve their political goals and the mortality rate of assassins is quite high.

Although we have not done as detailed and systematic a study of terrorism as we have of assassination, it seems evident in a preliminary sense at least that the near future will see a vast increase in its use, both officially by governments or their surrogates, and by private groups with private grievances. Terrorism will continue to be effective, just as single acts of assassination will continue to be ineffective, and will continue to prove difficult to combat. Terrorism is a new dimension of the political process; to modify and garble a famous quotation,

terrorism will become the extension of politics by other means! The
following constitute some of our major observations:

(1) Terrorism can be, and often is, a highly effective political
weapon for groups that are weak relative to their opposition. Major
political concessions were made, or are being made, in the examples
detailed above. These concessions almost certainly would not have
been "achieved" without the terroristic component. The whole corpus
of terrorism supports this conclusion, although in many actual in-
stances, goals have been so confused and the terrorist leadership so
fragmented as to disguise the tremendous power and leverage resident
in terrorism. A recent conference on "terrorism, pre-emption and sur-
prise" held in Hebrew University in Jerusalem[18] underlined this par-

18. The conference was sponsored by the Leonard Davis Institute of International Relations at Hebrew University. See the report of this conference by Terence
Smith, "Terrorism is a subject for study," *The New York Times*, June 15, 1975.
The quotation in the text is from this article. There were two other major conclusions of the conference. (1) Terrorists have more options today because of
the "development of portable, destructive weapons;" discussed, as it always is
at conferences of this kind, was the possibility that some terrorist group would
somehow obtain a nuclear weapon and hold a country at ransom. (2) A trend
exists "toward greater tolerance for acts of terrorism and a general laxness in
the punishment of terrorists." The explanation of the latter by Professor George H.
Quester of Cornell University that there is a "worldwide social tendency to place
more and more value on human life" seems highly questionable to say the least.
More likely is the fact that in a world highly fragmented politically and ideologically—and often highly excited about these differences as well—the terrorist
becomes a hero in another setting. Even a world populated only by the major
powers would be unlikely to agree on the punishment of *all* terrorists, but the
actual world, containing an individual such as Idi Amin of Uganda would abso-
lutely be unable to agree as to what should constitute punishable terrorists.
To pursue the remarks attributed to Professor Quester in the quoted article:
"Professor Quester also talked about the unique case of the Palestinian Liberation
Movement. Despite its consistent use of terror, it has won political recognition.
Palestinian terrorism, he suggested, is tolerated more than any other terrorism
because 'the Palestinians look more like an army, less like a criminal gang.' "
Moreover, the "Palestinians are 'literally getting away with murder,' the professor
observed, 'in part because they are converging on the normal legitimacy of an
established political movement, that is, a state and states do not "commit murder,"
they "wage war." ' " It is difficult to accept this sort of analysis. It is philosophical
fakery to distinguish morally between the minor deaths of political murder and
the major deaths of political war. If both are the policy decisions of a government, they are equally moral, or immoral. At any event, there is a failure in this
analysis to note that terrorism is in many ways just a form of war. It is unconventional war. It has been for the Palestinians the only form of war that they could
mount.

tially by concluding that the " 'technological vulnerability' of modern society has made terrorism more feasible and more profitable at less risk for the terrorists." Technology not only permits a synchronization of terrorist tactics on a world-wide basis but offers all kinds of variety in weapons and targets.

(2) Terrorism is a cheap device, in terrorists' lives and in money. Whatever goals the SLA possessed and whatever "achievements" they may lay claim to have effected, there is no question that it did not cost them much. A handful of individuals, a few weapons and hideouts and a great deal of imagination resulted in an overwhelming response. Lives were lost to be sure, but lives are often lost in violent encounters. There are those who believe that the results of war—some particular war of course—more than compensate for its costs. If this be true, the costs of terroristic success are even more startlingly small.[19] Because these costs are small, groups that are weak in numbers or resources, can often produce the leverage to achieve major political ends that they could never have ventured to seek in the more conventional ways. It must be remembered that conventional politics—electing an American president, for example—is enormously expensive in effort and money, if not always in lives. Terrorism is the politics of the unconventional.

Perhaps governments will resort more and more to terrorism as a substitute for war. In the days when war can escalate into nuclear destruction, the temptation to seek the ends of war in some less annihilating way is strong. Also the costs of conventional war itself, that is the costs of the military equipment necessary to carry on this conventional war, have risen so steeply as to preclude most nations from engaging in it. (The Egyptians and Israelis would hardly have a go at it as they do periodically if they were not the surrogates of richer patrons, the Russians and the Americans.) The result in the future may well be more terrorism.

(3) Terrorism generally results in enormous publicity, far out of proportion to the events themselves. The professions of news gathering

19. With respect to the comments in the above footnote, note that one of the options formally and apparently seriously discussed during the Cuban missile crisis in 1962 was a major air strike on Cuba. Perhaps indeed the nuclear option was discussed as well. If so, then the assassination of Castro and other Cuban leaders, of which the CIA has latterly been accused of planning, would indeed have been a more humane option. Whether or not governments often admit to such tactics, there can hardly be any question that they do indulge in them.

and reporting are fond of making much of the violent, the grotesque, the obscene. The worst kind of terroristic act, therefore, will be precisely the kind that will be widely reported and endlessly analyzed. Since a common goal of terrorist groups is publicity of their more substantive ends, they find it easy to disseminate their views and locate whatever sympathetic audiences may exist.

(4) It is difficult to counter terrorism within a polity. The often tiny size of the terrorist group permits its members to disappear "into the woodwork" after a terroristic attack. It is not unfair to say that the police in the United States have been generally unable to apprehend many terrorists, particularly the more publicized of them. The methods used by police to unearth and capture and/or punish terrorists are often so exceptional as to create sympathy for the terrorists themselves. When the police begin their own terroristic tactics this tendency is of course exacerbated.

But armies are not very good devices to combat terrorism either, as the French found out in Algeria and the British in other locales. Armies are organized to fight certain kinds of enemies in certain kinds of stylized ways. They are rarely effective in anti-terroristic activity. The overkill they generate often creates once again sympathy for terrorists. Perhaps the army success in Uruguay against the Tupamaros is an exception to this rule, but there are complicating factors in this example.

One device in "combatting" terrorists is to give in to their demands. This tendency has been well displayed in several European countries on whose territories acts of violence have occurred. For such a country catching a terrorist is even worse than not catching him. Catching him forces the government to deal with him and invites new retaliatory terrorist actions. So in the case of Palestinian terrorism at least more than one country has been glad to accede to the demands of terrorists and release their previously held comrades. On a more general level, there is little doubt that there are many who would counsel that whenever possible the demands of terrorists should be met. Thus, on a minor level, the Hearst family provided the food for the giveaway that the kidnappers of their daughter had demanded. On an international level the Austrian government agreed to Palestinian demands, although it did not entirely live up to its promises, to curtail the movements of Russian Jewish refugees, some of whom were on their way to Israel.

The Israelis in general have tried to adhere to a twinfold policy with respect to terrorist actions attributed to Palestinians. First of all, they try never to give in, never to accede to demands. The government has at times been sorely pressed to change this policy but in general it has adhered to it. Second, the Israelis have believed in the policy of terroristic retaliation. Since it is not always possible, indeed if ever, to pinpoint the terrorists who need retaliation, targets are chosen across some convenient border, often the Lebanese, and an action is carried out against them. The Israelis have been virtually as willing to engage in terrorism as have their Palestinian enemies.[20] But there is this difference. It is more difficult for the Israelis to establish their goals in terroristic terms, that is goals that can be achieved through terroristic action. Generally their biggest payoff has been in their own domestic political scene. Abroad the results have been frequently counterproductive.

(5) Terrorism is commonly employed by a wide variety of governments. It is only fair to say that we do not have hard evidence that every current government in the world has engaged in terrorism but the number that has is impressively large. It is not just the weak and unstable government that resorts to such tactics, nor is it necessarily the revolutionary and militant government. Despite pious disclaimers many democratic governments have indulged at times in terroristic methods. The British used terrorism in many of their overseas territories, usually without positive results. The French systematically carried out a terroristic campaign against the Algerian rebels in the long struggle there, again with failure the result. The record of the United States, we are discovering in the mid-1970s, is not very clean in this regard either.

The interesting thing is that almost every government official in every country will decry terrorism; he refers, of course, to the terrorism

20. It is not inappropriate, perhaps, to point out that one of the Israeli objects of negotiations between Egyptians and Israelis in the early summer of 1975 was the recovery of the bodies of the Jewish terrorist-assassins who killed Lord Moyne in Egypt in 1944. Upon recovery, the bodies were buried in Israel with full military honors.

employed by others. He feels compelled to state repeatedly that his own government does not engage in activities of this sort. For many people terrorism is an immoral thing; they certainly do distinguish it from the activities of war, even if we do not.[21] Yet it is difficult to find a rational basis for this. It is even more difficult to imagine a situation in which terrorism would be a uniquely useful device for government but that government would not be tempted to use it. But what most governments fear more than terrorism inspired by each other is the uncalculated terrorism promulgated by private groups. Most governments rule through popular acceptance of their legitimacy. If terrorism of private inspiration runs rampant, as in Argentina or Uruguay in the last few years, that legitimacy is sorely weakened. It is imperative that private terrorism be eliminated; every government must seek to do so. It is convenient while doing this to deny that public terrorism ever exists either.

Further Research on Assassination and Terrorism

When we prepared the first edition of this book we said that a necessary and important task was the preparation of a carefully compiled list of assassinations and their attempts. Our own list was compiled for the National Commission on the Causes and Prevention of Violence. But this list was only a sample; of necessity it was hurriedly put together and was incomplete. We estimated that for the period

21. See Tom Wicker, "Murder By Any Other Name," *The New York Times*, June 3, 1975. Wicker, in this column, was discussing the early reports that President Kennedy was implicated in assassination attempts. He asks whether a President of the United States, by "virtue of that title, can . . . be said under any moral, religious or ethical view of life to have had some right not previously his to order a specific human life extinguished in what he believed to be the national interest?" He goes on: "This is not the pacifist question whether any killing or any war can ever be justified. It is a question of simple decency—whether outside the exigencies and brutalities of warfare any political personage has the right to order the death of any other human being for the political purposes of the person who gives the order." He ends his column by quoting Senator George Smathers' discussions of conversations that he had with Kennedy over the political impact of Castro's assassination if it were to be carried out. The emphasis in those conversations was not the moral aspect, but the practical aspect, that is whether it would have any political embarrassments for the United States. Wicker then ends his commentary by saying, "Murder was not wrong; it was just ineffective—and by any other name would smell as rotten."

since 1918, assassinations at all levels must have numbered five or six thousand. Our point was that until a fairly accurate collection was assembled, many important questions could not be answered in any but speculative terms. Apparently some such collections are being put together although very little has been published. Some of the results are interesting. For example, one estimate for the ten-year period ending in 1975 of the total number of *politically* motivated incidents (armed attacks, arson, bombings, assassinations, hijackings, kidnappings and thefts) for the entire world number around 3000. Impressive as this may seem it is only 300 per year, less than one a day, for the entire world! Probably this collection is incomplete as well, for the reason that all such collections are incomplete. For the world, one is perforce reduced to examining newspaper files; such files are of necessity faulty. How does one compile such figures from mainland China, for example?

With respect to assassination we are interested in the types of societies or systems that seem to spawn them, or be immune to them. What connection does the incidence of assassination have with violence in general or with the existence of terrorism? It is inviting to speculate that assassination partakes in the general incidence of violence—that when riots, demonstrations, or attempted coups occur in any great numbers then assassination levels also rise.

What is the relationship between assassination, terrorism, and ordinary crime? Does the general incidence of murder, assault, robbery, rape, or other major crimes relate in any way to levels of assassination or terrorism? The data are very inconclusive. First of all it must be said that statistics on crime are far from complete. It is next to impossible to assert very confidently that we know what "crimes" have been committed, in what numbers and where. Completing and refining this information seems an essential first step in order to compare it usefully with the incidence of assassination. At present it is not possible even to assert that there is a connection.

We are also interested in discovering whether the distribution of assassination within a system is skewed in any way with respect to the *level* of the victims. At the highest political level there is no correlation between assassination and the general incidence of violence—there may be correlation with assassination at lower political levels.

It is also necessary to comment that our statistical summary of chief executives does not tell us all that we would like to know about either that political level or lesser levels. Chief executives are not equally vulnerable, nor are they equally protected, everywhere in the world. But they are certainly better protected than intermediate-level political figures. Although high-level leaders are more exciting targets, it may be that we will learn more about assassination from the intermediate level than from the high or low. The intermediate level is important enough to present *political* rather than *personal* targets (disentangling murder from assassination on the low level is a major task) and it is low enough to be without major security devices. Perhaps a more accurate gauge of assassination could be found here. Assassinations at this level occur in greater numbers and are more uniformly distributed geographically within countries. All of these considerations make the intermediate level an important and necessary one to study.

The intermediate level is also of crucial importance with respect to terrorism but in a somewhat different way. (We need not emphasize that although terrorism often includes assassination, an assassination need not be terroristic, nor have that effect.) In order for an isolated act of assassination to have any effect on the political system or on policy an individual whose level is commensurate with the implications of the desired effect must be chosen. For terrorism quite the contrary is possible. Targets can be chosen from all levels, and indeed are most effectively chosen from that level in which the terroristic acts are most easily carried out. Although this is sometimes at the lowest levels if the targets have other distinguishing characteristics— members of a police force or an army, white or black, and so on—the terrorists usually would want to choose those targets who are easily hit but whose capacity to generate publicity is high. This combination is again found in the intermediate level. Unfortunately the systematic research on terrorism is so modest in amount and so meager in conclusions that little can be said, a posteriori at least, about the general nature of the phenomenon of terroristic violence. Our own limited data on chief executives indicate very little. Single acts of assassination can occur anywhere. So can modest campaigns of terrorism, although major terroristic movements seem to exist only where there are groundswells of popular support. It is easy to commit an act of terrorism; it is not really difficult to produce a certain level of terrorism within a community. But to sustain it, to increase it, to derive "benefits" from it, require, we believe, something more than the dedication of a few score fanatics.

The methodological danger lies in deducing general principles from very small bits of evidence. We need further in-depth, country-by-country studies of terrorism and assassination. When such studies have been accumulated it may become possible to link general terroristic indices, or general indices of violence, with other kinds of indices, those whose orientation is cultural, economic or social. We can only honestly say that there are now many more questions to be asked than reasonable answers to be formulated. Our readers will not have to be reminded of the great difficulty that private researchers have in investigating things like the subject matter of this volume, as well as the major expense in conducting systematic research on this issue.

Some Additional References

The last five years have produced a plethora of books on violence, revolution and kindred subjects. With a few exceptions there has been very little on assassination and virtually nothing on terrorism. We append a few of the books published more recently that relate in some way to the themes of this volume:

Crotty, William J. (ed.) *Assassinations and the Political Order* (New York: Harper and Row, Publishers, 1971).

Dunn, John. *Modern Revolution: An Introduction to the Analysis of a Political Phenomenon* (New York: Cambridge University Press, 1974).

Feierabend, Ivo K., Rosalind L. Feierabend and Ted Robert Gurr (eds.). *Anger, Violence, and Politics: Theories and Research* (Englewood Cliffs: Prentice-Hall, Inc., 1972).

Hibbs, Douglas A., Jr. *Mass Political Violence: A Cross-National Causal Analysis* (New York: John Wiley & Sons, 1973).

Hirsch, Herbert and David C. Perry (eds.). *Violence as Politics: A Series of Original Essays* (New York: Harper and Row, Publishers, 1973).

Paynton, Clifford T. and Robert Blackey (eds.). *Why Revolution? Theories and Analyses* (Cambridge: Schenkman Publishing Co., 1971).

Quandt, William B., Fuad Jabber, and Ann Mosely Lesch. ·*The*

Politics of Palestinian Nationalism (Berkeley: University of California Press, 1973).

Russell, D. E. H. *Rebellion, Revolution, and Armed Force: A Comparative Study of Fifteen Countries with Special Emphasis on Cuba and South Africa* (New York: Academic Press, 1974).

Stansill, Peter and David Zane Mairowitz (eds.) *BAMN** (**By Any Means Necessary) Outlaw Manifestos and Ephemera, 1965–1970* (Baltimore: Penguin Books, Inc., 1971).

Wolf, Eric R. *Peasant Wars of the Twentieth Century* (New York: Harper Torchbooks, 1973).

In addition we call attention once again to a book listed in our original bibliography but the importance of which is now somewhat more sharply accented. This is Eugene Victor Walter *Terror and Resistance; A Study of Political Violence with Case Studies of Some Primitive African Communities* (New York: Oxford University Press, 1969). In the author's words it "is the first systematic effort to develop a general theory of terrorism." Whether it was entirely successful is somewhat uncertain, but that it was original, insightful and enormously valuable, cannot be doubted.

Bibliography

Abdel-Malek, Anouar. *Egypt: Military Society*. Translated by Charles L. Markmann. New York: Vintage Books, 1968.

Aron, Robert. *Histoire de Vichy, 1940–1944*. Paris: Librairie Arthème Fayord, 1955.

"The Assassination Cult in Japan." *The China Weekly Review*, LX, no. 5 (April 2, 1932), 137–40.

"Assassins' Victims." *Review of Reviews*, LXXXV, no. 538 (November, 1934), 15–17.

Barrett, R. T. "Political Assassination in Japan." *Great Britain and the East*, L, no. 1398 (March 10, 1938), 260.

Bennett, Lerone. *What Manner of Man: A Biography of Martin Luther King*. 3d rev. ed. Chicago: Johnson Publishing Co., 1968.

Blair, Clay. *The Strange Case of James Earl Ray*. New York: Bantam Books, 1969.

Bornstein, Joseph. *The Politics of Murder*. New York: William Sloane Associates, 1950.

Briggs, Lloyd V. *The Manner of Man That Kills: Spencer, Czolgosz, Richeson*. Boston: R. G. Badger, 1921.

Burgess, Alan. *Seven Men at Daybreak*. New York: E. P. Dutton and Co., Inc., 1960.

Conquest, Robert. *The Great Terror: Stalin's Purge of the Thirties*. New York: The Macmillan Co., 1968.

Corfe, T. H. "The Phoenix Park Murders: May 6th, 1882." *History Today*, XI, no. 12 (December, 1961), 828–35.

Cottrell, John. *Anatomy of an Assassination*. New York: Funk & Wagnalls, 1966.

Crassweller, Robert D. *Trujillo. The Life and Times of a Caribbean Dictator*. New York: The Macmillan Co., 1966.

de Launay, Jacques. "How Lumumba Really Died." *Atlas*, XII, no. 4 (1966), 16–19.

de Montmorency, Alec. *The Enigma of Admiral Darlan*. New York: E. P. Dutton & Co., 1943.

Deutsch, Herman B. *The Huey Long Murder Case*. Garden City, N.Y.: Doubleday & Co., 1963.

Dewar, Hugo. *Assassins at Large.* New York: Wingate, 1951.

———. "Murder Revisited. The Case of Sergei Mironovich Kirov." *Problems of Communism,* XIV, no. 5 (September–October, 1965), 75–80.

Dietze, Gottfried. "Will the Presidency Incite Assassination?" *Ethics,* LXXVI, no. 1 (October, 1965), 14–32.

Donovan, Robert J. *The Assassins.* New York: Harper and Brothers, 1955.

Dulles, John W. F. *Yesterday in Mexico: A Chronicle of the Revolution, 1919–1936.* Austin: University of Texas Press, 1961.

Fay, Harold. "Pistols and Political Plots in Japan." *China Weekly Review,* LXI, no. 10 (August 6, 1932), 355–56.

Feierabend, Ivo and Feierabend, Rosalind et al. "Cross-National Comparative Study of Assassination." Unpublished report prepared for the National Commission on the Causes and Prevention of Violence (edited version). Task Force I, Vol. I, chap. III. Mimeographed, 1968.

Feuer, Lewis S. *The Conflict of Generations: The Character and Significance of Student Movements.* New York: Basic Books, Inc., 1969.

Fine, Sidney. "Anarchism and the Assassination of McKinley." *The American Historical Review,* LX, no. 4 (July, 1955), 777–99.

Floris, George A. "'Nine Hours to Rama'—The Man Who Killed Gandhi." *Contemporary Review,* CCIII (April, 1963), 167–75.

Frankfurter, David. "I Kill a Nazi Gauleiter. Memoir of a Jewish Assassin." *Commentary,* IX, no. 2 (February, 1950), 133–41.

Friedrich, Paul. "Assumptions Underlying Tarascan Political Homicide." *Psychiatry. Journal for the Study of Interpersonal Processes,* XXV, no. 4 (November, 1962), 315–27.

Galbraith, W. C. "The Abode of the True Believers." *Blackwood's Magazine,* CCXCII, no. 1765 (November, 1962), 424–38.

Gales, Robert Robinson. "Notes. The Assassination of the President: Jurisdictional Problems." *Syracuse Law Review,* XVI, no. 1 (Fall, 1964), 69–81.

Gall, Norman. "How Trujillo Died." *The New Republic,* CXLVIII, no. 15 (April 13, 1963), 19–20.

Gilula, Marshall F. and Daniels, David N. "Violence and Man's Struggle to Adapt." *Science,* CLXIV, no. 3878 (April 25, 1969), 396–405.

Graham, Hugh D. and Gurr, Ted R., eds. *A History of Violence in America. A Report to the National Commission on the Causes and Prevention of Violence.* New York: Frederick A. Praeger, 1969.

Graham, Stephen. *Alexander of Yugoslavia. The Story of the King Who Was Murdered at Marseilles.* New Haven: Yale University Press, 1939.

Gribble, Leonard. *Hands of Terror: Notable Assassinations of the Twentieth Century.* London: Frederick Muller Limited, 1960.

Guttmacher, Manfred S. *The Mind of the Murderer.* New York: Farrar, Straus and Cudahy, 1960.

Harris, Christina P. *Nationalism and Revolution in Egypt; The Role of the Muslim Brotherhood.* The Hague: Mouton & Co., 1964.

Hastings, Donald W. "The Psychiatry of Presidential Assassination. I. Jackson and Lincoln." *Journal Lancet,* LXXXV, no. 3 (March, 1965), 93–100.

―――――. "The Psychiatry of Presidential Assassination. II. Garfield and McKinley." *Journal Lancet,* LXXXV, no. 4 (April, 1965), 157–62.

―――――. "The Psychiatry of Presidential Assassination. III. The Roosevelts." *Journal Lancet,* LXXXV, no. 5 (May, 1965), 189–92.

―――――. "The Psychiatry of Presidential Assassination. IV. Truman and Kennedy." *Journal Lancet,* LXXXV, no. 7 (July, 1965), 294–301.

Hepple, Alexander. *Verwoerd.* Baltimore: Penguin Books, Inc., 1969.

Hoptner, Jacob B. *Yugoslavia in Crisis, 1934–41.* New York: Columbia University Press, 1962.

Husaini, Ishak Musa. *The Moslem Brethren, the Greatest of Modern Islamic Movements.* Beirut: Khayat's College Book Cooperative, 1956.

Jackson, Donald. "The Evolution of an Assassin." *Life,* LVI, no. 8 (February 21, 1964), 68A–80.

Jászi, Oscar and Lewis, John D., *Against the Tyrant; The Tradition and Theory of Tyrannicide.* Glencoe: The Free Press, 1957.

Johnson, Francis. *Famous Assassinations of History from Philip of Macedon, 336 B.C., to Alexander of Servia, A.D. 1903.* Chicago: A. C. McClurg & Co., 1903.

El Jurado de Toral y la Madre Conchita. . . . México, D. F.: n.p., n.d.

Kaplan, John. "The Assassins." *Stanford Law Review,* XIX, no. 5 (May, 1967), 1110–51.

Kelly, Joseph B. "Assassination in War Time." *Military Law Review,* XXX (October, 1965), 101–11.

*Kirkham, James, Levy, Sheldon G. and Crotty, William J., eds. *Assassination and Political Violence. A Report to the National Commission on the Causes and Prevention of Violence* (Washington, D.C.: U.S. Government Printing Office, 1969).

Laney, Richard B. "Political Assassination: The History of an Idea." Ann Arbor: University Microfilms, 1966.

Leiden, Carl. "Assassination in the Middle East." *Trans-Action,* VI (May, 1969), 20–23.

Lemarchand, René. *Political Awakening in the Belgian Congo*. Berkeley: University of California Press, 1964.

Lewis, Bernard. *The Assassins. A Radical Sect in Islam*. New York: Basic Books, Inc., 1968.

Lumumba, Patrice. *Congo, My Country*. New York: Frederick A. Praeger, 1962.

MacDonald, Arthur. "Assassins of Rulers." *Journal of the American Institute of Criminal Law and Criminology*, II, no. 4 (November, 1911), 505–20.

Manchester, William. *The Death of a President, November 20–November 25, 1963*. New York: Harper & Row, 1967.

Marshall, John. "The Twentieth-Century Vehme. Terror by Assassination." *Blackwood's Magazine*, CCLVII, no. 1556 (June, 1945), 421–25.

Martin, John B. *Overtaken by Events; the Dominican Crisis from the Fall of Trujillo to the Civil War*. New York: Doubleday & Co., Inc., 1966.

Mazrui, Ali A. "Thoughts on Assassination in Africa." *Political Science Quarterly*, LXXXIII, no. 1 (March, 1968), 40–58.

Mikes, George. *Darlan. A Study*. London: Constable & Co., Ltd., 1943.

Minobe, T. "Measures to Protect Statesmen Are Urged." *Trans-Pacific*, XX, no. 10 (March 10, 1932), 4, 16.

Mitchell, Richard P. *The Society of the Muslim Brothers*. London: Oxford University Press, 1969.

Nieburg, H. L. *Political Violence. The Behavioral Process*. New York: St. Martin's Press, 1969.

Nomad, Max. *Dreamers, Dynamiters and Demagogues; Reminiscences*. New York: Waldon Press, 1964.

Opotowsky, Stan. *The Longs of Louisiana*. New York: E. P. Dutton & Co., 1960.

Osborne, Duncan E. "The Assassination of Anastasio Somoza." M.A. thesis, University of Texas, 1968.

Padover, Saul K. "Patterns of Assassination in Occupied Territory." *Public Opinion Quarterly*, VII (Winter, 1943), 680–93.

Palmer, Stuart H. *A Study of Murder*. New York: Thomas Y. Crowell Co., 1960.

Potter, John Mason. *Plots Against Presidents*. New York: Astor-Honor, Inc., 1968.

Report of the Warren Commission on the Assassination of President Kennedy. New York: McGraw-Hill Book Co., 1964.

Robert, H. "Les regicides." *Les Annales Politiques et Litteraires*, XCVIII, no. 2416 (June 15, 1932), 500.

Rosenberg, Charles E. *The Trial of the Assassin Guiteau; Psychiatry and Law in the Gilded Age.* Chicago: University of Chicago Press, 1968.

Rosenfeld, Albert. "The Psycho-biology of Violence." *Life,* LXVIII, no. 25 (June 21, 1968), 67–71.

Rothstein, David A. "The Presidential Assassination Syndrome." *Archives of General Psychiatry,* XI (1964), 245–54.

————. "The Presidential Assassination Syndrome. II. Application to Lee Harvey Oswald." *Archives of General Psychiatry,* XV (1966), 260–66.

Rummel, R. J. "Dimensions of Conflict Behavior Within Nations, 1946–59." *The Journal of Conflict Resolution,* X, no. 1 (March, 1966), 65–73.

Saunders, J. V. D. "A Revolution of Agreement Among Friends: The End of the Vargas Era." *The Hispanic American Historical Review,* XLIV, no. 2 (May, 1964), 197–213.

Schwartz, David C. "On the Ecology of Political Violence: 'The Long Hot Summer' as a Hypothesis." *American Behavioral Scientist,* XI, no. 6 (July–August, 1968), 24–28.

Sindler, Allan. *Huey Long's Louisiana: State Politics, 1920–1952.* Baltimore: The Johns Hopkins Press, 1956.

Slomich, Sidney J. and Kantor, Robert E. "Social Psychopathology of Political Assassination." *Bulletin of the Atomic Scientists. Science and Public Affairs,* XXV, no. 3 (March, 1969), 9–12.

Sparrow, Gerald. *The Great Assassins.* London: Long, 1968.

Stark, Freya. "Assassins of Syria." *The Cornhill Magazine,* CLXII, no. 972 (Autumn, 1947), 417–26.

Stokes, William S. "National and Local Violence in Cuban Politics." *Southwestern Social Science Quarterly,* XXXIV, no. 2 (September, 1953), 57–63.

Tanter, Raymond. "Dimensions of Conflict Behavior Within and Between Nations, 1958–60." *The Journal of Conflict Resolution,* X, no. 1 (March, 1966), 41–64.

Tischendorf, Alfred. "The Assassination of Chief Executives in Latin America." *The South Atlantic Quarterly,* LX, no. 1 (Winter, 1961), 80–88.

Toch, Hans H. *Violent Men: An Inquiry into the Psychology of Violence.* Chicago: Aldine Publishing Co., Inc., 1969.

Tomakoff, George. "Stolypin's Assassin." *Slavic Review,* XXIV, no. 2 (June, 1965), 314–21.

Tompkins, Peter. *The Murder of Admiral Darlan; Study in Conspiracy.* New York: Simon and Schuster, 1965.

Tuchman, Barbara. *The Proud Tower. A Portrait of the World Before the War, 1890–1914.* New York: Bantam Books, 1966.

186 Bibliography

Walter, E. V. *Terror and Resistance. A Study of Political Violence.* New York: Oxford University Press, 1969.

Waskow, Arthur I. *From Race Riot to Sit-in: 1919 and the 1960's; A Study in the Connections between Conflict and Violence.* Garden City, N.Y.: Doubleday, 1966.

Weinstein, Edwin A. and Lyerly, Olga G. "Symbolic Aspects of Presidential Assassination." *Psychiatry. Journal for the Study of Interpersonal Processes,* XXXII, no. 1 (February, 1969). 1–11.

Weisz, Alfred E. and Taylor, Robert L. "The Assassination Matrix." *Stanford Today* (Winter, 1969), pp. 11–17.

Wiarda, Howard J. *Dictatorship and Development: The Methods of Control in Trujillo's Dominican Republic.* Gainesville: The University of Florida Press, 1968.

———. "From Fragmentation to Disintegration: The Social and Political Effects of the Dominican Revolution." *América Latina,* X, no. 2 (April–June, 1967), 55–71.

Williams, T. Harry. *Huey Long.* New York: Alfred A. Knopf, 1969.

Wolfgang, Marvin E. *Patterns in Criminal Homicide.* Philadelphia: University of Pennsylvania Press, 1958.

Young, Crawford. *Politics in the Congo.* Princeton: Princeton University Press, 1965.

Zinman, David H. *The Day Huey Long Was Shot, September 8, 1935.* New York: Ivan Obolensky, Inc., 1963.

Appendix A

Assassinations and Attempted Assassinations of Chief Executives, 1918–68

Sidonio Paes	President	Portugal	Dec. 7, 1918	Attempt
Sidonio Paes	President	Portugal	Dec. 14, 1918	Assass.
Georges Clemenceau	Premier	France	Feb. 19, 1919	Attempt
*Habibullah Khan	King	Afghanistan	Feb. 20, 1919	Assass.
M. Paderewski	Premier	Poland	May 15, 1919	Attempt
Mohammed Said	Premier	Egypt	Sept. 2, 1919	Attempt
*V. Carranza	President	Mexico	May 20, 1920	Assass.
Droubi Pasha	Premier	Syria	Aug. 23, 1920	Assass.
*Eduardo Dato	Premier	Spain	Mar. 8, 1921	Assass.
Machado Dos Santos	Former president	Portugal	Oct. 19, 1921	Assass.
Nikola Pashich	Premier	Yugoslavia	June 29, 1921	Attempt
Alexander	Prince regent	Yugoslavia	June 29, 1921	Attempt
*Antonio Granjo	Premier	Portugal	Oct. 19, 1921	Assass.
J. Pilsudski	President	Poland	July 14, 1921	Attempt
J. Pilsudski	President	Poland	Sept. 27, 1921	Attempt
J. Andressy Pakovsky	Former president	Hungary	Sept. 24, 1921	Attempt
*Takashi Hara	Premier	Japan	Nov. 4, 1921	Assass.
*Michael Collins	Prime minister & general	Ireland	Aug. 22, 1922	Assass.
*Gabriel Narutowicz	First constitutional president	Poland	Dec. 16, 1922	Assass.
*Alexander Stambuliski	Premier	Bulgaria	June 12, 1923	Assass.
Ignatz Seipel	Chancellor	Austria	June 2, 1924	Attempt
Mario G. Menocal	Former president	Cuba	Oct. 6, 1924	Attempt
Zaghloul Pasha	Premier	Egypt	July 12, 1924	Attempt
Boris	King	Bulgaria	Apr. 14, 1925	Attempt
Boris	King	Bulgaria	May 1, 1925	Attempt
Carol	King	Rumania	Sept. 13, 1925	Attempt
Takaaki Kato	Premier	Japan	Jan. 10, 1925	Attempt
B. Mussolini	Premier	Italy	Sept. 11, 1925	Attempt
B. Mussolini	Premier	Italy	Nov. 4, 1925	Attempt
Alexander Tsankoff	Premier	Bulgaria	Apr. 17, 1925	Attempt

* An asterisk indicates a chief executive (president, king, prime minister, dictator, etc.) who was successfully assassinated while in power or in office in a state which was in existence throughout the fifty-year period being investigated.

Adolfo Diaz	President	Nicaragua	Dec. 23, 1926	Attempt
B. Mussolini	Premier	Italy	Apr. 7, 1926	Attempt
B. Mussolini	Premier	Italy	Sept. 11, 1926	Attempt
Simon Petlura	General & former president of Ukraina	Poland	May 25, 1926	Assass.
Alvaro Obregón	General & presidential candidate (former president)	Mexico	Nov. 13, 1927	Attempt
P. E. Calles	President	Mexico	July 17, 1928	Attempt
*Alvaro Obregón	President-elect	Mexico	July 17, 1928	Assass.
*Yuko Hamaguchi	Premier	Japan	Nov. 14, 1930	Assass.
Augusto Leguia	President	Peru	Apr. 24, 1930	Attempt
J. Pilsudski	Premier	Poland	Oct. 14, 1930	Attempt
P. Ortiz-Rubio	President	Mexico	Feb. 5, 1930	Attempt
Ismail Sidky Pasha	Premier	Egypt	Aug. 26, 1930	Attempt
Chiang Kai-shek	President	China	July 30, 1931	Attempt
Hsuan Tung	Former boy-emperor	China	Nov. 7, 1931	Attempt
Ismet Inonu	Premier of Turkey	Greece	Oct. 1, 1931	Attempt
Gerardo Machado	President of Cuba	U. S.	Feb. 24, 1931	Attempt
B. Mussolini	Premier	Italy	Feb. 2, 1931	Attempt
Zog	King of Albania	Austria	Feb. 20, 1931	Attempt
Subhi Barakat	Former president of federal council of Syria	Syria	Apr. 12, 1932	Attempt
Antonio Oscar de Fragoso Carmona	President	Portugal	Jan. 16, 1932	Attempt
Chiang Kai-shek	Former president & generalissimo	China	July 10, 1932	Attempt
Hans Luther	Former chancellor	Germany	Apr. 9, 1932	Attempt
*Paul Doumer	President	France	May 6, 1932	Assass.
Hirohito	Emperor	Japan	Jan. 8, 1932	Attempt
*Ki Inukai	Premier	Japan	May 16, 1932	Assass.
Gerardo Machado	President	Cuba	June 11, 1932	Attempt
B. Mussolini	Premier	Italy	June 6, 1932	Attempt
L. M. Sánchez Cerro	President	Peru	Mar. 7, 1932	Attempt
Ismail Sidky Pasha	Premier	Egypt	May 6, 1932	Attempt
O. P. Benavides	President	Peru	Oct. 22, 1933	Attempt
Carol	King	Rumania	Oct. 12, 1933	Attempt
Ramón Grau San Martín	President	Cuba	Oct. 3, 1933	Attempt
*L. M. Sánchez Cerro	President	Peru	Apr. 30, 1933	Assass.
Engelbert Dollfus	Chancellor	Austria	Oct. 4, 1933	Attempt

Appendix

E. Venizelos	Prime minister	Greece	June 6, 1933	Attempt
*Ion G. Duca	Premier	Rumania	Dec. 29, 1933	Assass.
*Nadir Shah	King	Afghanistan	Nov. 8, 1933	Assass.
Franklin D. Roosevelt	President-elect	U. S. (Fla.)	Feb. 15, 1933	Attempt
Ismail Sidky Pasha	Premier	Egypt	May 16, 1933	Attempt
*Alexander	King of Yugoslavia	France	Oct. 9, 1934	Assass.
Chiang Kai-shek	President	China	Nov. 9, 1934	Attempt
*Engelbert Dollfus	Chancellor	Austria	July 25, 1934	Assass.
Carlos Mendieta	President	Cuba	June 15, 1934	Attempt
Franz von Papen	Former chancellor	Germany	June 30, 1934	Attempt
Augusto Cesar Sandino	General & former chief of state	Nicaragua	Feb. 22, 1934	Assass.
Kurt von Schleicher	General & former chancellor	Germany	June 30, 1934	Assass.
Abdul Aziz	King	Saudi Arabia	Mar. 16, 1935	Attempt
Gabriel Terra	President	Uruguay	June 2, 1935	Attempt
Wilhelm II	Former kaiser of Germany	Netherlands	Jan. 17, 1935	Attempt
Bogoljub Yeftitch	Premier	Yugoslavia	Apr. 6, 1935	Attempt
Edward VIII	King	England	July 16, 1936	Attempt
Keisuki Okada	Admiral & prime minister	Japan	Feb. 26, 1936	Attempt
Saito Makoto	Viscount & former premier	Japan	Feb. 26, 1936	Assass.
Milan Stoyadinovitch	Premier	Yugoslavia	Mar. 6, 1936	Attempt
*Bakr Sidky	Military strongman	Iraq	Aug. 12, 1937	Assass.
P. E. Calles	Former president of Mexico	U. S. (California)	Jan. 1, 1937	Attempt
Mustafa Nahas Pasha	Premier	Egypt	Nov. 28, 1937	Attempt
A. Salazar	Prime minister	Portugal	July 4, 1937	Attempt
Getulio Vargas	President & dictator	Brazil	May 11, 1938	Attempt
*Armand Calinescu	Premier	Rumania	Sept. 21, 1939	Assass.
Adolf Hitler	Reichs-chancellor & dictator	Germany	Nov. 8, 1939	Attempt
Juan Almazan	Important presidential candidate	Mexico	Feb. 7, 1940	Attempt
Tiburcio Carías	President	Honduras	Oct. 24, 1940	Attempt
Nicolas Iorga	Former premier	Rumania	Nov. 28, 1940	Assass.
Arturo Alessandri	Former president	Chile	Dec. 6, 1941	Attempt
Pierre Laval	Former premier	France	Aug. 27, 1941	Attempt

Victor Emmanuel	King of Italy	Albania	May 17, 1941	Attempt
A. Enriquez	General & former dictator	Ecuador	May 30, 1942	Assass.
Hideki Tojo	Premier & dictator	Japan	June 17, 1942	Attempt
Abdul Ilah	Regent	Iraq	June 5, 1943	Attempt
*Boris	King	Bulgaria	Aug. 24, 1943	Assass.
Manuel Camacho	President	Mexico	Feb. 2, 1943	Attempt
Emile Edde	Former president	Lebanon	Nov. 14, 1943	Attempt
Pierre Laval	(Vichy) Premier	France	May 1, 1943	Attempt
Manuel Camacho	President	Mexico	Apr. 10, 1944	Attempt
Adolf Hitler	Reichs-chancellor	Germany	July 20, 1944	Attempt
Charles DeGaulle	Head of provisional government	France	Aug. 26, 1944	Attempt
*Ahmed Maher Pasha	Premier	Egypt	Feb. 24, 1945	Assass.
Mustafa Nahas Pasha	Former premier	Egypt	Dec. 6, 1945	Attempt
Nicolai Radescu	Premier	Rumania	Feb. 24, 1945	Attempt
*Ananda Mahidol	King	Thailand	June 9, 1945	Assass.
T. Monje Gutiérrez	President	Bolivia	Sept. 27, 1946	Attempt
*Gualberto Villaroel	President	Bolivia	July 21, 1946	Assass.
Nu Thakin	Prime minister	Burma	Nov. 6, 1947	Attempt
U Aung San	Prime minister	Burma	July 19, 1947	Assass.
Mustafa Nahas Pasha	Ex-premier	Egypt	Apr. 25, 1948	Attempt
*Mahmoud Nukrashy Pasha	Premier	Egypt	Dec. 28, 1948	Assass.
Yahya ibn Muhammad	Imam	Yemen	Jan. 14/15, 1948	Attempt
*Yahya ibn Muhammad	Imam	Yemen	Feb. 17, 1948	Assass.
Muhsin al-Barazi	Premier	Syria	Aug. 14, 1949	Assass.
*Francisco Javier Arana	Presidential candidate	Guatemala	July 18, 1949	Assass.
Husni Zaim	President	Syria	Aug. 14, 1949	Assass.
Mohammed Reza Shah Pahlavi	King	Iran	Feb. 4, 1949	Attempt
Abdul Husayn Hazhir	Former premier	Iran	Nov., 1949	Assass.
*Carlos Delgado Chalbaud	Head of provisional military government	Venezuela	Nov. 13, 1950	Assass.
Riad el-Solh	Premier	Lebanon	Mar. 9, 1950	Attempt
Sami al-Hinnawi	Ex-strongman of Syria	Lebanon	Oct. 30, 1950	Assass.

Harry S Truman	President	U. S. (District of Columbia)	Nov. 1, 1950	Attempt
Abdullah ibn Husain	King	Jordan	July 20, 1951	Assass.
Liaquat Ali Khan	Prime minister	Pakistan	Oct. 16, 1951	Assass.
*Ali Razmara	Premier	Iran	Mar. 7, 1951	Assass.
Riad el-Solh	Former premier of Lebanon	Jordan	July 16, 1951	Assass.
Konrad Adenauer	Chancellor	Germany	Mar. 27, 1952	Attempt
José Velasco Ibarra	President	Ecuador	Oct. 11, 1953	Attempt
Anastasio Somoza	President	Nicaragua	Apr. 3, 1954	Attempt
Muhammad	Sultan	Morocco	Sept. 11, 1953	Attempt
Juan Perón	President	Argentina	Apr. 15, 1953	Attempt
Ismail Azhari	Prime minister	Sudan	Oct. 27, 1954	Attempt
Muhammad	Sultan	Morocco .	Mar. 5, 1954	Attempt
Gamal Abdel Nasser	Premier	Egypt	Oct. 26, 1954	Attempt
Hussein Ala	Prime minister	Iran	Nov. 17, 1955	Attempt
W. S. Tubman	President	Liberia	June 22, 1955	Attempt
Adnan al-Malki	Strongman	Syria	Apr. 22, 1955	Assass.
J. Nehru	Premier	India	Mar. 12, 1955	Attempt
K. Nkrumah	Prime minister	Gold Coast	Nov. 10, 1955	Attempt
Juan Perón	President	Argentina	June 16, 1955	Attempt
*José Antonio Remón	President	Panama	Jan. 2, 1955	Assass.
Mao Tse-tung	Chairman of the Communist party	People's Republic of China	Feb. 13, 1956	Attempt
*Anastasio Somoza	President	Nicaragua	Sept. 21, 1956	Assass.
N. Azikiwe	Prime minister	Nigeria	Apr. 16, 1957	Attempt
Fulgencio Batista	President	Cuba	Mar. 13, 1957	Attempt
*Carlos Castillo Armas	President	Guatemala	July 26, 1957	Assass.
Ngo Dinh Diem	President	Vietnam	Feb. 22, 1957	Attempt
A. Sukarno	President	Indonesia	Nov. 30, 1957	Attempt
Abdul Ilah	Crown prince & former regent	Iraq	July 14, 1958	Assass.
*Faisal II	King	Iraq	July 14, 1958	Assass.
*Nuri al-Said	Prime minister	Iraq	July 16, 1958	Assass.
Sami el-Solh	Premier	Lebanon	Apr. 20, 1958	Attempt
Sami el-Solh	Premier	Lebanon	July 29, 1958	Attempt
S. W. R, Bandaranaike	Prime minister	Ceylon	Sept. 25, 1959	Assass.
Ismet Inonu	Ex-president	Turkey	May 1, 1959	Attempt
Rashid Karami	Premier	Lebanon	May 17, 1959	Attempt
Abdul Karim Kassem	Prime minister	Iraq	Oct. 7, 1959	Attempt

Abdul Karim Kassem	Prime minister	Iraq	Oct. 22, 1959	Attempt
Luis A. Somoza	President	Nicaragua	June 6, 1959	Attempt
Norodom Suramarit	King	Cambodia	Aug. 31, 1959	Attempt
Rómulo Betancourt	President	Venezuela	June 24, 1960	Attempt
Arturo Frondizi	President	Argentina	Mar. 28, 1960	Attempt
Nobusake Kishi	Premier	Japan	July 14, 1960	Attempt
Patrice Lumumba	Premier	Congo	Sept. 15, 1960	Attempt
Hazza Majali	Prime minister	Jordan	Aug. 29, 1960	Assass.
Henrik Verwoerd	Premier	South Africa	Apr. 9, 1960	Attempt
A. Sukarno	President	Indonesia	Mar. 9, 1960	Attempt
Charles DeGaulle	President	France	Sept. 8, 1961	Attempt
Patrice Lumumba	Ex-prime minister	Congo	Jan. 17, 1961	Assass.
*R. Trujillo	Dictator	Dominican Republic	May 30, 1961	Assass.
Louis Rwangasore	Crown prince and first premier	Burundi	Oct. 13, 1961	Assass.
Ahmad ibn Yahya	Imam	Yemen	Mar. 27, 1961	Attempt
Muhammad al-Badr	Imam	Yemen	Sept. 26, 1962	Attempt
Charles DeGaulle	President	France	May 25, 1962	Attempt
Charles DeGaulle	President	France	Aug. 22, 1962	Attempt
Ngo Dinh Diem	President	South Vietnam	Feb. 27, 1962	Attempt
Mahendra	King	Nepal	Jan. 22, 1962	Attempt
Kwame Nkrumah	President	Ghana	Aug. 1, 1962	Attempt
Kwame Nkrumah	President	Ghana	Sept. 9, 1962	Attempt
S. Olympio	President	Togo	Jan. 21, 1962	Attempt
A. Sukarno	President	Indonesia	May 13, 1962	Attempt
Rómulo Betancourt	President	Venezuela	June 12, 1963	Attempt
*Abdul Karim Kassem	Prime minister	Iraq	Feb. 8, 1963	Assass.
*John F. Kennedy	President	U. S. (Texas)	Nov. 22, 1963	Assass.
Ngo Dinh Diem	President	South Vietnam	Nov. 1, 1963	Assass.
Sylvanus Olympio	President	Togo	Jan. 13, 1963	Assass.
Savang Vathana	King	Laos	Oct. 31, 1963	Attempt
René Barrientos	Vice-president (strongman)	Bolivia	Aug. 13, 1964	Attempt
René Barrientos	Chief of air force (strongman)	Bolivia	Feb. 25, 1964	Attempt
A. Ben Bella	Premier	Algeria	May 31, 1964	Attempt
Jigme P. Dorji	Premier	Bhutan	Apr. 5, 1964	Assass.
Ismet Inonu	Premier	Turkey	Feb. 21, 1964	Attempt
Adib al-Shishakli	Former president of Syria	Brazil	Sept. 28, 1964	Assass.

René Barrientos	Provisional president	Bolivia	Mar. 21, 1965	Attempt
Fidel Castro	Prime minister	Cuba	July 27, 1965	Attempt
Mohammed Reza Shah Pahlavi	King	Iran	Apr. 10, 1965	Attempt
Hamani Diori	President	Niger	Apr. 13, 1965	Attempt
Diosadado Macapagal	President	Philippine Islands	Oct. 29, 1965	Attempt
*Hassan Ali Mansour	Premier	Iran	Jan. 21, 1965	Assass.
*Mario Méndez Montenegro	Presidential candidate	Guatemala	Oct. 31, 1965	Assass.
Pierre Ngendandumwe	Premier	Burundi	Jan. 15, 1965	Assass.
Sir Abubakar Balewa	Prime minister	Nigeria	Jan. 15, 1966	Assass.
J. T. V. Ironsi (Aguiyi)	Head of state	Nigeria	July 29, 1966	Assass.
*Henrik F. Verwoerd	Prime minister	South Africa	Sept. 6, 1966	Assass.
Etienne Eyadema	President	Togo	Apr. 24, 1967	Attempt
Leopold S. Senghor	President	Senegal	Mar. 22, 1967	Attempt
François Duvalier	President	Haiti	Apr. 15, 1967	Attempt
François Duvalier	President	Haiti	June 23, 1967	Attempt
Levi Eshkol	Premier	Israel	Sept. 27, 1967	Attempt
H. Boumedienne	President	Algeria	Apr. 25, 1968	Attempt
Camille Chamoun	Former president	Lebanon	May 31, 1968	Attempt
Abdul Rahman al-Iryani	President	Yemen	July 7, 1968	Attempt
George Papadopoulis	Premier	Greece	Aug. 13, 1968	Attempt
Mohammed Ayub Khan	President	Pakistan	Nov. 10, 1968	Attempt

Appendix B

Selected Assassinations
of Politically Prominent Individuals, 1918–68

Karl Liebknecht	Germany	Jan. 15, 1919
Rosa Luxemburg	Germany	Jan. 15, 1919
Emiliano Zapata	Mexico	Apr. 10, 1919
Talaat Pasha	Germany	Mar. 15, 1921
Walther Rathenau	Germany	June 24, 1922
Sir Henry Wilson	England	June 22, 1922
Pancho Villa	Mexico	July 20, 1923
Giacomo Matteoti	Italy	June 10, 1924
Sir Lee Stack	Egypt	Nov. 19, 1924
Louis Barthou	France	Oct. 9, 1934
Ernst Roehm	Germany	June 30, 1934
Gregor Strasser	Germany	June 30, 1934
Sergei Kirov	U.S.S.R.	Dec. 1, 1934
Huey P. Long	U. S. (Louisiana)	Sept. 8, 1935
Federico García Lorca	Spain	Aug. 19, 1936
Lev Trotsky	Mexico	Aug. 20, 1940
Jean Darlan	Algeria	Dec. 24, 1942
Reinhard Heydrich	Czechoslovakia (German Protectorate of Bohemia and Moravia)	May 27, 1942
Lord Moyne	Egypt	Nov. 6, 1944
Count Folke Bernadotte	Israel	Sept. 17, 1948
M. K. Gandhi	India	Jan. 30, 1948
Lavrenti Beria	Russia	Dec. 23, 1953
Dr. Khan Sahib	Pakistan	May 9, 1958
Ngo Dinh Nhu	Vietnam	Nov. 1, 1963
Che Guevara	Bolivia	Oct. 8, 1967
Robert F. Kennedy	U. S. (California)	June 5, 1968
Martin Luther King, Jr.	U. S. (Tennessee)	Apr. 4, 1968

Index

●